W9-DEI-230

Marriage and Inequality in
Classless Societies

Jane Fishburne Collier

MARRIAGE AND INEQUALITY IN CLASSLESS SOCIETIES

Stanford University Press 1988
Stanford, California

Stanford University Press
Stanford, California
© 1988 by the Board of Trustees of the
Leland Stanford Junior University
Printed in the United States of America

CIP data appear at the end of the book

IN MEMORY OF

Michelle Zimbalist Rosaldo

Preface

This book presents three ideal-typic models for analyzing inequality in classless societies. It stems from a project begun ten years ago, a study of the relationship between social stratification and legal processes. At that time, I was interested in the relationship between the amount and kind of power available to political leaders and the types of procedures leaders use in handling conflict.

In the early 1970's, as I prepared an article reviewing anthropological studies of legal processes (J. Collier 1975), I noted an apparent correlation between forms of dispute handling and ethnographers' descriptions of leaders' power. In foraging societies, where leaders have only authority, not power, many disputes are handled through physical contests between individual disputants. Simple horticulturalists, in contrast, tend to convene moots in which Big Men negotiate compensatory payments for victims of wrongdoing. And chiefdoms may have formal courts with judges.

Analyses of marriage (Goody 1973; Meillassoux 1972, 1973a, 1973b) suggested a reason for the first two correlations. In societies without classes or estates, where kinship organizes people's rights and obligations, marriage, as the basis of kinship, organizes social inequality. In such societies, disputes between men over rights to women are endemic. It thus seemed reasonable to expect that different forms of marriage might explain differences in leaders' powers and disputants' aims. In societies where men earn their wives through brideservice, for example, no man may provide another man with a wife. As a result, leaders have little power to reward or punish others, and men whose wives are stolen have no reason for seeking compensatory goods. Physical contests between men are the consequence. In societies where men marry with bridewealth, however, elders control the goods that allow juniors to marry. Political leaders may thus reward others for compliance, and cuckolded or deserted husbands have reason to demand the compensatory goods that will allow them to acquire replacement wives. In such societies, Big Men have both the power and the incentive to convene moots for negotiating compensatory payments.

I derived my first understanding of why forms of marriage might correlate with degrees of social stratification from Emerson's (1962) analysis of power-dependence relations. Emerson suggests that leaders' power is a function of followers' needs. He uses this formulation to analyze followers' strategies for minimizing power differentials. But his formulation also suggests that the amount of power available to leaders in any social system will be a function of the mechanisms available for putting some people in the position of needing what others can provide. Using Emerson's formulation, therefore, brideservice appears to be an inefficient mechanism for creating needs, since bachelors who are able to earn their wives need not incur long-term debts to others. Bridewealth is a more efficient mechanism. If young men cannot acquire for themselves the valuables they need to marry, then their need grants power to elders who control marriage-validating gifts.

In 1976, I received a grant from the National Science Foundation to test the internal consistency and empirical validity of the conceptual scheme I was developing. Because I was concerned with the relationship between stratification and legal processes, I began my research by reading ethnographic studies of law and of the societies whose legal systems were described. Information on stratification I classified under the headings of economic organization, political centralization, values, and conflicts; information on legal institutions I classified under the headings of forums, claims, legal norms, and patterns of dispute processing. I later divided the category of economic organization into production, exchange, and marriage, and added a category on the quality of the data.

In my reading, I focused on trying to understand systems of stratification. I asked, what does a man or a woman have to do or be—whether intended or accidental—to become a respected and influential member of this society? I read skeptically. Instead of accepting ethnographers' descriptions of native customs and beliefs as accurate representations, I asked why such customs and beliefs appeared to be the way they were described. What had ethnographers seen and heard that, given their theoretical frameworks, led them to reach the conclusions they did?

I assumed that natives impose their views on what an ethnographer writes. Because researchers obtain their information from the people they interview and observe, natives influence an ethnographer's perception of what is happening and what is important. A reader who analyzes the theoretical framework a researcher used in selecting and organizing material may therefore partially recover informants' voices and interpret them within a different theoretical framework.

I also recognized that English, as a language long associated with capitalism, is a problematic medium for describing classless societies. Because many English words presume the social institutions and cultural understandings of our social system, they necessarily misrepresent the institutions and beliefs of people who live in noncapitalist societies.

The problem of using English to describe noncapitalist social relations is one that I recognized in the writing of this book as well as when reading ethnographies written by others. Readers are therefore advised that many of the words used here to discuss noncapitalist social relations are intended to convey meanings that differ slightly from those preferred in dictionaries. Terms for kinship relations, such as "parent," "child," "brother," "sister," "wife's father," or "mother's brother," do not refer to genealogically defined bonds but to socially defined relationships. The words "man" and "woman" also refer to sociological gender, not to biological sex. Many English verbs that presume a market economy, such as "to possess," "to give," "to earn," and even "to marry," here presume a different set of social relations. And words connoting inequality, such as "rich" and "poor" or their synonyms, do not refer to the amount of wealth people possess but to the amount of goods they have given away.

After reading many ethnographic descriptions of social and legal systems, I decided to concentrate on two sets of monographs. First, I focused on studies of foragers and hunter-horticulturists among whom men appear to marry with brideservice or sister-exchange. I worked in collaboration with Michelle Rosaldo, who had noticed that such societies lack developed images of femininity (Rosaldo & Atkinson 1975). My study of legal processes suggested an explanation for this deficiency: in societies where conflicts between men are handled through physical contests, people lack contexts for discussing women's qualities and thus for developing concepts of femininity. Our collaboration resulted in a paper titled "Politics and Gender in Simple Societies," published in 1981 as part of *Sexual Meanings* and presented here in somewhat different form in Chapter 1.

Second, I focused on three nineteenth-century Plains Indian societies. After reading Hoebel's analysis of Comanche law (1940), Llewellyn and Hoebel's classic study of Cheyenne law (1941), and Richardson's analysis of Kiowa law (1940), I realized that these three contiguous societies, none of which was a developed chiefdom with courts and adjudicatory procedures, exemplified three different patterns of stratification and dispute handling. The Comanche, like most foragers and hunter-horticulturists, had powerless leaders and often handled disputes between men by means of physical contests. The Cheyenne, like many simple horticulturists, had Big Men who handled men's disputes over women by negotiating compensatory payments. And the Kiowa, like the *Gumsa* Kachin of Highland Burma described by Leach (1965), recognized named, hereditary ranks and required high-ranking people to pay larger fines than low-ranking ones. It thus became obvious to me that a comparison of the Comanche, Cheyenne, and Kiowa might illuminate the relationship between stratification and dispute handling that was the object of my research.

In 1977, after reading not only about the nineteenth-century Comanche, Cheyenne, and Kiowa, but also about other Plains societies, Plains history, and the history of anthropological theory, I wrote a preliminary paper on my findings titled "Women's Work, Marriage, and Stratification in Three Nineteenth-Century Plains Tribes." Basing my analysis on Lewis's description of a Blackfoot chief who declared that his eight wives working together could produce 150 dressed bison hides a year, whereas a single woman working alone could produce only 10 (1942: 39), I estimated the amount of goods available to leaders for use and distribution by ascertaining the relationship between ways of validating marriages and the structure of bison-hunting and -processing groups. In Comanche society, where each man earned his own wife, no man could draw on more produce than his wife or wives produced. In Cheyenne society, where marriages were validated by exchanges of gifts between the senior kin of a bride and groom, some seniors were able to accumulate many working juniors in their households. And in Kiowa society, where marriages among high-ranking people were accompanied by more lavish gift exchanges than marriages among lower-ranking ones, high-ranking families were able to draw on the labor and produce of lower-ranking households headed by socially defined brothers or sisters' husbands. I thus traced the connections between gift exchanges at marriages, the kinship relations established by such exchanges, and the organization of domestic production units that produced gifts.

I never submitted the paper for publication. It was too long and ultimately incomplete. I had examined the relationship between ways of validating marriage and the organization of social inequality, but left unanswered the question of why people married in the ways they did. Why did Comanche women, who apparently preferred lovers to husbands, marry at all? Why did Cheyenne youths and maidens submit to marriages arranged by elders rather than simply live together? And why did some Kiowa women allow their male kin to give them to poor youths in exchange for the youths' labor?

I was particularly struck by the fact that cultural prescriptions for male success did not mention men's rights to women. Ethnographers, for example, report that "the crucial status determinants on the Plains were military skill and the possession of horses" (Oliver 1962: 65). Yet my analysis of marriage and kinship revealed that, both within and between societies, men's power was a function of their rights to appropriate the products of women and, through women, the products of male bison hunters. High-status men did enjoy reputations for military skill and for acquiring many horses, but a man's opportunities to join raiding parties, and so to obtain such marks of success, were determined by his rights to the labor of women. If rights to women's labor, not "military skill and the possession of horses," was the crucial determinant of male status, why did ethnographers not report this fact? Could the natives who informed them have misrecognized the basis of social inequality in their societies?

I spent the next two years pondering and reading about the problem of misrecognition. The record of my thinking as I turned from trying to understand why natives apparently misrecognize the basis of social inequality to analyzing hegemony, as defined by Raymond Williams (1977), is set out in Chapter 4. That chapter first served as a bridge between two parts of a book-length manuscript, completed in 1980, on marriage and inequality in nineteenth-century Comanche, Cheyenne, and Kiowa societies. In the first half of the manuscript, I examined the effect of economic relations on political processes, expanding the analysis developed in the earlier paper on women's work. In the second half, I used the concept of hegemony to study the effect of political processes on economic relations, examining the role of power in structuring people's understanding of their social world.

The central premise of that manuscript was that marriage is a socially constructed bond. Few anthropologists would argue with this statement, but few have rigorously explored its implications. Sahlins, for example, in discussing the "domestic mode of production," treats households as natural, biological units consisting of parents and children (1972). He is thus led to question what prompts cooperation among households in societies with a simple sexual division of labor where each household has access to the tools, skills, and land needed for its own subsistence. His answer is that such societies need political processes to force cooperation. I, in contrast, consider the husband-wife bond not as an invariant biological given but as a socially created, variable bond that must be analyzed. Just as Marx did not search for the key to capitalism by studying relations between corporate production units but rather analyzed the capital-labor relations that made corporations possible, so I do not analyze relationships between households but focus on marriage as the political process that produces individuals who are appropriately categorized and motivated to assume family roles.

As I reviewed ethnographies of nineteenth-century Plains societies to explore the role of political processes in organizing marriage, I came to realize that I was pursuing two inherently contradictory aims. It is impossible simultaneously to analyze particular societies and to build ideal-typic models of social systems. To the degree that a society is analyzed as historically specific, it ceases to represent an ideal type, and to the degree that an ideal type is developed, it necessarily misrepresents any particular historical society.

The incompatibility of societal analysis and model building was brought home to me by Plains specialists who criticized me for misrepresenting Plains societies. They suggested that if my aim was to analyze marriage among the historical Comanche, Cheyenne, and Kiowa, I needed to go beyond published sources. I should do fieldwork on reservations and comb the archives for unpublished materials. But—as I then realized—my aim was not to study specific societies but to develop a conceptual scheme for understanding the relationship between stratification and legal processes. I needed to build ideal-typic models, not to describe specific historical peoples. Consequently, I stopped reading ethnographies of Plains societies and turned once again to reading ethnographic descriptions of societies around the world in order to develop the models presented here.

The present book was written in 1984–85, when I spent a year at the Stanford Humanities Center. As the reader will see, I have employed very little of the material I collected on nineteenth-century Plains societies. I present only brief examples from Comanche, Cheyenne, and Kiowa ethnographies to illustrate the models.

During the long process of researching and writing this book, I received help from many people. As I began the project in 1976–77, my thinking was influenced by George Collier, Donald Donham, Bridget O'Laughlin, Michelle and Renato Rosaldo, and Sylvia Yanagisako, who were my colleagues at Stanford. After I wrote the preliminary paper on "Women's Work, Marriage, and Stratification," I received helpful comments from these colleagues and others. I particularly wish to thank Paul Diener, Timothy Ingold, Martin Orans, George Spindler, Katherine Verdery, and Margery Wolf for their insightful criticisms.

While writing the book-length manuscript on Plains societies between 1977 and 1980, I again received help from my colleagues at Stanford, particularly Michelle Rosaldo and Donald Donham. I owe special thanks to E. A. Hoebel. His outstanding ethnographies of the Comanche and the Cheyenne stimulated my thinking and his encouragement gave me confidence in the project. I benefited too from the comments of Donald Collier and Jack Goody, who read particular chapters.

Several colleagues, including Louise Lamphere, Richard Maddox, Sherry Ortner, Karen Paige, Carol Smith, and Marilyn Strathern, offered useful comments on the completed manuscript. I owe particular thanks, however, to John Comaroff. His clear understanding of what I was trying to do informed his page-by-page comments. The present book owes much to his constructive criticisms.

The Plains specialists who criticized my analyses of Comanche, Cheyenne, and Kiowa societies, particularly Alice Kehoe, did me an invaluable service. Although I did not follow their advice to do fieldwork with Plains Indians and to consult the archives, that urging led me to understand the difference between studying historical societies and building ideal-typic models. I also want to acknowledge the modern Comanche, Cheyenne, and Kiowa peoples whose historical societies serve as examples to illustrate the models. Because I focus on social inequality and conflict, I emphasize aspects of these past societies that their present members may prefer to forget, even as I underemphasize aspects in which members must take pride. But I hope readers will recognize the positive qualities of classless societies. No known social system is without inequities, but in classless societies, where people value generosity over possession and achieve power and influence by collecting people rather than things, individuals enjoy an equality of lifestyle and show a respect for persons that members of capitalist society can envy.

While I was writing the manuscript for this book in 1984–85, Ann Swidler helped me to clarify my argument and Nancy Donham offered consistent encouragement coupled with intelligent criticism. Nancy Fraser, my colleague at the Stanford Humanities Center, renewed my faith in the project by understanding the argument and by helping me to think through several of the ideas. And Martha Roldán's penetrating questions on the completed manuscript stimulated me to revise some sections.

This book is dedicated to the memory of my friend and colleague Michelle Zimbalist Rosaldo. Her thinking permeates every page. As we jointly taught an undergraduate course on sex roles from 1973 to 1980, commented on rough drafts of each other's writings, and developed a model for understanding gender in brideservice societies (1981), I came to appreciate the cooperative nature of feminist scholarship and to understand how a focus on gender can transform our understanding of the world. Shelly Rosaldo died in 1981, but her ideas live on in her writings, in books and articles by her collaborators, and in the memories of those who knew her.

J.F.C.

Contents

*Marriage and Inequality in
Classless Societies*

Introduction

This book presents three ideal-typic models for analyzing social inequality in kin-based, nonstratified societies. Such societies, which lack classes or estates based on unequal access to the means of production, are often described as egalitarian. Indeed they are, particularly when compared with stratified societies. But even in societies where members of kin groups work and consume together, not all kingroup members have common interests. Nonstratified societies may lack "systematic exploitation of person by person or category by category" (Berreman 1981: 20), but within kin groups members enjoy different privileges and have different obligations, and within society as a whole some people enjoy more power and privileges than others. Labor in such societies may be divided only by sex and age, not by caste or class, but each person's privileges and obligations do not derive solely from obvious physical differences between men and women or between the old and the young (Wolf 1981). Kin-based, nonstratified societies have socially organized inequalities that merit analysis.

In each of the three models presented here, I explore the systematic connections between relations of privilege and obligation, the organization of economic activities, kinship and family forms, household composition, manifestations of discord, procedures for managing conflict, powers available to leaders, folk models of social structure, concepts of personhood and gender, rituals, and ideas of ultimate order. I do not argue that relations of privilege and obligation determine economy, kinship, polity, and culture. Rather I suggest that, by focusing on such relationships, we can understand how particular social divisions of labor are realized in institutions, activities, and ideas.

The concept of social system underlying the models is quite similar to that advocated by Bourdieu (1977; see also DiMaggio 1979). Like Bourdieu, I define social systems as systems of domination— although I prefer to use the word "inequality" in referring to the three types of classless societies modeled here. And, like Bourdieu, I analyze a social system not by positing an unseen, timeless structure but rather by focusing on how ordinary people, pursuing subjective ends, realize the structures of inequality that constrain their own possibilities. To analyze a social system is to elucidate the commonsense understandings available to people for monitoring and interpreting their own and others' actions. But to analyze commonsense understandings is, once again, not to posit an unseen, timeless culture but to explore how people's understanding of the world is shaped by their structured experiences. The analysis of a social system thus requires a dialectical movement between an analysis of social structure (as realized in institutions) and an analysis of social action (often realized in the guise of strategic behavior), each of which can be understood only in terms of the other (Giddens 1976, 1979).

Because I focus on kin-based, nonstratified societies, marriage is the central institution I examine. In societies where labor is divided primarily by sex and age, marriage organizes the distribution of privileges and obligations between the sexes and generations. I thus label the three models developed here with terms referring to how marriages are validated: *brideservice, equal bridewealth*, and *unequal bridewealth*. My use of the terms "brideservice" and "bridewealth," however, differs from that common among anthropologists.[1] Therefore, readers who find these labels distracting should feel free to substitute any terms they prefer.

The three models are based partly on Meillassoux's brief discussions of three types of precapitalist economies (1972; see also 1973a, 1973b, 1981). Although I base my models on analyses of marriage rather than on analyses of how people exploit their land, my brideservice model corresponds to his hunting band, my equal bridewealth model corresponds to his simple agricultural communities, and my unequal bridewealth model corresponds to his transformed simple agriculturists.

I note, for example, that men in brideservice societies, like Meillassoux's hunters, are "free from any further reciprocal obligations or allegiance" to others after distributing the meat from each hunt (1972: 99). In equal bridewealth societies, as in Meillassoux's simple agricultural communities, elders control the valuables young people use to validate their marriages, the family consisting of socially defined parents and children is "a productive and cohesive unit," and people are very concerned with "notions of seniority and anteriority" (1972: 99–100). And in unequal bridewealth societies, elites, like the "dominant class" in Meillasoux's transformed agricultural communities, "gain control over the matrimonial policy of the community" by controlling the valuables used to validate marriages (1972: 101).

The three models I develop also correspond to societal types identified by other anthropologists. Because theorists who classify societies use different criteria, such as means of social integration (Service 1962), mode of distribution (Fried 1967), productive system (Lenski 1966; Martin & Voorhies 1975), relationship to the means of production (Sacks 1979), or amount of energy captured (Adams 1975), they draw different boundary lines between categories. But the cores of their categories usually overlap even if the boundary lines do not. Anthropologists seem to recognize a limited number of distinctive clusters of elements. My three models, like the societal types proposed by others, reflect this fact.

I developed my brideservice model to analyze foragers and hunter-horticulturists that other theorists have classified as bands (Service 1962, 1979), egalitarian societies (Fried 1967; Leacock 1978), or hunter-gatherers (Lenski 1966; Martin & Voorhies 1975), or have described as having a communal mode of production (Sacks 1979). Similarly, the societies I analyze with the equal bridewealth model can be classified as tribes (Service 1962; Sahlins 1968), as simple horticulturists (Lenski 1966, Martin & Voorhies 1975), or as groups having a kin corporate mode of production (Sacks 1979). Finally, I developed the unequal bridewealth model to analyze ranked, but uncentralized, societies. This category does not correspond to a type isolated by other theorists, but it should be familiar from its best-known ethnographic example: the *Gumsa*

Kachin of Highland Burma (Leach 1965). In this book, I do not develop a model for analyzing the centralized, hierarchical societies commonly called chiefdoms (Service 1962, 1975).

Ideal-typic models of the kind I present in this book are necessarily simplifications of complex realities. No model can, or should, reflect the intricacies and peculiarities of a particular people. Every historical society is more complex than models can suggest, if only because the experiences from which people draw their understanding of the world are always affected by historical and local events not considered in models. The models presented here thus fail to capture the richness of particular societies and will seem more applicable to some societies than to others.

Not only do the three models presented here correspond to the three types of precapitalist economies discussed by Meillassoux (1972), but the concept of social system that underlies the models is an answer to questions raised by Meillassoux's analysis of inequality in simple agricultural communities. In analyzing African "segmentary lineage-based societies," Meillassoux (1972; see also Terray 1972 and Rey 1975) suggests that elders perpetuate their supremacy over juniors by controlling both the distribution of women and access to the valuables young men must present to women's kin to validate marriages. As a result of elders' dual control, young men in such societies must work for elders if they are to acquire wives and become elders in turn.

Although Meillassoux's analysis provides the starting point for my equal bridewealth model, his analysis raises serious questions, for one of its crucial elements is the proposition that elders control the distribution of women. Every reader of African ethnographies, however, knows that African elders do not control the distribution of women in any ordinary sense of the word "control." Far from controlling women, they seem to be constantly involved in litigation because unmarried girls have affairs and married women leave their husbands to run off with lovers or return home to mother (see Bohannan 1957; Gough 1971). It would thus seem far more accurate to say that women in such societies do what they want to do, leaving elders to negotiate with other elders over who owes what to whom.[2] But if elders do not control women, why do young men need valuables in order to marry?

The obvious answer to this question—that mating and marriage are not the same thing—raises another question: What is marriage?

An examination of the remedies available to elders whose unmarried kinswomen have run off with lovers, or whose wives have deserted them, suggests that the legal basis of marriage is primarily men's right to demand valuables from women's lovers. In other words, elders' right to dispose of women in marriage and husbands' right to have wives are evidenced primarily in the fact that wronged kinsmen and husbands may demand valuables from whomever a woman happens to be living with. Unmarried men thus need valuables primarily because the elder kinsmen or husbands of their lovers will demand them. But if this is true, why should young men pay?

Ethnographic evidence reveals that, in reality, young men do not pay (see Evans-Pritchard 1940; Bohannan 1957; Gulliver 1963). Rather, elders negotiate with one another. The elder who supposedly controls the woman demands valuables from the woman's lover, and another elder, representing the offending junior with or without his consent, agrees to pay. Juniors' "need" for valuables in order to marry is thus not a real need, for in most cases some elder will give valuables in a junior's name, whether or not the junior asks for such aid. But if elders provide valuables anyway, why should juniors work for them?

This is the question I faced in my fieldwork with the Maya of Zinacantan, Chiapas, Mexico, for Zinacantecos in the 1960's, like many African peoples, validated marriages with transfers of gifts from the groom's family to the bride's (J. Collier 1968, 1973). My initial response to the question of why juniors worked for seniors— as those juniors clearly did—was that young men might not need elders' help to marry, but they certainly needed elders' help if they were to keep their wives. Zinacanteco brides constantly returned home to mother, and a youth who was not supported by his kin had little chance of recovering his wife. Zinacanteco juniors thus "needed" elders' help to acquire wives, but not quite in the way suggested by Meillassoux's analysis of African segmentary lineage-based societies.

My observation that Zinacanteco grooms needed elders' help to recover runaway wives raises another question. If this was true, why did people not say so? Why did Zinacanteco informants tell me— as their counterparts in Africa apparently told ethnographers— that young men "had to" provide expensive gifts for bride's kin, and that once married, young couples worked for the husband's parents because they were "in debt" to them for having paid the groom's courtship and wedding expenses? Why did Zinacantecos talk about "needing courtship gifts" and "owing debts" when my analysis clearly revealed that young men did not need to borrow from parents, and that the parents of a groom who refused to recognize his debt could do little about it unless their daughter-in-law ran away? Why was there a discrepancy between what people said and what my analysis of remedies revealed?

I could, of course, have decided simply to dismiss what people told me. Anthropologists have long recognized that there is a difference between what people say and what they do, and that both are different from what people say they should do. In the past, anthropologists have tended to focus on what people say they should do (values) and on what an ethnographer's observations suggest they actually do (behavior). People's commonsense understandings have generally been considered a residual category.

But people have their being in the commonsense world. It is primarily in this world that people claim and resist unequal privileges and obligations. Common sense is what I want to understand. But if people's taken-for-granted assumptions about the nature of their society are not direct reflections of the remedies offered by sanctioning agencies, what is the relationship between common sense and sanctions? Or, stated in more general terms, what is the relationship between culture and power? That is the central question I ask in this book.

In brief, I answer the question by suggesting that the powers available to people are important, not because of what they allow power holders to do or to prevent others from doing, but because they structure the contexts in which people negotiate the consequences of actions and events. If "common sense" is defined as people's uncritical and largely unconscious way of perceiving the world (Gramsci 1971), then we can understand the unexamined assumptions that structure perception by examining the contexts in which such assumptions are created and used. We therefore analyze the powers people have, not to find out what they may or may not do, but rather to understand the shape of particular discourses.

I focus on discourses because it is in discourse that culture and power are joined. Power relations provide the necessity for, and the contexts of, ongoing and recurring conversations. At the same time, such conversations, by requiring and producing particular understandings of the social world, presume unexamined assumptions that grant power to some and not to others.

In the end, this is why I adopt an analytic strategy similar to that advocated by Bourdieu (1977). Because power and culture are joined in discourse, I alternately discuss how power relations elicit particular conversations and how the unexamined assumptions underlying those conversations distribute power.

The three models described in this book represent three different configurations of power and their associated conversations. In particular, I analyze the powers people wield when negotiating marriages to elucidate their understanding of what marriage entails, and I analyze peoples' understanding of marriage to elucidate the distribution of powers and constraints.

Because the three models presented here are intended to illuminate societal types, I should, ideally, illustrate each with examples drawn from several historical societies, chosen to display the model's range of application. This is the strategy Michelle Rosaldo and I adopted in first presenting the brideservice model (Collier & Rosaldo 1981: 281). We illustrated that model with examples drawn from the !Kung Bushmen of the Kalahari Desert, the Australian Aborigines of Northeastern Arnhem Land, and the Ilongot hunter-horticulturists of Northern Luzon, Philippines, to show that societies differing in amounts of stratification and utilizing different subsistence strategies might nevertheless be analyzed in similar terms.

But to illustrate each model presented here with examples drawn from three societies would lengthen the book considerably and would also obscure the differences among the models. I therefore chose a different strategy of presentation. Instead of illustrating each model with several examples selected to display its range of application, I draw most of my ethnographic examples from three societies chosen to illustrate the differences among them.

These three societies are the Comanche for brideservice, the Cheyenne for equal bridewealth, and the Kiowa for unequal bridewealth, as they lived during the nineteenth-century when men were bison hunters, warriors, and traders on the North American Great Plains. Although these three groups had tumultuous histories before and after they were confined to reservations at the end of the nineteenth-century, and although ethnographers working in the twentieth-century relied on informants' memories for analyzing pre-reservation social relations, ethnographies of these three historical groups offer unparalleled advantages for my purposes.

Anthropologists have long recognized that nineteenth-century native American cultures of the Great Plains provide a "natural laboratory" for testing anthropological theories (Oliver 1962: 1). Hoebel, for example, writes that the Comanche, Cheyenne, and Kiowa

offer a good comparative case study. Their geographical environments and economic systems were virtually identical. In familial structure they were quite alike (all three were clanless). Their fundamental religious ideas were essentially similar in the use of the vision quest to obtain supernatural power from guardian spirits. Their war patterns were one. They differed only in language, in minor details of their general cultures, and in the degree of integration of tribal government, control of the individual, and in the elaboration of their religious systems. Hence, with these three tribes we can look at the comparative effects upon the law of differing social emphases within a single cultural area. (1954: 130–31)

Whereas Hoebel stresses the social and cultural similarities of these three contiguous groups in highlighting differences, I suggest that the three offer a unique opportunity for illustrating societal differences because the apparently similar elements Hoebel lists are, in fact, very different.

The Comanche, Cheyenne, and Kiowa did share a common environment—all three lived on the Great Plains—but they occupied quite different niches in the Plains trading and raiding networks. Their economic systems were identical only in that all three practiced mounted bison hunting. Within each society, the groups who cooperated in hunting and processing bison were differently organized. None of the three societies had a developed system of clans, but their familial structures varied from nuclear to extended. People in all three societies used the vision quest to obtain supernatural power from guardian spirits, but they had different understandings of what constituted such power. And although all three had similar war patterns, different social rewards awaited the war hero.

Ethnographies of nineteenth-century Comanche, Cheyenne, and Kiowa societies thus illustrate the limitations inherent in any form of analysis that does not seek the meaning of a social institution or practice in the whole of which it is a part. It is not true that the three societies were similar in some ways and different in others.

They were complete transformations of one another. Elements that appear similar at first glance turn out to be profoundly different when understood within the context of total systems. Examples drawn from the nineteenth-century Comanche, Cheyenne, and Kiowa thus highlight, as comparisons of few other societies can, the insights to be gained from the kind of holistic analysis advocated here.

Comanche, Cheyenne, and Kiowa ethnographies are also useful for my purposes because they were written by similar, occasionally identical, ethnographers. Analyses of Comanche, Cheyenne, and Kiowa legal systems (Hoebel 1940; Llewellyn & Hoebel 1941; and Richardson 1940) were based on fieldwork carried out at the same time by ethnographers who used similar methods and theoretical frameworks. Hoebel, Llewellyn, and Richardson all visited reservations in the 1930's. All interviewed elderly informants about conflicts that occurred before the groups were confined to reservations in the last quarter of the nineteenth century. And all shared Karl N. Llewellyn's understanding of law. Therefore, differences in their descriptions of how the Comanche, Cheyenne, and Kiowa understood and handled marital disputes cannot be attributed to differences in ethnographers' timing, methods, or theoretical frameworks.

Finally, ethnographies of Comanche, Cheyenne, and Kiowa societies reveal that these three groups exhibited the three patterned relationships between marriage and inequality proposed by Meillassoux (1972) and affirmed by my reading of many ethnographies of classless societies. Lowie reports that in all nineteenth-century Plains groups, "the most generally approved form of marriage was by purchase" (1954: 79). But the Comanche, Cheyenne, and Kiowa differed in the means available to potential grooms for acquiring needed goods. They also differed in the organization of production units and in the type and extent of power available to political leaders.

Comanche men, who seldom married before the age of 25, reportedly purchased wives with horses the groom acquired by his own raiding. It was considered disgraceful for a groom to ask his father for horses to give to his in-laws (Wallace & Hoebel 1952: 132). Comanche men thus incurred no debts in marrying. Successful Comanche hunters distributed their meat throughout the band (Hoebel 1940: 119). Married women were responsible for the feeding and housing of their husbands and children. The Comanche had a very egalitarian society. Hoebel reports that their leaders lacked the power to give orders (1940: 19). As among Meillassoux's hunters, the basic social unit was "an equalitarian but unstable band with little concern for biological or social reproduction." Comanche men were "free from any further reciprocal obligations or allegiance" to others after distributing the meat from each hunt (Meillassoux 1972: 99).

Cheyenne marriage exchanges were more complex. If a groom's kinsmen approved of his choice of bride, they assisted him in bringing together "such items as clothing, blankets, guns, bows and arrows, and horses" (Hoebel 1978: 28) to present to the bride's brother. The bride's brother then distributed the gifts among his kinsmen, each of whom was obligated to return a gift of equal or greater value. These return gifts were later distributed among the groom's kinsmen (Hoebel 1978: 27–28). The Cheyenne are reported to have lived in extended uxorilocal households. Unmarried sons and the husbands of daughters hunted bison. The household women, working together under the mother's direction, transformed dead bison into food, clothing, and tipis (Eggan 1955: 61). A mother's husband thus had the right to appropriate the products of many workers. The Cheyenne are famous for their Council of Forty-Four Chiefs, made up of men chosen for their generosity who served ten-year terms (Hoebel 1978: 43). As in Meillassoux's simple agricultural communities, Cheyenne elders controlled the valuables juniors used for validating their marriages, people lived in extended family households, and rituals focused on ensuring reproduction, both human and cosmic (Meillassoux 1972: 99–100).

Information on Kiowa marriage exchanges is fragmentary, but ethnographies suggest that Kiowa affines exchanged gifts and that the number of gifts expected from a groom's family varied according to the standing of his bride. More gifts were required to validate the marriage of a high-ranking woman than of a woman of low rank. In Kiowa society, the entire band formed an economic unit (Mishkin 1940: 26). Bands were composed of brothers with their wives and children; their half, classificatory, and pact brothers; some sisters and their husbands; and some "poor" men living with daughters or sisters of the headman (Richardson 1940: 5–6). Because oldest brothers were regarded as heads of families (Richardson 1940: 12), and because wife-takers could not refuse wife-givers' requests (Richardson 1940: 66), a band headman could draw on the produce and labor of many socially defined younger brothers and sisters' husbands. The Kiowa were unique among Plains bison hunters in recognizing three named, apparently hereditary ranks (Hoebel 1954: 170). People born into high-ranking families never had to perform degrading tasks or to work for others; men could devote their time to raiding for honor and horses. Low-ranking men, in contrast, never escaped having to hunt and herd for others (Mishkin 1940: 62). In Kiowa society, as in Meillassoux's transformed agricultural communities, elite men, because of their ability to join many raiding parties, controlled access to the valuables (horses) used for validating marriages (Meillassoux 1972: 100).

Although ethnographies of the nineteenth-century Comanche, Cheyenne, and Kiowa offer several advantages for illustrating the models presented here, they also have disadvantages. As noted earlier, the descriptions from which I draw most of my illustrative examples (Hoebel 1940 and Wallace & Hoebel 1952 for the Comanche; Grinnell 1923, Llewellyn & Hoebel 1941, and Hoebel 1978 for the Cheyenne; and D. Collier 1938, Richardson 1940, and Mishkin 1940 for the Kiowa) were written by ethnographers working in the twentieth-century who had to rely informants' memories to reconstruct pre-reservation social relations. The ethnographies, although otherwise excellent examples of the genre, thus include all the distortions and omissions common to remembered narratives. In particular, they lack information on people who did not exemplify cultural ideals. Elderly, primarily male, informants probably had little reason to remember the lives of women, youths, and social failures. And the ethnographers who interviewed them in the 1930's focused on chiefs, priests, and famous warriors.

Because these ethnographers tended to use theoretical frameworks positing cultural integration and stability, it is important to point out that even before being confined to reservations, the Comanche, Cheyenne, and Kiowa had quite tumultuous histories. The nineteenth-century Comanche—from whom I draw examples to illustrate the brideservice model—were descendants of Shoshonean hunter-gatherers who entered the Plains from the west. They were one of the first groups to acquire horses, and during the eighteenth-century, they roamed widely, raiding other groups for slaves and booty to trade with whites. By 1805, the Comanche and their Shoshonean relatives were gone from the Plains of Wyoming and Montana. Groups that had both horses and guns had pushed them south of the Arkansas River (Hyde 1959: 194). During the nineteenth-century, the Comanche were a large ethnic group, numbering approximately 10,000 to 12,000 people (Ewers 1973). The bands they formed were scattered across the southern Plains and, unlike other bison-hunting groups, they did not come together for communal rituals during the summer months (Oliver 1962: 22). The Comanche did not have to produce bison products for trading with whites. Because of their southern location, they were within striking distance of Spanish settlements in the Southwest and northern Mexico and so were able to obtain needed manufactures by raiding for them or by trading raided goods (Jablow 1950: 70).

The Cheyenne—from whom I draw examples for illustrating the equal bridewealth model—were Algonkian speakers from the Northeast who, during the eighteenth century, lived in fortified earth-lodge villages on the Sheyenne river in South Dakota (Hoebel 1978: 7). During their sedentary period from approximately 1725 to 1782, Cheyenne women farmed maize, squash, and tobacco, while Cheyenne men, who acquired horses between 1760 and 1780, were traders and warriors who obtained meat in communal bison hunts (Hoebel 1978: 7–8). At the end of the eighteenth century, the Cheyenne abandoned their epidemic-prone agricultural villages to take up a nomadic life on the Plains. Cheyenne men became deeply involved in the horses-for-guns trade; they exchanged agricultural products and manufactured goods obtained from Missouri River villages for horses obtained from mobile hunters on the interior Plains (Jablow 1950). Cheyenne women, forced to give up farming, turned to processing bison meat and hides for use and trade. After 1840, the northern Cheyenne bands moved into Montana; the southern bands remained near Bent's Fort on the Arkansas River. "One of the last of the great ceremonial gatherings of the entire Cheyenne nation was held in late August, 1842" (Hoebel 1978: 10). At that time, the Cheyenne may have numbered around 4,000 people (Llewellyn & Hoebel 1941: 78).

Less is known about the Kiowa, from whom I draw examples for illustrating the unequal bridewealth model. No ethnographer writes about all aspects of Kiowa life, and Kiowa origins are shrouded in mystery. Their language, which is related to Tanoan, suggests a southwestern origin, but their myths tell of an earlier foraging life in Montana (Mooney 1898: 153; see also Lowie 1953).

By the 1740's, however, the Kiowa were already established on the Plains as long-distance traders. They exchanged "horses and Spanish articles from New Mexico for maize, vegetables, tobacco, and other Arikara products" (Hyde 1959: 139). After 1826, when raiding for horses replaced peaceful trade (Hyde 1959: 211), the Kiowa joined their Comanche allies in raiding until 1869, when they were confined, with some degree of success, to the Fort Sill reservation in southern Oklahoma (Mayhall 1962). The Kiowa were then a very small ethnic group, numbering only 1,600 people (Richardson 1940: 5).

Given their tumultuous histories, the nineteenth-century Comanche, Cheyenne, and Kiowa might seem inappropriate societies for illustrating ideal-typic models. However, their histories are probably no more tumultuous than the histories of most ethnic groups during the nineteenth and twentieth centuries, when the expansion of capitalism left no social groups untouched. Static societies appropriate for illustrating ideal-typic models do not exist. The ethnographic record contains descriptions only of historically located peoples whose reported activities and ideas provide data that are more or less useful for particular purposes.

Although I illustrate the models with examples drawn almost exclusively from ethnographies of the nineteenth-century Comanche, Cheyenne, and Kiowa, I do not offer analyses of these societies. The construction of ideal-typic models and the analysis of specific historical peoples are inherently incompatible tasks. To create an ideal-type is to abstract general propositions. To analyze a specific historical group is to focus on the particularities of their unique experience.

This book has three chapters (one on each of the ideal-typic models), followed by a chapter on theory and a Conclusion. Each of the chapters on an ideal-typic model begins with a preliminary description of the type that is intended to serve two purposes. First, it introduces each type in terms that should be familiar to most readers. Second, and more important, it raises the questions my ideal-typic models are constructed to answer. In particular, it reveals the failures of sociological analyses that do not consider how the people themselves understand their world. Reality is socially constructed (Berger & Luckmann 1966). If we are to understand the reality of any particular group, we must attend to how those people—women as well as men—talk about, and so constitute, the world they inhabit.

Each preliminary description is followed by two sections focusing on commonsense assumptions. The first examines marriage negotiations to uncover the presuppositions underlying negotiators' claims and arguments. The second, on production and circulation, is devoted to examining unstated assumptions about work, status, and the meaning of gifts. The next two sections, in contrast, are concerned with overt cultural idioms. In the first, I examine political discourse, as revealed in conflict-management procedures and leadership patterns. In the second, I examine concepts of personhood, particularly gender conceptions, and ideas of ultimate order as expressed in rituals. Each chapter ends with a brief reexamination of marriage, for marriages exist only as they are negotiated by socially created women and men.

Chapter 4, on approaches to understanding inequality, presents the concerns that guided my construction of ideal-typic models. Readers who are not familiar with the theoretical framework I use may wish to read this chapter first. In the brief Conclusion I examine the limits and uses of models.

I

The Brideservice Model

The brideservice model proposed in this chapter is most appropriate for analyzing groups of hunter-gatherers and hunter-horticulturists commonly known as bands (Service 1979) or as simple egalitarian societies (Fried 1967).[1] Michelle Rosaldo and I first proposed the model in our paper on "Politics and Gender in Simple Societies" (Collier & Rosaldo 1981). In this book, I discuss the same model, but I have rearranged the order of presentation for the purpose of making the model comparable to the equal bridewealth and unequal bridewealth models discussed in the next two chapters. For the same reason, I illustrate the model with ethnographic examples drawn primarily from Comanche society.

Preliminary Description of the Type

Ethnographers of societies appropriate for analysis with a brideservice model commonly report that these peoples have only a simple division of labor by sex. Men hunt, and perhaps clear land. Women gather and/or grow crops on the fields men clear. Or, in areas with few vegetable resources, women spend their time fishing and/or processing the large animals men kill.

Although men and women tend to perform different tasks and to produce different things, marriage is not the coming together of a male hunter with a female gatherer or grower of vegetable crops. Marriage does not involve a direct exchange, or even a pooling, of male and female products and skills. Nor is marriage a situation in which a male provider supports a dependent, helpless female with her young.

Anthropologists who generalize about simple egalitarian societies commonly fail to realize that marriage does not involve a direct exchange or pooling of resources between husband and wife. Most anthropologists expect such pooling. They belong to a society whose ideology casts marriage as the union of a male bread-winner and a female homemaker. And the theories of social structure they draw on do not require an examination of relations between spouses. Most of these theories focus on social rather than supposedly natural bonds. When anthropologists write about the economy of foraging peoples, for example, their observation that both sexes enjoy unfettered access to the means of production is usually followed by an analysis of forms of circulation outside the immediate circle consisting of husband, wife, and children. And when writing about kinship, they focus on the affinal or inter-generational relationships established through marriage, not on relations between husbands and wives. When such anthropologists ask why men and women marry, rather than simply assuming that they marry to gain access to the sexual services and economic products of the opposite sex, they commonly spell out what others take for granted. They conclude that the human division of labor by sex forces men and women to marry in order to gain regular access to the products and services they do not themselves create or provide (see Service 1979: 36; Lévi-Strauss 1969: 38–39).

Anthropologists who reach this conclusion, or spell it out, are only half right. Evidence indicates that men "marry" (i.e., seek to establish claims to specific women) in order to gain regular access to women's services and products. But ethnographic evidence also indicates that women do not have to marry. They have regular access to male products and sexual services whether or not they have specific men who claim to be their husbands.

When ethnographers of particular societies write about men's and women's obligations, as opposed to the sexual division of labor, they usually report that men and women have different responsibilities. Male hunters are commonly obliged to share their meat widely and to reserve the best portions for senior affines. A returning Comanche hunter was obliged to share his meat "with all who came for some," and he "had to give the best part to his wife to take to her father" (Hoebel 1940: 119). Married women, in contrast, are not expected to distribute their produce widely, and certainly are not expected to share it with their senior affines. Women are responsible for providing daily food, clothing, and shelter for their husbands and children, using the produce they gather, grow, or obtain when male meat and hides are distributed. Only if a woman has produce left over after feeding her family may she share it with others (see Collier & Rosaldo 1981: 282–83).[2]

A focus on the sexual division of labor might suggest that marriage is equally beneficial to husband and wife, but a focus on the sexual division of obligations suggests the opposite. Because men are obliged to distribute their meat widely, a woman does not have to have a husband to gain access to male produce. She simply has to be a member of a social group. But because women are responsible for feeding their husbands and children, a man must have a wife if he hopes to eat regularly and without having to demean himself. This difference in obligations by sex, and its consequence for the meaning of marriage, are the twin insights underlying the brideservice model presented in this chapter.[3]

When ethnographers of brideservice societies report that labor is divided by sex, they are simultaneously reporting that it is not divided by age or rank. Indeed, a striking fact about brideservice peoples is the reported laziness of children and unmarried young adults. Comanche youths seem to have performed little useful work. Wallace and Hoebel write that "a boy was allowed much liberty. . . . He was not expected to perform any menial labor about the camp and was always treated with great consideration, for 'he is going to be a warrior and he may die young in battle' " (1952: 127). Cheyenne youths, as we will see in the next chapter, were not treated with such consideration. They were required to herd the family horses, even though they, too, were going to be warriors who might die young.[4]

Because of the difference in men's and women's obligations, most of the societies appropriate for analysis with a brideservice model have two basic economic units: the separate hearths of individual women and the inclusive group within which male meat is shared. This inclusive group seldom comprises more than one hundred people, although several such groups may camp together during times of plenty. Inclusive groups are usually unstable. Groups move frequently, and people move in and out of them both as individuals and as families. As Meillassoux observes about foraging peoples, "the basic social unit is an equalitarian but unstable band" lacking "even the extended family organization" (1972: 99). Not only do people in these societies live in unstable groups, but they are widely reported to be improvident. They show little concern for property, movable or immovable. They neither accumulate possessions nor devote much attention to caring for the few things they have. Sahlins writes that foragers (and, I would add, many hunter-horticulturists) display "two complementary economic inclinations": (1) "prodigality: the propensity to eat right through all the food in the camp, even during objectively difficult times," and (2) "prodigality's negative side: the failure to put by food surpluses, to develop food storage" (1972: 30–31). They also "display a notable tendency to be sloppy about their possessions" (Sahlins 1972: 12).

The Comanche displayed all these "uneconomic" attitudes. Wallace and Hoebel describe them as an opportunistic people. A man "could demonstrate an amazingly gluttonous appetite when food was plentiful and no danger present," but "seldom were efforts put forth to make provision for the future other than preserving meat or wild fruits and nuts by drying such quantities as could be carried when the camp moved" (1952: 76).[5] The Comanche also had little "interest in sartorial splendor." Wallace and Hoebel report that "their work-a-day garb was simple and crude," as were most of their material possessions (1952: 77).

Ethnographers of brideservice societies commonly report that marriages are seldom marked by public celebration, and that divorce is both easy and common. Hoebel's description of the Eskimo, among whom "marriage is entered into merely by bedding down with the intention of living together; divorce is effected simply by not living together any more" (1954: 83), seems applicable to many groups. The Comanche had a simple ceremony in which a suitor tied his riding horse to the door of his desired bride's tipi. If she agreed to live with him, she drove his horse into the herd (Wallace & Hoebel 1952: 136). And Comanche marriages were brittle; divorce was frequent (Gladwin 1948: 86).

Although people in these societies seldom hold public ceremonies when a man and woman begin living together, that point is usually preceded and followed by negotiations between a man and his wife's kin. When ethnographers describe how men acquire wives, they usually mention one or more of the following ways: (1) hopeful grooms pay bridewealth to the wife's kin, but the bridewealth consists of valuables a groom is expected to acquire on his own; (2) young men perform required brideservice; (3) men exchange sisters for wives; (4) a bachelor may move in with a polygynous man who is socially defined as his older brother and gradually take over one of his wives; and (5) men move in with the kin of desired brides, giving rise to a pattern of uxorilocal residence.

The first four ways of acquiring a wife are all mentioned with reference to the Comanche. First, the Comanche had a form of bridewealth. Young men were expected to present gifts to the kin of girls they hoped to marry. As a result, bachelors "needed horses or other plunder to secure a wife." A Comanche youth might "persuade his father to furnish the necessary horses, but it was far more respectable for a young man to acquire his own" (Wallace & Hoebel 1952: 132). Second, some Comanche youths performed brideservice: "In a few cases a boy was known to work (hunt or raid) for the family of the girl he wanted for a wife for as much as one, two, or three years" (Wallace & Hoebel 1952: 134). Third, the Comanche practiced sister-exchange. "Brothers with their sisters formed a marriage group, which established relationships with another marriage group on the basis of inter-family exchange marriage" (Wallace & Hoebel 1952: 139). Fourth, young Comanche men could move in with polygynous older brothers. The Comanche practiced an attenuated form of polyandry that Wallace and Hoebel describe as "anticipatory levirate" (1952: 138). No ethnographer has reported that the Comanche evidenced a pattern of uxorilocal residence, but because most marriages took place within the band, men usually lived close to, if not actually with, their in-laws.[6]

Ethnographers of brideservice societies describe several ways men can acquire wives, but none of these requires a bachelor to borrow goods from his own senior kin. Instead of borrowing, men earn wives for themselves. But if bachelors can earn their own wives, it is also true that men's obligations to in-laws do not end once a man and his bride begin living together. In all brideservice societies, men are obliged to provide meat for, or give other gifts to, the wife's parents as long as the marriage lasts (see Wallace & Hoebel 1952: 134). As a result, most men spend many years living near or with the wife's kin, even if extended uxorilocal residence is not recognized as a requirement for marriage.[7]

When discussing leadership in brideservice societies, ethnographers commonly report that respected men give advice but lack the power to give orders. Fried writes that "it is difficult, in ethnographies of simple egalitarian societies, to find cases in which one individual tells one or more others, 'Do this!' or some command equivalent, [whereas] the literature is replete with examples of individuals saying the equivalent of 'If this is done, it will be good,' possibly or possibly not followed by somebody else doing it" (1967: 83). Fried further notes that "while men in these societies do not seem to display any drive for universal dominance within their groups, they do display a considerable drive to achieve parity, or at least to establish a status that announces 'don't fool with me' " (1967: 79).

The Comanche exhibited the leadership pattern noted by Fried. They had respected "peace chiefs" who had "a certain authority as counsellor-to-the-people-at-large," but whose advice was heeded only if others thought it right and proper (Hoebel 1940: 19). Comanche peace chiefs played an important role "in situations where the problem was a question of what *ought* to be done," but "under no circumstances had a peace chief the power to *order* an adjustment to be made" (Hoebel 1940: 19, italics his). Comanche men also displayed a considerable drive to achieve independence and to maintain that independence by reacting quickly and violently to perceived slights (see Wallace & Hoebel 1952: 146).

Ethnographers who write about conflict in brideservice societies report that people seldom quarrel over goods or land, but men do fight over women. Fried writes that "sexual tensions are the cause of much of the conflict" in simple egalitarian societies (1967: 75). Adultery and wife stealing, in particular, seem to be the major causes of public conflict between men. Wallace and Hoebel write that "forty-five cases of old-time legal actions arising from adultery and wife stealing alone were recorded from Comanche informants . . . of these, twenty-two were wife-absconding cases and twenty-three were cases of simple adultery" (1952: 225).

People in brideservice societies commonly handle conflicts by moving away. "Dispersal is in fact the most widely reported means of dealing with trouble" (Roberts 1979: 84). But if disputants do not disperse, and if quarrels are not immediately settled by the calming influence of elders or the preponderance of public opinion, "then some form of contest is held, preferably a game, that takes the place of an outright battle" (Service 1979: 53). Ethnographers commonly report that these people recognize few norms. Roberts concludes that although people in all societies need some social norms, "in hunting and gathering societies, these norms need not be very elaborate or wide-ranging" (1979: 82).

Most ethnographers who write about brideservice societies stress their egalitarian nature. The processes of production and circulation do not differentiate people. Labor is divided only by sex, and men distribute their meat widely rather than hoard it for personal consumption. Leaders lack the power to give orders. Social groups are fluid—people move in and out of them easily to gain advantages or avoid conflicts. And few norms constrain people from acting out their desires.

In short, brideservice societies seem most notable for what they lack. And, to most ethnographers, the cause of this lack is easy to find. A foraging or hunter-horticultural economy imposes few requirements and encourages nomadism. People who invest little labor in the land have no need to establish property rules or complex kinship groupings to ensure access to adequate labor. People who move frequently have no incentive to invest labor in making immovable or heavy objects. Nor do they need to develop elaborate norms to handle conflict. Finally, the lack of permanent settlements and large kinship groups limits possibilities for leadership. Hoebel emphasizes the "meagerness" of Comanche culture in comparison with that of the Cheyenne and Kiowa. He attributes this meagerness to Comanche descent from the foraging " 'Digger Indians' of the Great Basin" (1954: 128–29).

Most anthropologists who write about brideservice societies focus on what they lack; I am more interested in what they have. Such societies may be the most egalitarian ones known to us, but they nevertheless have socially created inequalities. The most visible one is that between married and unmarried men. In societies where women not only feed families but also build shelters, tend hearths, and provide sexual services, married men live very different lives than do bachelors and men whose wives have died or left them. Because a man who lives with a wife has a shelter, hearth, and a readily available sexual partner, he can avoid asking other men for anything. In contrast, the man who lacks a wife must either go without a shelter, hearth, and sex, or obtain goods and services from his mother, sister, or lover—a woman who is another man's wife or potential wife.

Ethnographic studies provide dramatic evidence that the bachelor and the man who loses his wife are sorry figures (see Lévi-

Strauss 1969: 39). Such men tend to eat irregularly and to sleep uncomfortably, because no woman is obliged to feed or shelter them. Bachelors have a particularly difficult time. Young, frequently handsome, and free, they are usually forced to live on the outskirts of camps by married men who reportedly fear seduction of their wives. In Comanche society, where the average age of marriage for men was between 25 and 30 (Wallace & Hoebel 1952: 133), bachelors were expected to spend most of their time away from camp hunting, raiding, and seeking visions. And when in camp, they lived in small tipis behind the lodges of their parents (1952: 130).

Given bachelors' sorry state, marriage is a major transition for them. The acquisition of a wife transforms unwelcome, wandering youths into settled, responsible adults. Once a man has a wife to provide food, shelter, and sex, he need no longer live outside the camp. Other married men no longer fear his presence. Marriage provides a man far more than a place in the camp and regular food, however. It also allows him to become a political actor—an initiator of relationships through generosity. A man who has a wife and a hearth can offer hospitality to other men. He can invite men without wives to share the shelter, food, and sexual services his wife provides. Because a married man has all his daily needs provided for, he can distribute his meat widely without having to ask for anything in return.[8] And because a married man has privileges to defend, his words take on new weight. As an individual with interests to protect, he is someone whom others must heed, or they will suffer the consequences.

This description of the lifestyle differences between married and unmarried men provides a context for understanding Fried's observation that men in simple egalitarian societies "display a considerable drive to achieve parity, or at least to establish a status that announces 'don't fool with me' " (1967: 79). "Parity" is the state of being married. A man who has a wife is truly the equal of other married men, for men with wives need never ask anyone for anything. As we will see, in the section on political processes, a status that announces "don't fool with me" is essentially a status that announces "don't fool with my wife."

Men in brideservice societies may need wives, but the fact that men can marry without incurring long-term debts to other men imposes limits on inequality. In societies where men appear to earn their own wives, the married man is truly independent. He owes no debts and need incur none. A focus on marriage thus illuminates Fried's observation that leaders lack the power to give orders. Because married men need nothing, and bachelors appear to earn their own wives, leaders have no means of rewarding or sanctioning other men. Respected men can offer only advice. Others may heed it or not, as they wish.

This first section of the chapter has consisted of a preliminary discussion of economy, marriage, and polity in brideservice societies that provides some insights into how marriage organizes social inequality. The difference between men's and women's obligations permits married men to enjoy a more privileged lifestyle than bachelors. This lifestyle difference constitutes the "parity" Fried describes all men as seeking to achieve. Yet the ability of men to apparently earn their own wives limits the power available to leaders. It is little wonder that men in simple egalitarian societies "do not seem to display any drive for universal dominance within their groups" (Fried 1967: 79).

This discussion leaves many questions unanswered, however. A basic question is, why do women marry? Because women are obliged to feed their families, it is easy to understand why a man would want a wife. But because men distribute their meat widely rather than bringing it home to their wives, it is hard to understand why a woman would want a husband. And if women do not want husbands, what does marriage mean to them? In the remaining sections of this chapter I offer answers to these questions. In particular, I explore the construction of commonsense meanings in an attempt to understand what marriage means to women and men.

Marriage

In societies appropriate for analysis with a brideservice model, marriage is primarily a relationship between men in respect to women. It is, of course, also a relationship between a man and a woman, but relations between spouses are best understood in the context of relations between men. The most visible inequality in lifestyle and privilege is that between married and unmarried men, and this inequality provides the context within which men and women relate to one another.

As noted in the previous section, ethnographers describe several ways men acquire wives, such as apparent bridewealth, brideservice, sister exchange, inheritance, and uxorilocal residence. I pointed out, however, that none of these methods requires a groom to borrow valuables from, and so incur debts to, other men. In that sense, grooms earn their wives.

In brideservice societies, however, men do not simply "earn" their wives in this negative sense. Rather, people seem to assume that men earn their wives as rewards for their own actions, and similarly to assume that men "earn" for themselves the privileges that having a wife entails. In this section, therefore, I will examine the meaning of a groom's gifts and services to his wife's kin in an attempt to reveal the senses in which men are understood to earn their wives.

The Meaning of Marriage Gifts

In societies appropriate for analysis with a brideservice model, men appear to earn their wives for three reasons. First, the gifts and services they give to women's kin are theirs to give. Men thus marry without incurring obligations to other men (or women). Second, the gifts a suitor gives are symbols of personal prowess. They are the products of his hunting and raiding—proof of his capacity to kill and fight. Third, the brides that bachelors acquire are not given to them by the women's kin. People may tell ethnographers that brothers "give" sisters or that women's parents "give" them to worthy bachelors, but these gifts of women do not grant the women's kin power over a bachelor's or husband's activities. Women's kin can "give" women, but they cannot withhold women or reclaim sisters and daughters if they do not like the recipient's behavior.

Men's gifts and services to in-laws are construed as earning a wife because the wider social context establishes that men must assert claims to women in competition with other men, and because women's kin have little power in situations where marriages are negotiated. Men's gifts to in-laws are construed as demonstrations to other men of their claims to women and their ability to defend them. And women's kin cannot consider suitors' gifts as their due because they lack the power either to give women or to take them back.

The obvious lifestyle difference between men who have wives and men who do not establishes a man's claim to women as the most important thing to be known about him. A man may need only one working wife to enjoy all the privileges of marriage, but both health and marriages are frail. Today's happily married man may be tomorrow's widower or deserted husband. As a result, people perceive a man's fate as resting on his claim to women. In brideservice societies, as we will see in the section on political processes, people understand all of a man's actions as statements about his claim to women.

And, in societies where men's claims to women are the final referent, all women—except, perhaps, the very old and the very young—appear to be taken. They all fall within some man's (or men's) orbit of claims. Brideservice societies vary in the extent to which men actively assert claims to women. In some, even unborn females are claimed (Hart & Pilling 1960); in others, men seem content with the wives they have (M. Rosaldo 1980). But in all these societies, women are a scarce good (see Collier & Rosaldo 1981: 291–92). In Comanche society, polygyny by older men apparently created a shortage of brides for younger ones. Wallace and Hoebel report that girls of 16 "were often married off to middle-aged men who could give a good bride-price," whereas boys had to wait until they were 25 to 30 before moving in with a woman (1952: 133).

This scarcity of women ensures that men who assert claims to women come into conflict with other men. To assert a claim to a particular woman is to deny a competitor's claim. In most human societies, of course, a man who marries declares that his wife is off limits to other potential marriage partners. But only in brideservice societies is marriage the most important determinant of a man's lifestyle and social possibilities. Only in such societies can one man's claim seriously prejudice the ability of his competitors to enjoy a reasonable life. A man who asserts a claim to a woman is not simply making a statement about his relationship to the woman and her family. He is simultaneously making a statement about his willingness and ability to violently defend his claim against the woman's other potential suitors.

Because a man's gifts and services to in-laws are understood as overt proof of this willingness and ability, those gifts and services do not stop when he moves in with his bride. They must continue for as long as he is willing to defend his claim to his wife. A Comanche husband, for example, "had to give the best part [of his meat] to his wife to take to her father" for as long as her father lived (Hoebel 1940: 119; Wallace & Hoebel 1952: 134). If a man were to stop giving gifts to a woman's kin, he would publicly proclaim his willingness to let her go.

Since grooms' gifts and services symbolize their willingness and ability to fight other men who contest their claims, grooms have to provide the gifts and services themselves. They cannot obtain the gifts from senior kin, as grooms do in equal and unequal bridewealth societies. It is not surprising that the Comanche considered it "far more respectable" for a groom to acquire his own horses to give to in-laws (Wallace & Hoebel 1952: 132). Were a bachelor to obtain horses from his father, he would publicly proclaim his failure as a warrior and raider. Therefore, it seems no accident that in most brideservice societies, a suitor's most publicized gifts to in-laws are the products of his hunting and raiding. I would imagine that suitors help in-laws with mundane tasks, but I know of no brideservice society whose ethnographers report that men "earn" brides by helping in-laws build houses, dig fields, or repair tools.

Although men appear to earn their brides by giving things that are theirs to give and that represent proof of their physical prowess, ethnographers of some brideservice societies report that elders arrange marriages or that women's kin give them to selected suitors. These reports seem to contradict reports that men earn their brides (for how can men both earn their brides and be given women), but they are easily reconciled. In a society where all women appear to be claimed, the bachelor who seeks a wife does not survey an open field of eligible marriage partners. Rather, he confronts a complex array of overlapping claims. Because elders and women's kin can support the claims of one suitor over another, they can appear to arrange marriages and to give away daughters or sisters. Women's kin cannot, however, provide a man with a wife. If a woman refuses to cooperate with her kin, there is little they can do. But a woman's kin can give her to a man in the limited sense of agreeing to accept that man's gifts instead of another's.

The Negotiation of Marriage

The wider social context may explain why men's gifts to in-laws are understood as proof of their willingness and ability to fight other men who contest their claims, but we need to examine the specific contexts in which marriages are negotiated if we are to understand why women's kin cannot consider suitors' gifts as their due. In brideservice societies, the conversations carried on in contexts where men acquire wives stress a groom's capacities and activities. They focus on what a groom does for his in-laws, not on what a man's in-laws do for him. The discourses establish men as "earning" brides. They do not establish women's kin as "having" daughters and sisters to give away. The discourses thus establish married men as being independent. A married man may be obliged to give the best portions of his meat to his wife's parents because if he neglects to do so, others will assume that he no longer cares to claim the woman as his wife. But a husband is not obliged to feed his wife's kin in the sense that his wife's kin have a recognized right to the products of his labor.

To understand why these conversations do not portray women's kin as having rights to the labor and products of men who marry kinswomen, we need to examine the powers available to people in contexts where marriages are negotiated. In brideservice societies, men appear to earn brides because women's kin have very little power. Women's kin can accept or refuse a man's gifts, and so publicly support or deny his claim against the claims of all other men. They can beat daughters or sisters who refuse to cooperate. But women's kin cannot "give" brides to hardworking suitors nor take back a daughter or sister from a husband they consider unworthy.[9]

The powerlessness of women's kin is revealed by two striking omissions in Hoebel's description of Comanche marriage law (1940). First, Hoebel does not discuss elopement, as he and Llewellyn do when describing Cheyenne marriage practices (1941: 1972–73), and as ethnographers of Kiowa society do (D. Collier 1938: 52; Richardson 1940: 112).[10] Second, Hoebel does not report instances of Comanche husbands asking their in-laws to return their wives to them, as he and Llewellyn do when writing about the Cheyenne (1941: 181) and as Richardson does when discussing Kiowa divorces (1940: 65).

My analysis suggests that Hoebel omitted a discussion of elopement from his description of Comanche law because the Comanche themselves did not differentiate between elopement and wife stealing. Because women's kin in brideservice societies cannot give them to husbands, the man who elopes with a girl is not thereby committing an offense against her kin. Rather, he is only stealing another man's wife or potential wife. And most brideservice societies lack recognized procedures that enable a husband to retrieve his wife from her kin because people lack contexts for developing the concept that a woman's kin may take or keep a woman from her husband.

In societies appropriate for analysis with a brideservice model, the inability of women's kin to give women to husbands is a result of their inability to shelter a daughter or sister from an abusive husband or from one who wishes to reclaim her. The reasons why women's kin cannot shelter them are complex. They are discussed briefly here and will be elaborated in the remainder of this chapter.

First, women's kin cannot shelter them because deserted husbands are cuckolded husbands. In societies where all women are, in some sense, claimed, the waning of one man's claims represents the waxing of another's. In brideservice societies, sexually mature women are, by definition, sexually active women. Women's kin, therefore, cannot keep a woman away from her husband without leaving themselves open to charges of furthering a rival potential husband's claim or of committing incest (see Hoebel 1940: 66–67). A sexually mature woman can live peacefully with her kin only so long as no man tries to assert husbandly claims to her.

Second, rejected sons-in-law perceive their rejection as an insult, not as an exercise of legitimate authority on the part of in-laws. In societies where men strive to establish and maintain a status that announces "don't fool with me," men interpret attempts to take things from them as questioning their capacity to take and keep what they want. Often they react violently and try to prove their capacity to obtain what they want by repossessing it. In brideservice societies, a disgusted husband can return his wife to her kin. But disgusted kin cannot keep a wife away from her husband—at least not without risking his violent revenge.[11]

Because a woman's kin cannot shelter her if she wants to leave her husband, women perceive their opportunities in life as determined by their own abilities and sexual attractiveness. Hoebel suggests that the only avenue of escape open to an unhappy Comanche wife "lay in absconding" with another man (1940: 73). A woman's kin thus have nothing to offer her to obtain her cooperation in marrying the man of their choice.

The weakness of women's kin in contexts where men assert

claims to women creates a situation in which grooms emphasize what they do for and give to the bride's kin, not a situation in which women's kin emphasize what they give to sons-in-law. Grooms emphasize what they give to in-laws because such gifts publicize both their claims to their brides and their capacity to defend those claims. But women's kin are not in a position to assert that suitors owe them gifts and services in return for being allowed to live with sisters or daughters. Because women's kin can neither give a woman to a worthy suitor nor take back a sister or daughter from an unworthy one, they can only announce their expectation of gifts and graciously accept those that are offered.

The conversations carried on when men assert claims to women thus establish men as "earning" their brides without incurring any long-term obligations to others, either their own kin or their in-laws. In brideservice societies, men appear to earn for themselves all the privileges available in their society—bachelors do not need help to acquire wives, and married men whose wives provide daily food and shelter need never ask anyone for anything. Once married, a man can appear truly independent. No one has any claim to his labor or its products.

The conversations also establish that women can be earned. Women, as we will see in the section on political processes, enjoy considerable autonomy in everyday life, but in the discourses surrounding marriage they are considered objects rather than subjects.

Production and Circulation

In brideservice societies, men "earn" not only their wives but also all the privileges that marriage brings. The dominant cultural representations of such groups do not portray men's privileges as deriving from the services of their wives. Rather, they portray men as earning shelter, hearth, and children. These representations portray people as having what they have because of their personal qualities, not because of their relationships with others. So men are portrayed as having wives because they earned them and are able to fight any man who contests their claim, not because their wives consent to live with them. And older men's qualities of hospitality, generosity, and political wisdom are portrayed as inherent, not as deriving from their positions as polygynous elders with growing daughters.

Anthropologists who write about the economies of foraging peoples tend to stress the lack of restrictions on access to the means of production (e.g. Fried 1967: 58) and the distribution pattern of "generalized reciprocity" (see Fried 1967: 64; Service 1979: 16–17). Such anthropologists suggest that neither the production nor the distribution system in these economies provides grounds for the unequal allocation of rewards. In a society where all members have unrestricted access to what they need in order to produce, and where produce (i.e. men's meat) is distributed widely without expectation of immediate return, no one enjoys privileged access to the labor or products of others. The inequalities in prestige that do exist, these anthropologists suggest, are a result of natural inequalities in abilities and skills. When brideservice peoples tell ethnographers that good hunters earn respect and extra wives, they seem to be reporting an obvious truth (see Fried 1967: 66).

Unlike most anthropologists, I do not stress the egalitarian nature of social relations in brideservice societies. Rather, I focus on the social bases of inequalities in prestige and privilege. People in brideservice societies do enjoy virtually unimpeded access to the means of production, and men do distribute their meat widely without expectation of return, but inequalities in prestige and possibilities do not therefore reflect differences in natural capacities. Everyone in brideservice societies gives things to other people, but the privileges and prestige that accrue to the giver are less a function of the gift than of the giver's social status. Women who are wives cannot earn wives, whatever their hunting skills.[12] And young men and women cannot reap the same benefits as older men from generosity, however much they give away.

The Meaning of Work

A striking fact about societies appropriate for analysis with a brideservice model is that people of all ages and of both sexes appear to have what they produce. Married women may be obliged to feed their families, and men may be obliged to distribute their meat widely after reserving the best portions for their in-laws, but the products that people have created or obtained are theirs to give. A woman's produce does not belong to her husband, nor do the choice portions of a hunter's kills belong to his in-laws. Because people's ability to earn privileges depends on having what they produce, I begin my analysis of how the circulation of things structures relations between people by examining the contexts in which people negotiate the meaning of work and its products.

In brideservice societies, there are no social contexts in which parents emphasize what they do for children; thus no contexts exist in which it makes sense for parents to construe children's labor and products as being owed to them. Marriage negotiations, as just noted, are contexts in which men discuss their claims to women, not in which parents discuss their claims to children. Nor do parents have the power to determine their children's futures. They can arrange marriages for growing boys by making agreements with the kin of eligible girls, but because men establish claims to wives in opposition to other men, each man must prove his own ability and willingness to fight others who threaten his claims to a woman. Similarly, parents cannot help daughters in quarrels with their husbands. Because women's kin lack the power to keep a married sister or daughter from her husband, women, like men, perceive their futures as dependent on their own abilities and resources.

Ethnographers commonly report that parents in these societies are indulgent toward children and demand little work from them. As already noted, Wallace and Hoebel write that Comanche boys were always treated with consideration and never given menial tasks (1952: 127). In a society where parents have no context in which to talk about how important their support will be for their children's futures, parents have no context in which to stress what their children should do for them. As a result, parents may ask children to perform tasks, but parents have no grounds to assume that children are obliged to obey.

If parents appear to demand little work from children, they also seem to provide little care for children past the ages of six or eight. Girls tend to remain with adult women, but boys often go off on their own. In Comanche society, boys went naked until the ages of eight or nine (Wallace & Hoebel 1952: 77); when older, they ran loose in gangs, rustling their food from the camp (1952: 130). In most brideservice societies, boys in their preteen and teen years fend for themselves. They run naked or dress in rags. They sleep in the open or in makeshift shelters. And they roam with friends, eating the small animals they kill and the vegetables they gather.

Boys thus grow up in a world where the few privileges they enjoy appear to result from their own efforts. No one provides for them, and no one makes demands on them. Boys control their own labor and its products. Consequently, when boys begin courting, the goods or labor they give to in-laws are theirs to donate. These young men are in a position where the most practical thing to do with their products is to give them away. Boys usually eat the small animals they kill, but once a youth begins killing large game, he and his cronies cannot consume all the meat themselves. They have to give some away. In Comanche society, a bachelor probably lacked the ability to process a whole bison. It would thus seem logical for him to give his kills to his future in-laws, or to a polygynous "older brother" who let the bachelor live with one of his wives. Similarly, a Comanche bachelor probably gave away most of the horses he acquired on raids. A man who had no wife to feed and care for the captive and slave children who herded horses in Comanche society (see Hoebel 1940: 15) probably had no way of keeping more than a couple of animals. As a result, a Comanche bachelor who lived near his desired bride's kin probably did "hunt and raid" for his in-laws, in the sense that he regularly gave them the products of his hunting and raiding.

In brideservice societies, everyone gives things away, but the meaning of peoples' gifts varies according to the context. Because such societies lack political agencies capable of protecting an individual's right to property, it is illogical for people to keep more things than everyone else has. But for the giver, the consequences of giving vary according to his or her life situation. The effect that gifts have on the relationship between giver and receiver is not determined by the intrinsic qualities of the gift or the giver's intentions, but by the giver's socially constituted characteristics. My analysis of circulation must thus be preceded by an analysis of existing statuses.

The Content of Statuses

Anthropologists commonly write that age and sex are the only criteria used to differentiate status in brideservice societies. Fried defines an "egalitarian society" as "one in which there are as many positions of prestige in any given age-sex grade as there are persons capable of filling them" (1967: 33). Age and sex are, indeed, the primary criteria used to differentiate status, but the privileges and possibilities of each category of age and sex are socially determined; they do not simply reflect biological differences between the sexes and ages.

Wallace and Hoebel report that the Comanche recognized five age groupings. For women these were infant, girl up to adolescence, adolescent girl, grown woman, and old woman. For men they were infant, boy up to adolescence, "young, unmarried brave," grown man, and old man (1952: 145). The Comanche reportedly expected different behaviors of men in the three adult age groupings. Young, unmarried braves were expected to be preoccupied with proving themselves as warriors, and grown men were expected to behave very differently from old men.

In the case of men, the ascribed status for old age differed radically from that for adults. The adult male was a warrior, vigorous, self-reliant, and aggressive. He took what he could get and held what he had without much regard for the abstract rights of those weaker than himself. A ready willingness to arbitrate differences or to ignore slights was a sign of weakness resulting in loss of prestige. The old man, on the other hand, was expected to be wise and gentle, willing to overlook slights, and, if need be, to endure abuse. It was his task to work for the welfare of the tribe, giving sound advice, smoothing down quarrels, and even preventing his tribe from making new enemies. Young men strove for war and honor; old men for peace and tranquillity. (1952: 146–47; see also Linton 1936: 121)

The Comanche were somewhat extreme in expecting such different behaviors of grown and old men. Nevertheless, ethnographers of other brideservice societies report similar, if less extreme, expectations about the behaviors of young, grown, and old men. Young, unmarried men are commonly expected to be concerned with proving themselves as hunters and killers. Grown men are expected to be concerned with maintaining a status that announces "don't fool with me." And old men are expected to be generously concerned with social welfare.

Although the behaviors brideservice peoples expect of young, grown, and old men correspond more or less to the male behaviors expected by people in industrialized capitalist societies and thus might appear to be natural, they are not. The three male age groupings, and their associated behavioral expectations, reflect socially constituted differences in privileges and possibilities that are determined by the organization of marriage.

As already noted, the most visible inequality in brideservice societies is that between married and unmarried men. Men who have wives never have to ask other men for anything. Men without wives must either live without women's products and services or obtain them from another man's wife. Therefore, in order to understand the privileges and possibilities available to men of different age groups, we need to examine the constraints and incentives that shape women's lives.

The conversations conducted during marriage negotiations may portray men as earning their wives and the privileges that marriage brings, but in fact, a man may enjoy the privileges of marriage only so long as his wife cooperates. A man has a place in the camp, the freedom to distribute his meat widely, the possibility of offering hospitality, and a voice in political affairs only so long as his wife tends her fire and provides daily food. The three stages of the male life cycle, therefore, do not correspond to male abilities or hormones, but rather to the timing of the socially constructed constraints and incentives that shape women's lives.

Marriage in brideservice societies is an achievement for men. It transforms excluded, wandering bachelors into settled, mature adults. But marriage is not an achievement for women. Unmarried girls, unlike bachelors, are not deprived; they are fed, desired, and courted. Girls thus think of marriage as imposing restrictions on their pleasures and freedoms. A girl who lacks a husband may play and flirt. But once a girl has a husband, she is expected to build a shelter, tend a hearth, and restrict her flirtations with other men. Husbands expect daily food and care, they beat wives they suspect of adultery, and instead of saving choice tidbits of meat for their wives, they give the best portions of their kills to a woman's parents.

Ethnographic evidence suggests that girls in brideservice societies want lovers but not husbands; they want sex, not marriage. Ethnographers report numerous instances of girls who are reluctant to marry, say they are too young, run away, take lovers, kill first babies, or refuse to work (see Turnbull 1961: 106; Thomas 1959; Shostak 1981; Siskind 1973; Murphy & Murphy 1974; Goodale 1971). Hoebel reports that Comanche brides escaped unwanted husbands by running off with lovers (1940: 49), or by shirking household duties until their husbands threw them out (1940: 73).

Because girls resist assuming the responsibilities of wifehood, marriage is actually a slow process rather than an event. Seniors may arrange marriages, or a girl's brothers may give her to a man, but these arrangements come to naught unless the girl cooperates. A girl's kin may beat her, and they frequently do. But if she keeps running away from her husband, openly courts lovers, or does nothing but cry all day, her kin usually give up. Ethnographers often report that first marriages have a high failure rate.

Girls may successfully resist particular unions, but they cannot resist marriage altogether, for their flirtations and affairs are too disruptive. In societies where men establish claims to women in competition with other men, women's affairs provoke violent confrontations between men. People may be indulgent toward the whims and flirtations of an adolescent girl, but no one—male or female—has much sympathy for the adult woman whose refusal to settle down endangers the lives of loved sons or brothers.

Although the conversations carried on during marriage negotiations may portray men as earning their wives by demonstrating their prowess, men actually acquire wives by being there when a girl gives up her adolescent flirtations. A bachelor may hope to persuade a girl to live with him, but in a society where all girls are potentially claimed and resist settling down, the most practical way for a bachelor to acquire a wife is to obtain the favor of an eligible girl's kin by giving them the products of his hunting and raiding. This enables him to hang around her until she grows up and to enlist the support of her kin in discouraging the attentions of other suitors.

In most brideservice societies, the birth of a child who is allowed to live marks the turning point in conjugal relations. Once a woman has a child to rear, she must provide daily food and shelter. Women with infants and toddlers also find it difficult to meet lovers in the bush (see Goodale 1971). Therefore, the presence of a child changes the context of a husband's demands for food, shelter, and sexual fidelity. He no longer appears to be asking his wife to do things she would not otherwise be doing. And he now has something to offer her in return. Ethnographers commonly describe fathers as actively and lovingly participating in child care.

In brideservice societies, marriage organizes the privileges and possibilities available to young, grown, and old men. The cultural category of "young, unmarried men" consists of those who lack wives or whose wives have not yet become mothers. "Grown men" are fathers of growing children. And "old men" are those with grown daughters or extra wives who are being courted by younger men. Men's status is a function of their relations with women, and these relations establish the context within which people assign meaning to men's and women's gifts.

The Meaning of Gifts

Ethnographers of brideservice societies seldom describe adult women as generous. Adult women do give things away. They share the food they gather, and they give away ornaments, baskets, and other objects they make or acquire. But married women can never give everything away. Because they are obliged to feed and care for their families, they must always hold back some of the vegetables they gather, the meat they receive, or the things they make. Married women must also ask others for things they need or want. When a woman is ill, she must ask other women to help feed her family. Women occasionally ask men to go hunting or to make the tools women need. And when meat is being distributed, it is usually women who ask for the family's share. Married women thus appear to be forever keeping things for themselves and asking others for things. It is little wonder that no ethnographer has written about women's generosity.

Men, in contrast to women, can appear to be generous. A man's ability to appear generous, however, varies according to his age/ status group. When ethnographers of brideservice societies write that young men are concerned with proving themselves, that grown men are concerned with maintaining a status that announces "don't fool with me," and that old men are concerned with generously helping others, they are accurately describing the meanings that people in brideservice societies assign to men's actions and gifts.

In Comanche society, young, unmarried braves were probably preoccupied with proving themselves as warriors. That is undoubtedly what everyone expected them to be doing. In brideservice societies, men in their late teens and early twenties who lack wives are expected to be concerned with acquiring them and therefore with demonstrating their prowess as hunters and raiders. It is also true that unmarried men have little else to do. They are not welcome in camp. When they are not off hunting and raiding, they are, by society's definition, being lazy or looking for trouble (i.e. for a woman to seduce).

Because of bachelors' obvious need for sex and wives, they inevitably appear selfishly concerned with their own affairs. When they give things to others, they appear to want something in return. Their gifts to lovers, potential in-laws, or polygynous elders who offer hospitality are understood as direct exchanges of meat for sex. Similarly, the gifts of a newly married man to his in-laws appear to be direct efforts to secure their goodwill and cooperation in maintaining his marriage. Young men, therefore, never seem generous, either to members of their own society or to ethnographers, even though they give away almost everything they produce.

Grown men, in contrast to younger ones, do not appear to be concerned with proving themselves and acquiring wives. A married man must maintain a status that announces "don't fool with me" to discourage other men from seducing his wife or wives, but he need not seek out occasions to prove his prowess. People assume that a man who has a wife must have already proven his vigor, self-reliance, and aggressiveness, and they have no reason to doubt his abilities as a hunter and warrior unless his wife is stolen or he stops hunting and raiding. People seek more immediate explanations for the hunting and raiding activities of married men.

Grown men and women appear to be concerned, not with acquiring things for themselves, but with fulfilling their acknowledged family obligations. They give away only what is left over after these have been fulfilled. Women work to feed and care for their families. Men hunt to provide meat for children and in-laws, and they fight to protect loved relatives. Men who have wives and growing children no longer appear to be irresponsible or engaged in direct exchanges of meat for sex. They, like their wives, seem preoccupied with family affairs. A man with young children who cry for meat appears to be hunting for his family and, in giving meat to his wife's parents, he appears to be fulfilling husbandly obligations. Marriage may start out as an inegalitarian relationship between a girl who is expected to feed her husband and a husband who hunts and raids for his in-laws, but marriages that last and produce children soon appear to be egalitarian.

Ethnographers commonly report that brideservice people practice "generalized reciprocity." Hunters, in particular, appear to distribute their meat widely without seeming to anticipate an immediate or a specific return. It is easy to understand why. Once a man has a wife who takes care of him, he does not need anything in return for his gifts. Similarly, a married woman who has kept back enough food and other basic necessities for her family can give the rest away without appearing to want an immediate return from the recipient.

When ethnographers write about what grown men and women expect to receive in return for their gifts, they stress men's and women's concern with establishing and maintaining cooperative relationships with others. Such men and women do not need direct returns from their gifts, but they do benefit from maintaining ties with others who will share work or help them in times of need. Women benefit by maintaining ties with kin, friends, and lovers who will share food with them or who will shelter them in times of warfare, or when husbands become abusive, or when they are widowed and want to escape from unwanted suitors supported by kin. Both men and women benefit by establishing ties with other parents of growing children. In brideservice societies, parents whose children marry within the group can look forward to being surrounded by supportive kin in their old age. And men benefit by asserting or maintaining claims to possible secondary wives. Men and women in their middle years may not expect direct returns from their gifts, but they do appear to hope for cooperation and eventual returns from recipients.

Old men, in contrast to young and grown men and all women, can appear to be truly generous. Once a man reaches the age of 40 and has daughters whose suitors or husbands give him meat, and in-laws who are either dead or dependent on his goodwill to remain near their daughter, he appears to have neither obligations nor needs. He can thus give things away without appearing to be fulfilling obligations or wanting anything in return. Not all old men are generous. But in brideservice societies, only old men can appear to be completely altruistic.

More important, old men are in a position where they no longer appear to be competing with other men for wives. Old men do marry secondary wives, but they can present their acquisitions as rightfully theirs. First, the claims of older men usually antedate the claims of younger ones. Second, it seems right that men who plan and lead war parties should have first pick of captured women. And third, social customs such as the levirate and sororate, which are frequently found in brideservice societies, permit married men to rightfully claim dead brothers' wives and wives' younger sisters.

Instead of competing with other men for women, old men appear to be concerned with helping other men to acquire wives. Once a man has secondary wives, he can generously offer hospitality to unmarried "brothers." Once he has claims to several women, he can generously cede his claims to others. And once he has growing daughters, he can generously help bachelors acquire wives.

In societies where (as we will see in the next section) all conflicts between men appear to be over women, old men emerge as natural leaders. If they no longer appear to be competing for women, then it is difficult for people to blame them for starting fights. And if they generously help other men acquire wives, they appear to actively promote peace. People can thus credit old men with establishing and maintaining the cooperative relationships that are so necessary—yet seem so fragile—in brideservice societies.

As old men begin to retire from active hunting and raiding, those who have acquired reputations as peacemakers appear to have the image confirmed. To the extent that an old man spends more time in camp and less time away demonstrating his capacity for violence by killing animals and enemies, he appears to be concerned with ensuring group welfare rather than with maintaining a status that announces "don't fool with me." Because he has neither needs nor wants, generously helps other men acquire wives, and appears to be concerned with the general welfare, an old man becomes eligible to tell others what they should do. His advice can appear to be selfless. It is the kind of advice that a grown man may heed without appearing to sacrifice his self-reliance. In short, old men are the political leaders. They may not be able to give orders, but they can tell others what they ought to do.

This brief analysis of how marriage organizes people's interpretations of men's and women's gifts in brideservice societies provides the context for understanding Wallace and Hoebel's description of the Comanche as recognizing three age groupings for adult men with associated behavioral expectations. It also suggests an explanation for a puzzling feature of Comanche society. Although all ethnographers describe the Comanche as egalitarian, available information suggests that horses were unequally distributed. Wallace and Hoebel report that some prestigious warriors had no horses because they had given them all away (1952: 131), and Hoebel tells of a man who died leaving an estate of 1,000 to 1,500 horses (1940: 123; see also Linton 1936: 297). How could a society with such an unequal distribution of the means of production lack inequities in the distribution of prestige, power, and privilege? The analysis of marriage suggests an answer.

Elders could accumulate huge herds because younger men had many reasons for giving them horses. Courting bachelors gave horses to in-laws. Young men gave horses to medicine men in return for their help in seeking supernatural powers. And seducers gave horses to husbands they cuckolded. Young men also had good reasons for not keeping more than one or two animals. Bachelors and newly married men lacked the several wives necessary to feed and care for the captive children who herded horses in Comanche society. It was prestigious for a man to give away horses he captured on a raid; ethnographers report that a man who distributed all his captured horses thereby proclaimed his power to acquire more (Wallace & Hoebel 1952: 131; Linton 1936: 143). And because horse raiding was prevalent on the Plains, it was unwise for a grown man—who needed to maintain a reputation for taking what he wanted and keeping what he had—to have more easily rustled horses than he used on a daily basis.

Old men were also in a position to maintain large herds. Polygynous elders had the wives necessary to feed and care for the captive children who herded horses. And such elders probably did not have to worry about maintaining a status that announced "don't fool with me." If horses were rustled from a polygynous elder who could recite many heroic deeds, or if one of his wives were seduced, people would probably blame his losses on the cleverness of horse thieves or the fickleness of women; they would not question his willingness or ability to kill his enemies.

The old men who accumulated large herds, however, were not able to enjoy the power, prestige, and privilege that such apparent ownership of the means of production would grant in a capitalist society, because younger men had no reason to ask senior men to give them horses, nor could they accept them if offered. Young men could easily care for or borrow (see Linton 1936: 297) the one or two horses they needed to hunt and raid. The Comanche did not consider it appropriate for a courting youth to ask his father to provide the horses he gave as gifts to in-laws. Nor did junior men ask their kin for horses to placate lovers' husbands. Outraged Comanche husbands commonly demanded a seducer's favorite horse; if the seducer lacked horses, the husband might ridicule or whip the seducer instead (Hoebel 1940: 58–59).[13] Young and grown men also had reason to refrain from accepting gifts of horses. If giving horses indicated a giver's power to acquire more, then accepting horses without giving a woman or providing help in obtaining supernatural power must have been taken as a sign of the accepter's inability to acquire animals on his own. The horses that entered old men's herds thus stayed in them. Horses were unequally distributed in Comanche society. But power, prestige, and privilege were not.[14]

Up to this point, I have discussed how the socially constituted characteristics of individuals determine the meanings that people assign to their gifts and actions. The constraints and incentives that shape women's lives structure what people assume actors and givers intend by their behaviors. The people who live in brideservice societies, however, seldom have reason to discuss the role of women's possibilities in structuring the meaning of actions and gifts. They take this role for granted. Instead, people talk about the consequences that a person's gifts and actions have for his or her relations with others. In their conversations, therefore, people misrepresent the relationship between a person's socially constituted characteristics and the person's gifts and actions. Instead of recognizing the role of socially constituted characteristics in determining the motives they assign to the behaviors of givers and actors, people portray a person's gifts and actions as determining his or her social characteristics. Ethnographers faithfully record this misrepresentation.

In brideservice societies, dominant cultural representations portray men as earning both their wives and the self-reliance available to a married man whose wife provides all his daily needs. It is obvious to everyone that the reason a married man need never ask anyone for anything is because his wife provides him with a shelter, hearth, and sexual services. Therefore, the role of women in providing the services that privilege married men over bachelors requires no discussion. But people frequently have occasion to wonder whether a particular bachelor will acquire a bride, or if a particular married man will keep his wife. And when they wonder, they focus on the actions of men. They assume that each woman will perform wifely services for some man; they merely wonder which man the woman will provide services for. They thus discuss a bachelor's or married man's ability to assert or enforce his claims against other men who might try to steal the woman. As a result, they represent their social world as one in which bachelors earn their wives, and married men keep them, through demonstrations of personal prowess.

This cultural representation is apparently confirmed by everyday experience. In brideservice societies, men who have wives tend to be more active hunters and raiders than bachelors, thus establishing an obvious correlation between a man's record in killing animals and enemies and his right to women.

Ethnographers frequently report that bachelors are reluctant hunters (see Siskind 1973) and that they turn back from raids complaining of sore feet or intestinal troubles (see Chagnon 1968: 130). It may seem odd that young men are reluctant hunters and raiders, given that the cultural representations of brideservice societies commonly portray hunting and raiding as the way to acquire a wife. Bachelors, however, have no reason to kill more animals or enemies than they need to satisfy the immediate demands of potential in-laws and to establish their reputations as men who can hunt and raid if they wish. The bachelor who kills more animals and enemies does not earn more wives. Meat can be traded for sex, but not for wives. And when women are captured on raids, they are usually taken into the households of senior men. It is thus not surprising that bachelors are reluctant hunters and warriors. They have little to gain from appearing industrious, and it is dangerous to chase animals and enemies.

Nor is it surprising that people in brideservice societies usually blame bachelors for their wifelessness. Their youth, freedom, and frequent handsomeness may earn them many lovers, but because bachelors also tend to be lazy, cowardly, irresponsible, selfish, and moody, people have no difficulty finding a ready explanation for why bachelors lack wives and for why no one pays much attention to what they say.

Married men, in contrast, have good reasons for hunting and fighting. They have children who cry for meat, and they have wives and families to protect. As a result, most married men hunt frequently, and they do not turn back from raids. And because the number of animals bagged and enemies killed tends to correlate with the amount of time a man spends hunting and raiding, married men also appear to be more successful hunters and raiders than bachelors. People in brideservice societies thus have no difficulty finding an explanation for why married men have wives, and for why others listen to them when they speak.

The cultural representations of brideservice societies also portray political leaders as earning their authority to advise others about what they ought to do. Because not all men who live past the age of 40 are successful hunters or give women away, people who wonder why a particular old man enjoys prestige focus on what differentiates this man from his age mates. They have no reason to discuss how the constraints and incentives that shape women's lives determine the possibilities open to old men. They need only wonder why some men realized those possibilities when others did not. As a result, dominant cultural representations portray respected old men as earning the esteem they enjoy through their wisdom and their generosity in helping other men acquire wives.

This portrayal is confirmed by people's everyday experience. Old men do appear wiser than younger men because others accept their suggestions. As men who are no longer actively hunting and raiding, old men can offer the apparently selfless advice that a grown man may heed without seeming to sacrifice his self-reliance. Successful political leaders also appear to give women to other men. In societies where men seek to maintain a status that announces "don't fool with me," it is illogical for a man to assert claims to more women than he is willing to defend. A man with too many adulterous wives must endure a life of constant battle. As a result, most old men who acquire several wives, and assert claims to many women, generously cede their extra wives and claims to other men. The cultural representation that political leaders earn respect by displays of generosity is also confirmed by the few old men who do not give women away but try to collect them instead. Such men are not respected. The Comanche thought they were witches (Wallace & Hoebel 1952: 147).

Not only do the everyday experiences of people in brideservice societies appear to confirm the cultural representation that men earn and keep their wives through demonstrations of personal prowess, but such experiences also provide people with few occasions for questioning the accuracy of this representation. People may say that men earn their wives through hunting and raiding, but successful hunters and raiders do not put this proposition to the test. They have the good sense not to claim the rewards their behavior supposedly earns. Bachelors who perform prodigious feats of bravery, for example, do not demand wives in return for their exploits. Nor do successful hunters try to trade their meat for wives. As a result, people who live in brideservice societies seldom have to provide explanations for why someone who performed a valued behavior did not receive the posited reward.

Political Processes

The everyday experiences of people in brideservice and in all societies may confirm dominant cultural representations and provide people with few occasions for questioning their validity, but it is in situations of conflict that such representations become self-fulfilling prophecies and so become established as guides for behavior. When people come into conflict, cultural assumptions about how to succeed, or fail, have real consequences for their lives. In brideservice societies, the understanding that men earn and keep their wives through demonstrations of personal prowess becomes established as truth in conflicts between men over women. As discussed in the previous section, men do not earn their wives through hunting and raiding. They acquire wives by being there when a woman settles down, which usually occurs when she has a living child to rear. But in conflicts between men over women, the man who fails to demonstrate sufficient prowess tends to lose his wife to another man.

Hoebel, in discussing Comanche law, writes that Comanche legal principles were greatly influenced by the male ideal of the warrior who realized himself in "striving for accumulated war honors, horses, and women" (1954: 131). Hoebel thus suggests that law and values are analytically separate domains. In every society, there are people who do wrong and who must be corrected, punished, or removed. And every society has values that determine how these measures are effected.

In contrast to Hoebel, I treat law and values as two sides of the same coin. In every society, people have systems of meaning that shape their perception of conflict and their understanding of how to handle it. The Comanche did not have a legal system that could be analytically separated from their values. They had recurring conflicts, engendered by inequalities in the organization of privileges and responsibilities, and perceived as arising from challenges to some man's reputation for bravery.

The Causes of Conflict

Ethnographers commonly report that sex, not property, is the major cause of conflict in simple egalitarian societies (see Fried 1967: 75). Adultery and wife stealing are the most commonly mentioned reasons for fights among men. A careful reading of ethnographies, however, reveals that these people quarrel over a variety of issues. They resent each others' stinginess, laziness, or carelessness; they fight over objects; women fight other women who flirt with their husbands or lovers. But none of these conflicts has as serious consequences for interpersonal relations as men's conflicts over women. In brideservice societies, "sexual tensions" appear to be the cause of most conflict, because all conflicts between men, no matter what the precipitating event, can be interpreted as being over women.[15]

In societies where the most visible inequality in lifestyle and privilege is that between married and unmarried men, a married man's loss of his wife, particularly if she was his only wife, is the most terrible thing that can happen to him. No other event can so dramatically affect his possibilities and relations with others, for it means a radical change in his lifestyle and influence. The widowed or abandoned husband whose daily needs were met and who was assured a secure place in the camp becomes an untended wanderer. A man who formerly offered hospitality to other men becomes a beggar who must either go without women's services or obtain them from another man's wife. A political actor whose words were heeded becomes an outcast, suspected of wanting to seduce other men's wives and blamed for his sorry state.

Women in these societies can never suffer an equivalent loss of privilege or influence. Because women provide their own food and shelter and receive meat when it is distributed, loss of a husband does not result in a drastic change in lifestyle or loss of respect. Women are never in a position to fail (see Siskind 1973); nor are they ever in a position to succeed. Because women never experience the misery of bachelorhood and cannot marry wives, they can never be credited with earning a shelter, a hearth, and a place in the camp.

As a result, a husband's adultery does not threaten a woman in the same way that a wife's adultery threatens her husband's claim to the influence and privileges of adult status. Ethnographers com-

monly report that women resent their men's affairs with other
women. Gladwin reports that Comanche wives staged jealous
scenes (1948: 86). But however jealous or angry a woman may be,
her husband's or lover's affairs have a very different meaning to her
than hers do to him. Not only do men need wives in a way that
women do not need husbands, but men must earn brides in competition with other men. Men are not scarce goods as women are.

Because of the importance of wives in men's careers, it is easy to
understand why men perceive adultery and wife stealing as serious
threats. Since dominant cultural representations credit men with
earning their wives, people commonly blame men for losing them.
Adultery and wife stealing are perceived less as fights over a particular woman than as challenges to the cuckolded husband's
reputation for being able to keep what he claims as his. Hoebel writes that in Comanche society, "adultery and taking another's
wife were direct attacks upon the prestige of the wife's husband.
Both acts were unmistakable challenges which could not be ig-
nored by the man who would maintain enough face to make life
liveable" (1940: 50).

When a man loses his wife, and so loses his home, shelter, and
hearth, it is obvious to everyone why he appears hungry, unkempt,
and unwanted. The interesting question is not, why is this man
miserable? but rather, why did this particular man, not some other
one, lose his wife? People do, of course, blame the woman, but
more important, they begin to question the husband's ability to
keep what he claims as his. In societies where overlapping claims to
women mean that men must earn wives in competition with other
men, the man who loses his wife appears to lack the abilities that
other men—particularly his cuckolder—possess. The man who
loses his wife is thus put in the position of having to prove that the
fault was not his. He must show that he possesses capacities equal
to those of his cuckolder. He must prove that he is capable of
defending what he *wants* to defend.

In the end, it is a man's reputation, not his claims to particular
women, that determines his possibilities. The man who establishes
a reputation for not being able to keep what he claims as his becomes vulnerable to attempts by other men to seduce his wives,
sisters, and daughters (see Chagnon 1968). The man with a reputation for bravely defending his claims, in contrast, can afford to give
away troublesome and adulterous wives without people questioning his ability to take and keep the women he wants.

In brideservice societies, the man who maintains a status that announces "don't fool with me" (see Fried 1967: 79) has control over his life and possibilities. He seldom has to defend his claims because other men think twice before fooling with him. The man who allows himself to be suspected of cowardice, however, loses control over his life. He becomes vulnerable to being treated as if he did not count; other men seduce his women, and people ignore his words. The man who establishes a reputation for responding violently to suspected insults can live peacefully with others. The man who becomes known as a coward cannot. He faces continual insults until he fights back.

Hoebel, in writing about the Comanche, attributes the apparent prevalence of adultery and wife stealing to (1) a romantic ideal of marriage for love that ran counter to the custom of arranged marriages between young girls and older men, and (2) male status competition that was expressed "in the taking of women from their husbands" (1940: 49).

But a reported prevalence of adultery and wife stealing can be explained without resorting to speculations about men's motives for seducing or stealing other men's wives. In brideservice societies, all conflicts between men, whatever event precipitates them, can be interpreted as being over women. Any incident that calls into question a man's ability to take and keep what he wants calls into question his ability to acquire and keep women. And because all women are in some sense claimed, people can always find a woman in whom the two contestants' claims overlap.

The Handling of Conflict

The procedures people use to manage conflict are not influenced by a separate set of values, as Hoebel implies in writing about the Comanche. They derive from peoples' understanding of the causes and consequences of conflict. If a conflict between men is understood as a challenge to some man's reputation for bravery, then all subsequent events are interpreted as indications of the challenged man's ability to maintain a status that announces "don't fool with me."

In writing about Comanche men's reactions to being cuckolded, Hoebel distinguishes between brave men and cowards (1940: 51–53). "A real man" went alone to confront his wife's seducer; he did not ask other men to accompany him (Hoebel 1954: 135). In brideservice societies, people interpret a challenged man's actions as indications of his bravery, a quality they presume existed before he acted. But this interpretation reverses cause and effect. The correlation between bravery and chosen procedure does not result from the fact that brave men and cowards choose different options when cuckolded. It results from the fact that people assess a man's bravery on the basis of which option he chooses. In Comanche society, "a real man" went alone because if he did not, he was obviously not "a real man."

Ethnographers of brideservice societies commonly report that when conflicts cannot be defused by talk, "then some form of contest is held" (Service 1979: 53). It is easy to understand why. If conflicts between men are interpreted as challenges to one man's reputation for bravery, then those that are not defused can be settled only by utilizing mechanisms that allow the challenged man to reestablish his reputation as someone who is not to be fooled with. Conflicts are necessarily contests between the two men involved. They cannot be mediated, arbitrated, or adjudicated by outsiders. Only the challenged man can repair his damaged reputation. If he allows another man to intercede for him, he merely proves his inability to keep what he claims as his.[16]

Hoebel reports that "the immediate goal" of a cuckolded Comanche husband "was to get restitutive damages" in the form of horses from his wife's seducer (1954: 135). Horses, however, could not have served as restitution for the lost wife. A man could not use the horses to acquire another woman. He could give the horses to potential in-laws, but those in-laws could not guarantee the woman's cooperation in return. In any case, the Comanche probably interpreted a groom's gifts of horses as proof of his prowess as a raider, not as payment for a woman.

Taking a horse could reestablish a husband's reputation, however. If a cuckold was, by definition, someone from whom something had been taken, thus calling into question his ability to take and keep what he wanted, then his most appropriate response was to prove that ability by taking something away from the person who had taken something away from him. Hoebel reports that a cuckolded Comanche husband often demanded the seducer's favorite horse, which he then killed (1940: 56). Taking a seducer's favorite horse was an excellent way for a cuckolded husband to publicize his ability to take what he wanted. And killing the horse both demonstrated the husband's lack of need (he took the horse because he wanted to, not because he needed a horse) and ensured that the cuckolder could not humiliate the husband again by taking the horse back.[17]

This interpretation of what the Comanche thought cuckolds were aiming to do when they demanded "restitutive damages" is supported by Hoebel's observation that "the one outstanding factor around which the settlement of a dispute turned was not the question of the right or wrong of the situation, but rather the relative bravery in warfare of the two parties involved" (1940: 54). The Comanche did not think that the number and quality of horses a man extracted from his wife's seducer reflected the nature or extent of the seducer's wrong, the value of the woman, or the quantity of gifts and services the husband had provided for his in-laws. But in interpreting the outcome of disputes between men as determined by their relative bravery, the Comanche were, once again, reversing cause and effect. Relative bravery did not determine the outcome; the outcome provided people with the evidence they used to assess contestants' bravery.

In all three of the Plains societies I use as examples for the models presented in this book, cuckolded husbands demanded horses from wives' lovers, but such demands had a profoundly different meaning in each society. An outside observer who never asked people what they were doing might conclude that adulterers in all three societies incurred liability to pay restitutive damages to husbands they cuckolded. But the cuckolds in all three societies were only superficially performing the same act (demanding horses from wives' lovers). As I argue throughout this book, meaning does not inhere in acts; it inheres in contexts. The cuckolded Comanche husband who demanded horses from his wife's lover was thought to be reestablishing his reputation for bravery. He was not presumed to be seeking compensation for his loss, as his Cheyenne counterparts were presumed to be doing, or validation of his rank, as was presumed of Kiowa cuckolds.

Ethnographers often assume that contests in brideservice societies, like contests in our own society, have winners and losers. This assumption is reflected in Hoebel's observation that the outcome of Comanche confrontations turned on "the relative bravery in warfare of the two parties involved" (1940: 54). I, however, do not believe that contests in brideservice societies differentiate winners from losers. Such contests are most effective when they allow both sides to demonstrate appropriate bravery. A contest may have a winner in the sense that one man may seem more aggressive, agile, or intelligent than his opponent. But if a contest is to promote peace, there cannot be a loser. Each contestant must be allowed to prove his ability to aggressively defend what he claims as his.

If men in brideservice societies need to establish and maintain a status that announces "don't fool with me," then contests that have losers promote conflict, not peace. If a contest ends with one man's reputation for bravery cast into doubt, then that man must stage another confrontation if he is to reestablish his reputation. Contests promote peace only if they end with both contestants having established their reputations for bravery. Indeed, contest audiences in these societies are probably less concerned with deciding which contestant is braver than with seeing whether each contestant has the capacity to defend what he claims as his. This need for both contestants to demonstrate prowess suggests an explanation for the reported role of leaders in managing contests. A leader may not be able to mediate, arbitrate, or adjudicate a dispute. But he can intervene in a contest to ensure that both sides fight fairly and that each man has ample opportunity to demonstrate his prowess (see Chagnon 1968: 95).

Leadership

Men's need to maintain a status that announces "don't fool with me" also suggests an explanation for Fried's observation that men in simple egalitarian societies "do not seem to display any drive for universal dominance within their group" (1967: 79). In the preceding section on production and circulation, I noted that brideservice societies have respected leaders—men who have established reputations for wisdom and generosity and who exercise considerable influence. But respect is not gained by dominating other men. The reverse is, in fact, true. The man who tries to dominate others provokes conflict and fear. The man who boasts of being a better hunter or warrior than his fellows arouses their desire to prove their equality with him. The senior man who tries to keep women, rather than giving them away, is feared as being evil. And the man who aggressively tries to take women or things from other men risks being assassinated by his angry fellows.

But if men do not display any drive to dominate other men, "they do display a considerable drive to achieve parity" (Fried 1967: 79). Equality is a positive value in brideservice societies because inequality is the condition that breeds strife. And equality is realized in a status that announces "don't fool with me" because only after a man has established a reputation for being able to keep what he claims as his can he cooperate—rather than fight—with other men.

As I noted in the beginning of this chapter, ethnographers of brideservice societies commonly report that leaders lack the power to give orders. Hoebel, for example, writes that the Comanche peace chief had "a certain authority as counsellor-to-the-population-at-large," but his advice was heeded only if others thought it was right and proper (1940: 19). This lack of power is easy to understand. In a society where attempts to dominate others provoke conflict, the leader who tries to give orders encourages resistance rather than compliance. And in a society where each man must establish and maintain a status that announces "don't fool with me," a man can heed a leader's advice without having his reputation called into question only if he appears to accept the leader's advice because he believes it is right.

In brideservice societies, the man who lacks a wife, and thus is visibly not equal with his fellows, is feared as a source of conflict—not simply because people believe he will attempt to seduce other men's wives, but because they believe he will undoubtedly seek occasions to prove his capacity for violence. Consequently, bachelors are not trusted, and people shun the abandoned husband. As long as a man lacks a wife, he cannot be counted on to cooperate with other men.

This attitude explains why "giving wives" is the prime political act in brideservice societies. By "giving wives" to bachelors, senior men turn unreliable and uncooperative bachelors into responsible, cooperating adults. "Giving wives" is perceived as the act that turns competitors into allies. Lévi-Strauss's (1969) "alliance theory" may or may not be useful for analyzing all kinship systems, but it does explain the perceptions of people in brideservice societies, such as the Amazonian groups he studied. In these societies, the man who gives up his sister by observing the incest taboo does "give a wife" to another man. The bond between brothers-in-law who give each other sisters as wives is the symbol of cooperation. The bond between brothers, whom incest taboos cast as competitors for women, is the symbol of conflict. Hoebel reports that a Comanche cuckold addressed his wife's seducer as "brother" (1954: 135). Many brideservice peoples appear to elaborate the distinction between "brothers-in-law" and "brothers" into a moiety system. Brideservice peoples do not seem to divide the social world into unequal "male" and "female" (or "high" and "low") halves. But they often divide it into equivalent, intermarrying halves. For a man in many brideservice societies, all same-generation men are either "brothers" or "brothers-in-law," and all same-generation women are either "sisters" or "wives."

The development of factional politics has not been observed in all brideservice societies, but where it has been reported, the factions appear to be composed of men who help each other acquire and keep wives. Faction cores consist of brothers-in-law who exchange sisters and close brothers who share women instead of competing for them (see Chagnon 1968). The Comanche may have had such factions. Wallace and Hoebel write that "brothers with their sisters formed a marriage group, which established relationships with another marriage group on the basis of inter-family exchange marriage" (1952: 139). And Comanche brothers did "[lend] each other their wives" (1952: 138).

If the Comanche had factions, then the famous Comanche champion-at-law (see Hoebel 1940: 62–65)—the outstanding warrior who reclaimed lost wives for brotherless cuckolds but received neither horses nor women in return—would appear to have been a faction leader. In Comanche society, the cuckold who did not go alone to face his wife's seducer necessarily appeared less brave than his opponent. But if the cuckold's wife had been taken by one of the most feared men in the group, people probably would have understood the cuckold's reluctance to face his enemy. Nevertheless, the man whose wife was taken from him must have become a liability to his allies. Because he lacked a wife, he must have appeared unreliable, uncooperative, and volatile. It would therefore have made sense for the faction leader to try to recover the wife—or at least to maintain the prestige of his faction—by facing the seducer in the cuckold's stead. This interpretation suggests that the champion-at-law was not "acting in the interest of the general social welfare" and "upholding the law of marriage," as Hoebel writes (1954: 137), but that he was acting in the interest of his own faction. The glory he acquired in facing a renowned warrior was not his only reward.[18]

Folk Models of Social Structure and Human Agency

Ethnographers commonly report that people in simple egalitarian societies recognize few rules. The explanation they usually give is that nomadic foragers have little need for rules (see Roberts 1979: 82), for they live in small family groups, lack marked inequalities, and have little to fight over. My analysis, however, indicates that people in brideservice societies lack established bodies of rules because their understanding of the causes and consequences of conflict focus attention on the intentions and prowess of the contestants; the rights or wrongs of their cases are perceived as irrelevant to the outcome of a dispute. Because people in brideservice societies have no contexts in which to develop and articulate rules, they are unable to recite lists of rules to visiting ethnographers.

This lack of rules is also reflected in ethnographers' reports that people "follow their hearts" (see M. Rosaldo 1980; Shostak 1981). When members of brideservice societies talk about behavior, they usually portray action as motivated by desire, not as dictated by rules, duties, obligations, or the rational contemplation of ends and means. Hoebel writes that Comanche "accounts of their war parties as often as not [began] with a laconic 'once there was a bunch of Comanches out looking for trouble' " (1954: 133). Instead of talking about retaliation, revenge, or a need for plunder, the Comanche described war parties as simply resulting from the unmotivated desires of participants.

The tendency of brideservice peoples to talk of following their hearts may explain Hoebel's description of Comanche behavior as "adolescent," in contrast to the "maturity" of Cheyenne behavior (1954: 130). The everyday American understanding, like that of people in brideservice societies, defines desire, not duties or obligations, as the cause of action. But according to the American understanding, the mature person, unlike the adolescent, stops to think about the consequences of an action before acting. Because the Comanche did not describe consideration of consequences as intervening between desire and action, they would appear adolescent to an American observer.[19]

Hoebel writes that among the Comanche, "personal power was the recognized basis of social relations between men" (1954: 137). This statement could be made about most brideservice peoples. In societies without established bodies of rules, where people appear to "follow their hearts," and where leaders can give only advice, not orders, people can be expected to perceive the ability to prevail despite resistance as depending on a person's forcefulness. Among the Comanche, "*ability* to possess was 'nine points of the law' " (Hoebel 1940: 66, italics his).

In brideservice societies, violence is exhorted and admired. The man who would maintain face sufficient to make life liveable must be ready to maintain a status that announces "don't fool with me." In a society where ability to possess is "nine points of the law," a man must be willing to fight for what is his. And if personal power is recognized as the basis of social relations, a man who would establish relations with others must demonstrate a willingness and a capacity to use violence.

Violence is also decried and condemned. The same people who exhort and admire violence in some contexts will avoid and deplore it in others. Violence appears to be an ever-present threat to the cooperative relations on which social life depends. In societies where people talk of "following their hearts," leaders lack the power to give orders, and goods cannot compensate individuals for their losses, nothing appears to intervene between anger and its expression in violence. In brideservice societies, people perceive no alternatives to fighting, with its consequent injuries and deaths (see Thomas 1959: 22).

Because violence is perceived as an ever-present threat, cooperative bonds—thought necessary for survival—appear fragile. As a result, cooperation takes on the semblance of an achievement. Senior men, who turn violent competitors into cooperative allies by appearing to give women, seem to have almost mystical powers. They make social life possible. Thus people have reason to respect their words. Cooperative bonds, I suggest, are no more fragile in brideservice societies than in any society. Humans are social animals. It is an irony of history that because people in brideservice societies perceive cooperative bonds as fragile, the apparently simplest human societies provide appropriate examples of a Hobbesian state of nature.[20]

This ever-present threat of violence provides a basis for understanding apparently contradictory reports about the status of women in brideservice societies. Ethnographers of some groups describe women as the powerless and abused pawns of men (e.g. Hoebel 1940; Chagnon 1968). Ethnographers of others describe women as autonomous (e.g. Leacock 1978; Draper 1975). While the amount of abuse women endure or the autonomy they enjoy varies from society to society, both aspects coexist in every group appropriate for analysis with a brideservice model. The ever-present threat of violence provides both a cultural justification for men to abuse women and a practical reason for men to respect women's autonomy.

In societies where "giving women" appears to be the act that turns enemies into allies, women have to be defined in political discourse as giveable. Hoebel writes that the Comanche woman was "a chattel, first to her father and brother, later to her husband" (1940: 119). Comanche women, however, could not have been chattels in the same way Roman slaves were. Hoebel's description of girls' unwillingness to settle down suggests that Comanche parents, like parents in most brideservice societies, had little control over their daughters. But Hoebel's choice of word does reflect, I think, Comanche political discourse. Because the nineteenth century Comanche were engaged in constant warfare, they had many occasions to talk about men giving women to, and stealing them from, potential enemies.

The definition of women as giveable suggests an explanation for reports of violence against women in brideservice societies. Because "giving women" is perceived as the act that turns enemies into allies, women's refusal to cooperate is perceived as the act that turns allies into enemies. If men who "give women" appear to make social life possible, then women who refuse to be given seem to destroy the bonds of cooperation on which everyone depends. If all fights between men, whatever their precipitating event, are perceived as being over women, then logically, men would not fight if women were not there to provoke them. The cultural logic of brideservice societies thus provides a justification for blaming all conflict, violence, and social disruption on women.[21]

Men in these societies—either individually or in gangs—occasionally rape, beat, torture, or kill uncooperative or unfaithful women. If a young woman refuses to settle down with one man and, in so doing, appears to cause fights among men, then it makes sense for men to join together to "tame" such a woman by raping her (see Murphy & Murphy 1974). And if an unfaithful wife causes a confrontation between her husband and her lover, then it seems reasonable for a husband to beat or torture the unfaithful wife whose affairs may cause him to lose his life. Women have no comparable justification for beating men. In brideservice societies, even women seem to blame other women for causing the fights that endanger the lives of loved sons, brothers, and husbands (see Hoebel 1940: 113).

In societies where conflict leads inevitably to violence, and where political leaders lack the power to settle disputes or arrange compensation, removing the presumed cause of a conflict may seem to be a logical way to avoid the violence everyone fears. Men may thus kill the sisters or wives whose adulterous affairs threaten to disrupt tenuous political alliances. And a husband may kill or mutilate an adulterous wife whom he can neither control nor give to her lover without losing prestige. Hoebel reports that "in seven of forty-five Comanche adultery and wife-absconding cases the women were slain by their husbands—one in seven! Three of these were adulteresses; four were absconders. Of the twenty other adulteresses five were mutilated by their husbands; four had their noses cut off, and one had the soles of her feet slashed so she could not walk" (1954: 139).

In brideservice societies, people may kill or destroy what is defined as theirs, but a man who would maintain a reputation for bravery cannot afford to have things taken from him. A woman, because she is defined within political discourse as giveable, may be killed by the men who give or receive her—her kin or her husband. But a man, because he is never defined as giveable, cannot be killed without having his murder perceived as an affront to his kinsmen. They must avenge his death if they are to maintain their reputations for bravery. Hoebel reports that Comanche women and men had very different legal personalities. "Any willful killing [of a man] required a revenge killing of the slayer," whereas "for a Comanche husband to kill his wife—with or without good cause—was not murder." The woman's kin did not seek vengeance (1954: 139). In brideservice societies, no man is obliged to avenge the murder of a woman who is killed by her husband (see Shostak 1981: 311–12), although someone may wish to do so.

Men's need to maintain a status that announces "don't fool with me" limits the aid a woman's kin may offer her in quarrels with her husband. A woman's kin may give her to a man, but they cannot take her away from him without casting doubt on her husband's ability to keep what he claims as his. Because men are perceived as earning their wives through demonstrations of personal prowess, cultural logic dictates that a man whose wife is taken or kept from him against his will—even if she is reclaimed by her parents or brothers—is perceived as someone whose reputation for bravery is called into question. Hoebel suggests that Comanche parents were powerless to protect their married daughters from the brutality of their husbands. He describes an instance in which a father begged his son-in-law (even offering him gifts) not to harm his daughter, who had been caught in the act of adultery (1940: 73, 102).

Practical Action

Nineteenth-century Comanche society, as described by Hoebel, provides an excellent example for illustrating the cultural logic that encourages and condones men's abuse of women. But because the Comanche were very aggressive and violent, and because the ethnographers who describe Comanche society rely on remembered accounts rather than personal observations, the Comanche provide a poor example for illustrating the autonomy that women enjoy in many, perhaps most, brideservice societies. In groups who are at peace with their neighbors, or for whom warfare is intermittent, women appear to control their own lives and activities. And ethnographers who have observed daily life in brideservice societies report more cooperation and less violence than ethnographers who rely on informants' memories.[22]

The ever-present threat of violence that provides a cultural justification for men to abuse women also provides a practical reason for men to respect women's (and other men's) autonomy. In a society where nothing appears to intervene between anger and its expression in violence, people are understandably reluctant to fight with, and perhaps kill, those whom they care about. Ethnographers commonly report that people try to forget their anger (see M. Rosaldo 1980). If angry or upset, they go off by themselves. They would rather separate than fight (see Turnbull 1968). Spouses who quarrel and family members who cannot get along move apart. A nomadic or semisedentary lifestyle makes separation easy. A sedentary lifestyle, however, does not prevent separation, because angry individuals may pay extended visits to distant kin or entire factions may move away to form new villages (see Biocca 1971; Chagnon 1968).

This fear of violence organizes relations between husbands and wives. Ethnographers generally report that married couples who stay together love one another. Men may have a cultural justification for beating, mutilating, or killing their wives, but in a society where conflicts lead to killings and separations, good sense suggests that the man who would keep a wife should treat her with kindness and consideration. The sensible man does not demand things from his wife, for what is he to do if she refuses? And he pretends not to notice her adulteries unless they are publicly called to his attention. As a result, women in most brideservice societies enjoy considerable autonomy, even though they are constrained by men's willingness to fight over them. The woman who cares about her husband's safety, however, is discreet in her love affairs and publicly attends to her husband's needs. In most brideservice societies, couples who stay together visibly demonstrate the concern and affection for each other that Westerners interpret as love.

Because women's husbands and kin are reluctant to tell them what to do, women in many brideservice societies seem to hold "decision-making power over their own lives and activities to the same extent that men [do] over theirs" (Leacock 1978: 247). In daily life, neither sex commands the other, and both sexes appear subject to similar social demands. As adolescents and young adults, both men and women are exhorted by elders to assume adult responsibilities. Young women are urged to tend their hearths and husbands, young men to hunt and fight enemies. In middle age, both sexes are concerned with feeding and caring for their children and aging parents. And in old age, women are as likely as men to serve as rallying points for younger kin. As long as people in brideservice societies manage to forestall or defuse conflicts, gender appears to have very little effect on a person's possibilities.

People in brideservice societies have many ways of forestalling and defusing conflicts. As noted above, the ever-present threat of violence makes it practical for people to forget their anger by leaving the scene, either temporarily or permanently. Avoidance is the most common means of handling conflict in simple egalitarian societies (see Roberts 1979: 84).

People also refrain from provoking others. This would seem to explain the reported informality, or absence, of marriage ceremonies in brideservice societies. No one wants to dramatize a girl's loss of freedom and thus grant importance to her resistance. A reluctant bride's kin or husband may beat her, but they do not want to kill or mutilate her. As a result, women usually have as much say as men about whom they will marry, even though political discourse portrays men as earning their wives, and women as objects in transactions between men.

Avoidance of provocation would also explain the reported improvidence of people in brideservice societies. Because they believe that conflict leads directly to violence, they are reluctant to provoke others' anger by refusing their requests. It is not unusual for individuals to "eat right through all their food in camp," even during difficult times and not to "put by food surpluses" (Sahlins 1972: 30–31) unless everyone does so. The person who has nothing worth requesting is seldom put in the position of having to refuse others' requests. There is also little reason to take care of possessions if a person knows they will have to be given away as soon as someone asks for them. People in brideservice societies may hide things from one another, but if hidden things are discovered and requested, they usually give them away.

In societies like the Comanche, where "*ability* to possess [is] 'nine points of the law' " (Hoebel 1940: 66), the sensible man takes care not to possess more than he is willing to defend. A man can more easily maintain a status that announces "don't fool with me" if he has little that can be contested. In Comanche society, "the self of the male" may have been "realized in striving for accumulated war honors, horses, and women" (Hoebel 1954: 131), but Comanche men gave away all three. They, like men in other brideservice societies, needed to demonstrate their ability to take and keep what they wanted. But they probably knew it was illogical to keep more potentially adulterous wives or easy-to-rustle horses than they needed to appear self-reliant.

People in brideservice societies also find it practical to give things away. Those who try to keep things that others lack are suspected of desiring the conflict and violence their behavior provokes. Comanche elders who tried to keep women instead of giving them to needy bachelors were suspected of witchcraft (see Wallace & Hoebel 1952: 146–47). Giving things to others also establishes and symbolizes cooperative relations. The improvidence that ethnographers condemn is simultaneously the generalized reciprocity they admire.

The fear of violence that leads people in brideservice societies to avoid provoking conflicts also stimulates them to intervene in the conflicts that do occur. Leaders may not be able to mediate, arbitrate, or adjudicate disputes, but they can ensure that contestants fight fairly. They can also urge the use of nonlethal weapons. Most interventions are carried out by kin and friends, however. When conflict erupts, noncombatants scurry to hide knives and spears. People throw themselves between contestants or try to pull them apart. Bystanders may grab the arms of men who are about to throw spears in an attempt to deflect their aim. Everyone talks a great deal. Elders, in particular, commonly try to persuade combatants that perceived competitors are actually kin with whom they should cooperate.

In the end, however, the practical actions that people take to avoid or defuse conflicts serve to confirm their belief that conflict leads inevitably to violence. If individuals try to forget their anger, people doubtless think that it is only because anger is forgotten that violence is avoided. Since everyone in brideservice societies readily gives things away, the common perception must be that givers do not want to keep the things they give and so have no reason to be angry when another person requests or takes them. And since bystanders intervene in the conflicts of others and hide contestants' weapons, people must assume that angry men fail to kill each other only because they are not able to find their weapons or reach each other before their anger cools.

People's interventions in fact probably encourage men to threaten violence. If angry men can expect others to hide their weapons or deflect their aim, then they can reach for their weapons with a reasonable assurance that they will not have to kill anybody. They can appear willing to fight without actually having to do so (see Warner 1958: 167). Ironically, the effectiveness of people's strategies for avoiding and defusing conflicts ensures that men and women in brideservice societies live in a social world where the threat of violence appears ever-present.

Cultural Representations

When writing about the values, or ethos, of societies appropriate for analysis with a brideservice model, ethnographers commonly report a cultural emphasis on masculine activities and attributes. Wallace and Hoebel, for example, begin their book on the Comanche by noting their reputation as "The Spartans of the Prairies," who "fought and whipped" the Texans and various Indian groups (1952: 3). And the first two "basic postulates" of Comanche culture listed by Hoebel are "the [male] individual is supreme in all things" and "the self of the male is realized in striving for accumulated war honors, horses, and women" (1954: 131).

Man the Hunter, who both kills and provides (see Lee & DeVore 1968), is a myth of capitalist society, but he is also a myth of brideservice peoples (see Collier & Rosaldo 1981). Contrary to Simone de Beauvoir's (1953) assumption that people everywhere recognize a symbolic opposition between Man the Life-Taker and Woman the Life-Giver, people in brideservice societies credit men with both taking and giving life (see Rosaldo & Atkinson 1975). Men kill enemies and animals; they make babies and nourish people. Woman the Mother and Source of All Life is absent, as is Woman the Gatherer. Women may give birth to babies and provide well over half of the food eaten, but these facts are not celebrated in myth and ritual.

Gender Conceptions

As discussed in the previous section, social processes in brideservice societies provide people with numerous occasions to emphasize male prowess. In a society where each man must establish and maintain a status that announces "don't fool with me," a man's bravery is the most important thing to be known about him. To people who live in such societies, male prowess does appear to order social life. Bachelors apparently earn wives by proving their ability to hunt and kill. Personal power seems to be the basis of social relations among men. And male elders appear to make social life possible by giving women to the bachelors and enemies whose hostility would undermine the cooperative relations that seem necessary for survival.

When these people talk about male prowess, they appear to emphasize its acquisition. In male initiation rituals, youths *acquire* the qualities or marks that make them adult men. They are not portrayed as having to shed childish or feminine qualities. Nor are they portrayed as needing help from others to acquire male prowess. In Comanche society, for example, a young man who went on a vision quest fasted during his vigil, "but unlike some Plains people, inflicted no self-torture. The Comanche was confident of himself as a man: he was reverent toward the power-giving spirits, but he felt no need to debase himself before them, to lacerate and mutilate himself in sacrificial appeasement. He was quietly humble before the sources of spiritual power, but he saw no call to demean himself in lamentation and self-pity. He called not for mercy" (Wallace & Hoebel 1952: 157). A youth apparently perceived himself as acquiring power—not as needing the power he sought or as being inferior to other men or the spirits because he lacked something that they had. The Comanche man did not demean himself. Undoubtedly, he felt no cause to be demeaned.

In brideservice societies, there are no contexts in which men talk about, and thus come to perceive themselves as needing, the things they lack. Because a man is supposed to take what he wants and keep what he has without much regard for the abstract rights of those weaker than himself, a man who expresses a need simultaneously expresses his inability to take. No man concerned with establishing and maintaining a status that announces "don't fool with me" would be foolish enough to express such a thought. And such a man would have to react violently to its expression by others.

Even children's obvious need for parental care is not used as a justification for portraying children as needing their elders' guidance and material support. Comanche boys were taught to hunt and fight. They were not—as far as I can tell from ethnographers' descriptions—told how helpless they were or how much they needed seniors' aid. Children may "have no sense" (see Shostak 1981: 49; M. Rosaldo 1980) and lack adult skills, but people seem to assume that children will acquire sense and skills as they grow older. Children's deficiencies are a justification for parental indulgence. Adults do not impress upon children how deeply they need the care their parents give them (or how much they owe their parents in return).

Since masculinity is something that boys are believed to inevitably acquire as they grow older, boys do not have to worry about being sissies. They expect to learn to hunt and bravely fight, and to acquire signs of adult masculinity such as spiritual power, tattoos, war records, semen, and brides. These acquisitions, as we will see shortly, differentiate men from women. Women in brideservice societies are considered to be like men except that they never acquire the skills, qualities (such as bravery), spiritual powers, or wives that signify that youths have become adult men.

The social processes of brideservice societies provide few occasions for people to discuss femininity. Man the Hunter is accompanied by a curiously undefined wife. In such societies, women are described not as *having* qualities that make them inferior to men[23] but as simply never *acquiring* the male qualities and skills that everyone celebrates.

As mentioned, political discourse in brideservice societies portrays women as objects of male transactions. The Comanche woman was a "chattel," passed from her father and brother to her husband (Hoebel 1940: 119). Women are portrayed as giveable in contexts where men talk about turning enemies into allies, and irresponsible bachelors into responsible adults, by giving them women. As noted, however, men have very little success in giving women unless the woman cooperates. And husbands who want to keep their wives must treat them with kindness and respect. Women may be cast as objects of male transactions in contexts where men negotiate with one another, but they enjoy autonomy in everyday cooperative relations.

Brideservice societies differ greatly in the importance they attribute to gender. Some peoples, particularly those who are at peace with their neighbors, regard men and women as basically similar. In these societies, the gender difference does not greatly affect social life. Among peoples who are engaged in active warfare, however, the gender difference is often dramatized. In such societies, the constant need to turn enemies into allies by giving them women provides many occasions for people to differentiate between wives and those who need them.

It seems reasonable to conclude, however, that even in societies where the gender difference matters, girls, like boys, grow up thinking of themselves as autonomous human beings. All children are said to lack sense and adult skills, but these obvious deficiencies of childhood are not emphasized to give girls the impression that they are inferior to boys. Children of both sexes know that they will gradually acquire the sense and skills possessed by adults. Neither girls nor boys need things. Girls are considered equal to boys, except that girls never acquire the extra "something" that boys ultimately do. Because girls do not acquire wives to feed and care for them, they are never credited with acquiring the abilities and skills that supposedly earn wives for men. A girl may kill an animal, but her hunting skills have no social significance. A boy's kills are celebrated. A girl's are eaten.

A striking feature of brideservice societies is that they appear to lack derogatory images of women. It is true that women appear selfish and demanding in contrast to older men, who generously give everything away, but brideservice peoples appear to lack contexts in which to develop an image of women as inferior beings who need men to control and provide for them. Men do not take from women anything that women could use to further their own plans. A man's ability to establish relationships with other men depends on his reputation for bravery, not on the quantity of goods and services he can extract from his wife. As a result, men have no contexts in which to develop elaborate cultural justifications for forcing women to work or for using women's products in ways that women do not want.

Brideservice societies provide few contexts in which to develop a concept of femininity. When men fight over a woman, people may blame her for causing the fight, but their attention is focused on the prowess and intentions of the contestants; they have no reason to discuss the woman's qualities. Her age, beauty, fertility, and capacity as a worker are all irrelevant to the outcome of the dispute.

Nor do women have any contexts in which to emphasize their own virtues. Women may gather or grow far more food than men, and they may talk about their gathering abilities when claiming equality with men. But women never have to justify enjoying privileges that other people lack, for they have none. Marriage is not an achievement for a woman. It is an unavoidable consequence of a girl's growing up. Man the Hunter gains a wife, and so must justify his privileged position relative to bachelors and women. But Woman the Gatherer acquires a husband whether she wants one or not.

Women also have no contexts in which to emphasize their role as mothers. In brideservice societies, children do little useful work, and when they do begin working, their work benefits others. Young women feed their husbands and children, and young men give the products of their hunting and raiding to the parents of girls they hope to marry. There are thus no occasions when it makes sense for a woman or her kin to stress how much a mother does, or suffers, for her children.

This lack of emphasis on motherhood would seem to explain ethnographers' reports of an absence of ritual surrounding childbirth. In Comanche society, for example, "giving birth to a child was ordinarily a simple affair." If the band was on the march, the woman just dropped behind, and if the band was settled, a woman gave birth in a tipi with a medicine woman in attendance (Wallace & Hoebel 1952: 142). People in brideservice societies want children, and pity people who do not have them, but sterility is not a tragedy. Men and women are respected for the work they do, not for how many children they have. Women, in fact, tend to have few children (see Wallace & Hoebel 1952: 142).

Motherhood may receive little attention, but fatherhood is often culturally elaborated. In many brideservice societies, the birth of a man's first or second child is celebrated as marking a youth's transition to manhood. It is easy to understand why. The birth of a child who is allowed to live usually marks the point at which a young woman settles down to her wifely duties. It is at this point that a man finally acquires a wife.

Men also benefit from talking about their claims to children, for such claims simultaneously publicize a man's claim to the child's or children's mother. In the cultural representations of many brideservice societies, men are credited with making babies, by dreaming them into existence or by providing the sperm that people believe congeals into babies. Men frequently name children and often cure them. Men may even receive credit for mother's milk in societies where people believe women need meat to lactate. Hoebel records a Comanche story about a man who adopted an abandoned baby. The baby's mother later regretted having abandoned her child and went to live with the man who had adopted it (1940: 107–8). This story illustrates a common perception of people in brideservice societies: men acquire wives by becoming fathers.

When women in brideservice societies celebrate their femininity, they appear to emphasize their health and sexuality. Girls' puberty rituals dramatize neither the polluting qualities of menstrual blood nor a girl's newly acquired capacity to give birth. Rather, they celebrate a girl's capacity for work and her sexual attractiveness to men. The Comanche did not regularly hold puberty rituals for girls, but when they did, the ritual demonstrated a girl's agility. She ran across the prairie hanging onto the tail of a fast horse (Wallace & Hoebel 1952: 125–26).

Women celebrate their health and sexuality because these are the qualities that appear to offer them autonomy. Women are usually proud of their ability to provide for themselves and their families. And in a society where a woman can escape from an unwanted husband or suitor only by absconding with another man, a woman's sexual attractiveness is the basis of her ability to control her living conditions.

In many brideservice societies, women appear to think of their sexuality as a potent, mystical force (see Shostak 1981: 288). Because people believe that men fight primarily over women, women's sexuality appears to lie at the heart of social life. A girl's sexual maturity is justifiably celebrated; it is the cause of all action, the source of all meaning. Man the Hunter and Life-Taker is not balanced by Woman the Gatherer or Life-Giver, but he is accompanied by a sexy mate.

Rituals

The symbolic opposition most commonly found in societies appropriate for analysis with a brideservice model is not between male and female, for the concept of femininity is not elaborated, but between a harmonious unisexual (male) world and a heterosexual world marked by conflict. If, in cultural logic, men fight over women, then people conclude that without women to fight over, men would live in peace with one another.

The possibility of a harmonious all-male world, is, of course, inevitably cast into doubt by everyday experience. In brideservice societies, where young men often reach the age of 30 before acquiring a sexually mature wife, bachelors perceive their deprivation as resulting not from women's deficiencies but from the fact that all sexually mature women are monopolized by older men. The difference in the lifestyles of bachelors and married men is both the most obvious and the most potentially disruptive inequality in brideservice societies.

The rituals of brideservice societies are complex and varied, but most societies seem to have at least one important ritual that dramatizes the notion of a harmonious all-male world. In these rituals, senior men display their abilities or marks of achievement and help junior men to emulate them, while women are excluded or allowed to participate only in a group. Men can make peace with one another only if women are not there as individuals to divide them and make them fight. Most male initiation rites take this form. At initiations, senior men make junior men their equals by helping them acquire the war records, skills, knowledge, semen, tattoos, or whatever the culture defines as marking the difference between adult (i.e. married) and subadult (i.e. bachelor) men. Women are usually excluded from participation. They may be required to emphasize their absence by closing themselves in their huts, hiding under mats, or singing in an absent choir. If women are present, they form a massed chorus or audience. Only men may dance and sing alone.

Comanche rituals to send off or welcome home raiding parties may have taken such a form. On these occasions, senior men recited their war deeds and displayed their superior war records in a context where they were visibly encouraging junior men to emulate them. Women appear to have constituted an undifferentiated audience to this display of male achievements and solidarity (see Wallace & Hoebel 1952: 252).

In some brideservice societies, myths and rituals portray the harmonious all-male world as based on elaborations of direct-exchange marriage. In societies where the most obvious inequality is that between married and unmarried men, the orderly exchange of women between groups of men is a symbol of social order, for it results in equality and cooperation among men. Just as men who give women to untrustworthy bachelors receive credit for turning potential troublemakers into cooperating adults, so groups of men who exchange women appear to establish themselves as cooperating allies. Elaborations of sister-exchange marriage, such as bilateral cross-cousin marriages, exogamous moieties, or section systems, may thus appear to be the foundation of social order. Public rituals may dramatize relations between brothers-in-law or exogamous moieties.

The notion of a harmonious all-male world based on elaborations of sister-exchange marriage would at first appear to conflict with the notion that men earn their wives through demonstrations of personal prowess. Elaborations of sister-exchange marriage imply prescriptive marriage rules; particular men and women are destined for each other from birth. The notion that men earn their wives implies achieved rather than ascribed privilege.

Although the two notions conflict, the logic of sister-exchange marriage complements, in at least two ways, the notion that men earn their wives through demonstrations of personal prowess. First, direct exchange has meaning for individuals, because if a man needs only a wife to become the equal of other adult men, then one woman is the equivalent of another. The married man who gives a sister to his wife's brother thus affirms his independence from, and equality with, his affines—even though he continues to give his wife's parents the products of his labor to prove his continuing claim to his wife. The married man who gives his sister to his wife's brother also strengthens his claim to his own wife by giving her brother a vested interest in preserving the marriage. Finally, the gift of a sister to a wife's brother establishes the recipient as a married adult, and therefore a worthy ally.

Second, the logic of sister-exchange marriage complements the notion that men earn wives through demonstrations of personal prowess because people perceive the lack of a wife as giving rise to conflict and violence. If the inequality between married men and bachelors is the cause of conflict, then the equality between men who exchange women will result in peace and cooperation. That the notion of a harmonious all-male world is linked with elaborations of sister-exchange marriage is therefore understandable.

People in many brideservice societies emphasize the link between brothers and sisters. Women, if they are thought to belong to any kinsman, are identified more closely with brothers than with fathers. Fathers may receive the best portions of a daughter's suitor's meat, but a bachelor may perceive his sister as the foundation of his own claim to a wife and to adult independence. The denial of reciprocity by a sister's husband may, in this context, dash a youth's hopes of marriage. Hoebel quotes a Comanche informant's story about two unmarried men who went on a suicide mission after they were refused food by their sister's husband. The story ends with the statement that "many young men in the same circumstances courted death at enemy hands" (1940: 116).

In societies where people believe elaborations of sister-exchange marriage are the basis of social order, brother-sister incest is a powerful symbol of disorder, as is the idea that women choose their own lovers. Men who mate with their sisters destroy their possibilities for relating to other men. And women who choose their lovers create the inequalities between men that breed conflict. Many brideservice peoples thus charge enemies and witches with incest. And many groups have myths of former societies ruled by women. Such myths inevitably emphasize the asocial nature of women-dominated societies and relate how men stole the source of women's power so that they could exchange women and establish the social order that prevails (see Bamberger 1974).

Because people in most brideservice societies both advocate sister-exchange marriage and assume that men earn their wives through demonstrations of personal prowess, the validity of the complex cosmologies that ritual specialists construct from elaborations of direct-exchange marriage is inevitably called into question by people's attempts to account for their everyday experiences. Proponents of complex cosmologies may claim to detect a basic order underlying the chaos of ordinary life, but the cosmologies they elaborate are founded on an inconsistency. Direct-exchange marriage, based on the notion of ascribed status, ultimately conflicts with the notion that men earn their own brides. People in brideservice societies thus have a rich language, full of contradictions, for talking about men's claims to women—the claims that organize inequality in their societies.

Marriage Revisited

I began my discussion of brideservice societies by asserting that everyday conversations portray men as earning their wives in three senses: (1) the gifts and services they give to in-laws are theirs to give; (2) the gifts are proof of a groom's ability and willingness to fight any other man who contests his claim; and (3) men are not given wives by their own or the women's kin. My analysis reveals, however, that these three senses are merely three ways of stating the same thing.

In societies appropriate for analysis with a brideservice model, both men and women perceive themselves as autonomous agents. Both have free access to the means of production and both have what they produce. Neither men nor women consider themselves dependent on others for fulfillment of their earthly or spiritual needs. Both perceive themselves as responsible for establishing their own relationships with others, perhaps within the range of possibilities offered by a moiety or section system. Men distribute their produce widely to publicize their claims to women and to establish relations with other adults, including wives. Women provide daily food for their hungry children and also distribute food to others who give them things in return: husbands, brothers of husbands, parents, co-wives, daughters' suitors, and guests. And women understand their possibilities for escaping from unwanted husbands as depending on their ability to attract lovers.

Anthony Giddens writes at the conclusion of his book *New Rules of Sociological Method* that "the production or reproduction of society . . . has to be treated as a skilled performance on the part of its members" (1976: 160). In this chapter, I have discussed the assumptions and skills, often unrecognized, that people in brideservice societies draw on in producing and reproducing a social world in which no individual can own another—a society in which husbands earn wives rather than one in which parents give away daughters. Men's gifts to in-laws buy nothing. Rather, they testify to a suitor's or husband's willingness and ability to fight any man who tries to take what he claims as his. The man whose wife is taken from him, either by another man or by her own kin, is incensed. Because his ability to take what he wants has been questioned, he demands blood. He does not total what he gave to his in-laws and demand compensation. In short, men in these societies marry with brideservice, not with bridewealth.

2

The Equal Bridewealth Model

The equal bridewealth model proposed in this chapter is most appropriate for analyzing societies commonly identified as "tribes without rulers" (Middleton & Tait 1958)—acephalous, primarily horticultural societies whose political leaders are variously described as Big Men (Sahlins 1963), lineage elders (Bohannan 1957), notables (Gulliver 1963), and even chiefs (Hoebel 1978). Such societies are found in many parts of sub-Saharan Africa, Melanesia, and North America.[1] They correspond closely to those Sahlins (1968) describes as "tribes," and to those Rey (1975) analyzes with his concept of the "lineage mode of production."

Preliminary Description of the Type

In societies appropriate for analysis with an equal bridewealth model, production is carried on within extended family households headed by elders who organize the work process and decide how to allocate the produce. Among the nineteenth-century Cheyenne, for example,

the general custom of matrilocal residence gave rise to an extended domestic family . . . , consisting of a man and his wife, their married daughters and husbands, their unmarried sons, their daughters' children, and any adopted or dependent relatives. The Cheyenne called such a group a 'camp' and usually named it after the male head of the family. While each elementary family in the camp occupies a separate lodge, the camp represents an economic unit. The sons-in-law assist in the hunting and work; food is prepared in the mother's lodge, each daughter taking her share to her own lodge where each elementary family eats as a unit.[2] Such an arrangement lasts as long as the sons-in-law carry out their duties. (Eggan 1955: 61)

As this quotation reveals, Cheyenne hunters, in contrast to their Comanche counterparts, were not obliged to share their meat with all who so requested. Rather a Cheyenne hunter delivered his meat directly to the lodge of his mother or wife. Cheyenne children also contributed more labor to their households than Comanche children. Cheyenne teenage boys herded the family horses (Grinnell 1923; 1:117–18)—a task the Comanche delegated to captive children (Hoebel 1940: 15).

Although households in equal bridewealth societies usually have access to all the tools, land, and skills needed for production, they vary in size, and hence in productivity. Households that have many workers produce many goods; households that have few workers must occasionally rely on neighbors and kin to replace exhausted supplies or to meet extraordinary needs. In many equal bridewealth societies, cooperation increases productivity. The women who processed bison hides on the nineteenth-century Plains could apparently double the output per woman by working together (see Lewis 1942: 39).

Equal bridewealth peoples, unlike members of brideservice societies, are seldom portrayed as improvident. Ethnographers attribute shortfalls to natural disasters or lack of workers, not to prodigality. Hoebel describes the Cheyenne as "anything but improvident." They constantly used "the drying power of the High Plains sun . . . to preserve meat and vegetables for leaner times" (1978: 72).

These people commonly validate marriages with exchanges of valuables between the kin of bride and groom; youths who are unable to obtain required gifts may work for in-laws instead. In some equal bridewealth societies, the gifts appear to pass only in one direction, from the kin of the groom to those of the bride. In other societies, nearly equal gifts are exchanged; or few or no gifts are exchanged at the time a bride and groom begin living together, but gifts to affines may be required later at births, funerals, or initiation rituals.

Among the Cheyenne, whose marriage exchanges are described by Grinnell (1923, 1: 139–40) and Hoebel (1978: 27–28), the kin of the bride and groom exchanged nearly equal gifts. A youth who wanted to marry told his parents, who then assembled their relatives. If the youth's kin approved of his choice, they gathered the necessary gifts: "such items as clothing, blankets, guns, bows and arrows, and horses" (Hoebel 1978: 28). These gifts were loaded onto horses, which an emissary led through the camp to the tipi of the girl's family. If the girl's family agreed to the marriage, they called their relatives together and distributed the groom's gifts among them. Each relative of the bride who accepted a gift was obligated to return a gift of equal or greater value. Several days or weeks after these return gifts had been assembled, an emissary from the bride's family led both the bride and the loaded horses back through the camp to the tipi of the groom's family. The groom's parents welcomed the bride with a feast, and later they divided the return gifts among their own relatives. After a few days of living with the groom's family, the newlyweds moved to a small tipi in the bride's camp, made and furnished by the bride's mother (Hoebel 1978: 28).

In equal bridewealth societies, the valuables used in validating marriages constitute what Goody (1973) calls a "circulating societal fund" that passes from elders to elders. This fund appears to guarantee the dependence of juniors on seniors. Because gifts pass from elders to elders, young people have difficulty acquiring marriage-validating goods before they become elders themselves. Grooms in equal bridewealth societies thus appear to need seniors' help to marry, unlike grooms in brideservice societies, who seem to earn their own brides.

In equal bridewealth societies, generosity is usually the prime requisite for leadership status. Hoebel, writing in the present tense about the nineteenth-century Cheyenne, states that "the personal requirements for a tribal chief, reiterated again and again by the Cheyennes, are an even-tempered good nature, energy, wisdom, kindliness, concern for the well-being of others, courage, generosity, and altruism. These traits express the epitome of the Cheyenne ideal personality. In specific behavior, this means that a tribal chief gives constantly to the poor. 'Whatever you ask of a chief, he gives it to you. If someone wants to borrow something of a chief, he gives it to that person outright' " (1978: 43). The Cheyenne, like most equal bridewealth peoples, valued giving over having. Renunciation of material goods was a culturally valued behavior.

In order to be generous, however, would-be givers in equal bridewealth societies first have to acquire the items they give to others. Because men achieve leadership status by giving things away, they become leaders by collecting many workers in their households: leaders acquire wives, children, orphans, and strays, whose produce they may appropriate for giving to others. "The first duty of a Cheyenne chief . . . was that he should care for the widows and the orphans" (Grinnell 1923, 1: 336). In capitalist society, a man derives little advantage from caring for widows and orphans. But in Cheyenne society, where youths herded horses and household women working together produced dressed bison hides for trade and giving, a man who took in widows and orphans increased his access to valuables for giving away.

Because men become leaders by accumulating workers in their households, leaders in equal bridewealth societies are best described by the Melanesian term "Big Man" (Sahlins 1963), although most ethnographers stress leaders' wisdom and generosity rather than portraying them as swaggering, selfish, or calculating. A leader uses the produce of the many workers he accumulates in his household to generously help less successful household heads, who then owe him a return for his generosity. Because a leader has many workers in his own household and many people who owe him return favors in other households, he is able to assemble the large quantities of goods and the crowds of people needed to stage important ceremonies, manage warfare, and conduct interregional trade.[3] Leaders in equal bridewealth societies, unlike their brideservice counterparts, can get things done.

In many equal bridewealth societies, the male life cycle appears to be divided into definite stages, sometimes codified as age grades. All young men start out with an equal need for valuables that will enable them to marry and set up households of their own. All recently married men are in debt to those who helped them marry, but since they have the right to appropriate the labor products of wives and children, they may use the products of their incipient households to repay creditors and begin acquiring debtors. Finally, male elders with marriageable children have many workers in their households whose products they can appropriate; they also receive valuables from members of other households when juniors marry.

The dependencies established in the kinship system are frequently replicated in the ritual and legal systems. In many equal bridewealth societies, elders control the transmission of ritual knowledge. A young man who seeks knowledge must accompany his request for enlightenment with a gift of valuables for the elder to whom he applies. Because few young men have the necessary valuables, they must request them from senior kin. The valuables used to validate the acquisition of ritual knowledge, like the valuables used to validate marriages, thus pass from elders to elders. Hoebel, writing about the nineteenth-century Cheyenne in the present tense, reports that spirits taught the great rituals

to the legendary knowledge seekers who in turn carefully taught them to their fellow Cheyennes. So it is that one who has learned a ritual becomes a teacher in the later performance of that ritual. The Pledger of an Arrow Renewal or a Sun Dance, the Quiller of a first robe, is taught step by step the performance of the rite. Even the leader of a first war party must learn the preliminary rites from a knowledgeable priest. Every Cheyenne ritual of consequence has at least a Teacher and a Novice in its personnel. (Hoebel 1978: 89)

In Cheyenne society, the teacher provided the knowledge; the novice provided gifts for the teacher and the goods required for staging the ritual.

The legal systems of most equal bridewealth societies also establish the dependency of young men on their senior kin. Most offenders in cases of fornication, elopement, adultery, and wife-stealing are young men who must obtain the valuables they need for paying fines from their senior kin. The offended parties who expect compensation are invariably men who are already married and often fathers of mature daughters.

As this brief discussion of economy, kinship, religion, and polity suggests, equal bridewealth societies appear to have two salient inequalities—between juniors and seniors, and between successful and unsuccessful seniors.[4] All young men start out in need of the valuables that will enable them to marry, acquire ritual knowledge, and possibly pay compensation for misdemeanors. All elders, by virtue of being or having been married, receive valuables that they may generously use to help needy juniors. All seniors are not equal, however. Some men succeed in collecting many wives, children, and strays in their households, whereas, at the other end of the social scale, a few lose their wives and children to the households of more successful elders. Some elders have many valuables and much esoteric ritual knowledge to give away. Because they control valuables and ritual knowledge, they are able to negotiate marriages and legal settlements and to control the timing and organization of important rituals. They become the Big Men of their local groups.

This preliminary discussion would seem to explain how marriage transactions organize inequality in equal bridewealth societies. Young men's need for valuables to marry and set up households of their own puts them in a position where they must obtain elders' support. Consequently young men work in the households of those elders who can provide valuables to validate their marriages. After marriage, young men remain in debt to those seniors who helped them marry, but they gradually repay their creditors as they mature and their children become productive. Some men are ultimately more successful in acquiring wives, children, orphans, and ritual knowledge. Such men establish large, productive households and receive many valuables from wives' lovers, sons-in-law, and seekers of ritual knowledge. They may then build a following among less successful household heads by lending them the valuables they need to help their children marry, acquire ritual knowledge, and possibly pay compensation for misdemeanors.

The discussion also provides an explanation for the egalitarian nature of equal bridewealth societies. Privilege and prestige cannot be inherited. Because leadership is a creation of followership (Sahlins 1963), a Big Man's household and following dissolve upon his senility or death. The sons of a Big Man may have a slight advantage in the competition for valuables, wives, ritual knowledge, and followers, but each would-be Big Man must make his own marriages, acquire his own children, learn ritual knowledge on his own, and organize his own following.

Equal bridewealth societies also seem egalitarian because, for most of these people, increasing age brings increasing power, privilege, and prestige. Almost all men and women who live past middle age become respected household heads and can devote their time to politics and ritual while younger people perform the arduous routine tasks.

Although this preliminary discussion provides some insights into how inequality is organized in societies appropriate for analysis with an equal bridewealth model, it is ultimately problematic. In the Introduction to this book, I noted that elders do not control the distribution of women as Meillassoux (1972) suggests. Women are, in fact, almost entirely missing from this discussion. Nor is it true that young men are unable to acquire marriage-validating gifts on their own. Some Cheyenne bachelors, for example, were spectacularly successful in obtaining horses on raids. And there is evidence that Cheyenne bachelors were able to acquire women's products by trading with their sisters (Llewellyn & Hoebel 1941: 159). Yet, as I will discuss later in this chapter, the young men in equal bridewealth societies who acquire valuables do not validate their own marriages without help from senior kin. In what sense, then, do young men need valuables to marry?

It also seems wrong to conclude that young men work for elders because they need elders' help to validate their marriages and acquire ritual knowledge. Such a conclusion suggests that young men have their labor to allocate to particular uses. But informants' accounts provide no evidence that young men in equal bridewealth societies have their labor and products in the way that young men in brideservice societies do. It therefore seems more logical to conclude that young men work for elders because that is what they and everyone else think they should be doing.

In short, the preliminary discussion is deficient because it does not explain how people living in equal bridewealth societies understand their own actions and those of others. What do people mean by their statements that women's kin can give them in marriage? What is marriage and how does it differ from a relationship between lovers? How do people come to be recognized as having the valuables they give to others as gifts? These are the kinds of questions I answer in the sections that follow. In particular, I focus on the cultural idiom that I call "respect" which is parallel to the idiom of "bravery" in brideservice societies. As in Chapter 1, I begin with an analysis of marriage negotiations.

Marriage

Marriage in equal bridewealth societies is necessarily a different relationship than marriage in brideservice societies. In equal bridewealth societies, people can appropriate the labor and products of others. As a result, the amount they can give away is not a function of how much they produce, but rather of their claims to others. In brideservice societies, as noted in the previous chapter, a man enjoys the benefits of marriage only so long as his wife performs her daily tasks. In equal bridewealth societies, a man can reap the benefits of marriage even after his wife has died or departed. Kinship organizes labor obligations, and kinship bonds outlast the people whose marriages establish them.

Men in equal bridewealth societies, like men in brideservice ones, usually give gifts to, and perform services for, the kin of women they hope to marry, but these gifts and services have different meanings in the two types of societies. In brideservice societies, as discussed, a man's gifts and services to his in-laws represent his continuing claim to his wife vis-à-vis other men. They are proof of his willingness and ability to fight any other man who tries to take his wife from him. In equal bridewealth societies, a man's gifts and services to in-laws validate a kinship bond—marriage. A man need give only a finite (although frequently disputed) amount to validate his marriage, and he expects to realize the benefits of this bond regardless of what happens to the woman.

Although kinship organizes labor obligations in all equal bridewealth societies, such obligations can vary. In some societies, sons-in-law are expected to live with, and work for, the wife's parents, as has been reported for the nineteenth-century Cheyenne. In others, men live with and work for their own parents. Or newlyweds set up a separate household but are expected to obey senior kin or perform specific services for them. Descent systems also vary, ranging from patrilineal to matrilineal with varieties of dual claims in between. One similarity, however, unites all equal bridewealth societies: kinship obligations are theoretically the same for everyone. People may recognize that some individuals and some families are better than others (see Hoebel 1978: 29), but there is rarely a concept of rank. Not all tribal societies have what Goody calls "standard bridewealth," but most share the equality he associates with it (1973: 12).

Marriage transactions can include apparent exchanges of women, as among the Tiv (Bohannan 1957); exchanges of "standard bridewealth" (Goody 1973), gifts, or mere tokens; or apparently no exchanges at all. As a result, we cannot understand marriage by focusing on what people do. We cannot begin by asking who gives what to whom and whose work went into the gifts. Rather, we must ask what gifts mean, for only when we know that will we be able to understand the consequences of variations in the content, provenience, or destination of gifts. We need to focus on discourses. Equal bridewealth societies may exhibit great variation in what grooms are expected to do for, or give to, their in-laws, but beneath this diversity there is an essential similarity, for all acts take their meaning from the contexts in which they are negotiated.

The Meaning of Marriage Gifts

In equal bridewealth societies, men are not credited with earning their wives; they are given wives by elders.[5] A brief comparison of brideservice and equal bridewealth societies will reveal the senses in which this is true.

First, in equal bridewealth societies, most of the gifts a groom gives to his in-laws are not his to give. They belong to his senior kin who contribute them on his behalf, and they usually pass directly from elders to elders. In Cheyenne society, as described, marriage-validating gifts were exchanged between the relatives of the bride and groom. Grooms probably never touched some of the gifts. Unlike the Comanche groom, for whom it was "far more respectable" not to ask his father for help in acquiring horses for giving to in-laws (Wallace & Hoebel 1952: 132), a Cheyenne groom was expected to obtain the assistance of his senior kin (Hoebel 1978: 28). It was far more respectable for a Cheyenne groom to marry with the aid of his kin than without it.

Second, the gifts are a sign of what the groom's elders think of him and the marriage. In all societies, women's suitors are evaluated in terms of their personal qualities, but societies vary in the qualities desired and the means for proving them. In brideservice societies, a groom's gifts constitute proof of his personal prowess— his individual ability to hunt and fight. He must provide the gifts himself to prove his capacities. But in equal bridewealth societies, a groom's senior kin presumably know him, so their willingness to provide the gifts he needs to validate his marriage is taken as a sign of his worthiness and their commitment. If a suitor's elders do not provide gifts, the suitor may have to prove his own worthiness and value as a son-in-law through long years of hard labor. In equal bridewealth societies, unlike brideservice societies, real work is required of the groom who does brideservice.

Third, and most important, a woman's kin can apparently give her away. Unlike women's kin in brideservice societies, a woman's parents and brothers in equal bridewealth societies are not limited to supporting one suitor's claims against those of other suitors, and to beating daughters or sisters who refuse to cooperate. Rather, women's kin can portray themselves as giving daughters because they can keep a married woman away from her husband if they do not approve of his behavior. As will become clear in this chapter, it is this ability of women's kin to shelter married sisters and daughters that structures the discourses constituting marriage and therefore structures the organization of inequality in equal bridewealth societies.

The ability of women's kin to shelter them from their husbands is clearly illustrated in Llewellyn and Hoebel's description of divorce in Cheyenne society (1941: 181). They report that "a wife displeased with her husband's conduct went 'home to mother.' " If her husband requested her return by giving a horse to her kin, "it was the prerogative of the [woman's] brother and any of his 'brothers' who had been in the gift exchange at the marriage to decide the woman's fate. They put her through a cross-examination to determine her grounds for divorce. If they were weighty, the disunion was allowed" (Llewellyn & Hoebel 1941: 181). The reasons why women's kin can "allow a disunion" are complex and will be elaborated in this chapter. I will begin by summarizing them.

In many equal bridewealth societies, women's kin obtain direct benefits by taking in sisters and daughters who want to separate from their husbands. Cheyenne elders could "maximize property" by collecting "working women in [their] own [camps]" (J. Moore 1974a: 87). The Cheyenne, like many other nineteenth-century Plains societies, produced dressed bison hides for the capitalist world market. When several women divided processing chores among themselves, they could produce almost twice as many dressed hides in a year as a woman who worked alone (see Lewis 1942: 39).

But even in societies where women's kin derive no immediate benefits from accumulating women in their households, women's kin still welcome home unhappy sisters and daughters—at least temporarily. In societies where elders acquire power and prestige by establishing claims to juniors, women's kin and women's husbands are in continual competition for the loyalty and labor of women's children. Taking in children's mothers validates claims to children. However unilineal the descent system may be, men in equal bridewealth societies maintain claims to both wives and sisters.

Married women also maintain ties with their natal families. In equal bridewealth societies, as in brideservice societies, the conjugal relationship is initially unequal and thus unstable. It is one in which a woman works for her husband while her husband works for seniors. In brideservice societies, as discussed in the previous chapter, the relationship becomes more equal and stable after the birth of a child. When a woman must provide food and shelter for her baby, and restrict her extramarital affairs, she no longer finds her husband's demands so onerous. In equal bridewealth societies, however, the birth of a child appears to weaken the conjugal bond, at least initially. A woman's fate is bound up in the fate of her children. They provide her household labor, and they are the basis of whatever power she comes to enjoy. Because a woman's fate depends on her children, a mother courts the man most able to advance her children's careers. However unilineal the descent system may be, women inevitably play off brothers against husbands to gain advantages for their children and for themselves.

Women's kin in equal bridewealth societies seldom need fear violent reprisals if they keep a married sister or daughter from her husband. As suggested by the preceding quotation on Cheyenne divorce, the discourses surrounding the dissolution of marriage focus on a woman's reasons for leaving her husband, not on the husband's inability to keep what he claims as his. In equal bridewealth societies, an abandoned husband is someone who stands accused of wrongdoing. He is expected to defend himself against his wife's accusations, and perhaps to beg her pardon and that of her kin. Unlike his counterpart in brideservice societies, he is not expected to demand blood in order to reestablish his reputation for bravery.

Finally, women in equal bridewealth societies are more giveable than their brideservice counterparts. In brideservice societies, a woman's kin may beat a sister or daughter who refuses to marry the man they have chosen, but if she is adamant they must either kill her or let her have her way. In equal bridewealth societies, a woman's kin have something to offer a cooperative bride: shelter, when disputes arise with her husband, and help in furthering her children's careers.

The Negotiation of Marriage

The power of women's kin to keep married sisters and daughters from their husbands structures the arguments people make when negotiating marriages, and therefore structures the commonsense understandings that organize social inequality. In particular, the arguments that people advance when trying to make or break marriages assume, and so establish, (1) the affinal bond as determining each side's rights and obligations; (2) the "parent-child"[6] bond as one in which socially defined parents generously provide more support than parental obligations require, thus rendering their socially defined children as forever in debt; and (3) a gender difference that establishes women as being more giveable than men.

Although women's kin are assumed to give brides to sons-in-law and/or brothers-in-law, the rights and obligations of each side are not negotiated by the parties. They are determined by the affinal bond. The arguments that people advance when trying to make or break marriages define the content of this bond. Marriage is not a market transaction. Women are not commodities to be bought and sold. In providing valuables for his in-laws, a groom does not buy a wife. He merely assumes the already defined obligations of a husband and son-in-law.

The rights and obligations of affines vary from society to society, but in all cases they are understood to derive from the nature of the affinal bond, not from the amount and quality of goods exchanged. In equal bridewealth societies, "property law . . . defines not so much rights of persons over things, as obligations owed between persons . . . related in specific long-standing ways" (Gluckman 1968: 75). In many of these societies, ancestral gods are credited with having defined the obligations affines owe one another.

The Cheyenne provide a particularly good example of how the affinal bond, defined in the course of negotiations, determines rights and obligations. As Llewellyn and Hoebel's (1941: 181) description of divorce indicates, the negotiations between an abandoned husband and his wife's kin centered on whether the woman's kin should allow a "disunion," a decision based on whether the woman had "grounds" for divorce. Discussions, therefore, must have centered on whether the woman's husband had behaved badly, a subject that necessarily assumed the prior existence of standards defining the proper conduct of a husband, son-in-law, and brother-in-law.

Men cannot buy wives; nor can women's kin sell a daughter or sister. They do not have the ability to withhold young women from bachelors. They have only the power to shelter unhappily married sisters and daughters. As a result, women's kin seldom have reason to tell a bachelor what he must do to obtain a bride. But they must frequently justify keeping a man's wife from him by arguing that he did something wrong.

Because the obligations of sons-in-law and brothers-in-law are already defined, it is easy to understand why suitors in equal bridewealth societies do not appear to earn their wives. Their gifts and services to in-laws validate a relationship; they do not create obligations on the part of in-laws. A man who gives more gifts or services than another man does not put his potential in-laws under a greater obligation to reciprocate with a wife or to demand less of him should he become their son-in-law. In theory, it takes only a finite number of gifts, or set of exchanges, to validate a marriage. Suitors who cannot obtain the gifts may have to work instead, but—again in theory—their labor obligations are finite. Once the labor has been performed, such a suitor is married and has only the obligations ordinarily expected of any husband and son-in-law.

The power of women's kin to keep unhappily married sisters and daughters also structures the discourses that define the relationship between seniors and juniors within kin groups—particularly within household production units. The arguments that people advance when trying to make or break marriages define the parent-child kinship bond, in the abstract, as one involving a balanced exchange of parental support for children's obedience. In each concrete situation, however, the parents are defined as having overfulfilled their obligation to support, whereas the children are defined as having underfulfilled their obligation to obey. In all societies, of course, parents are obliged to support their children, and children are expected to obey their parents, but in most societies the obligation of adolescent and adult children to obey their parents does not constitute the most significant form of labor appropriation.

Socially defined parents are inevitably cast as providing more support than required because marriage negotiations are occasions when youths request parents' help. Although parents are commonly expected to help sons marry as part of their ordinary obligation to provide support, parents are not obliged to help in any particular instance. In Cheyenne society, for example, if a youth's parents did "not agree that the match [was] a good one, they [would] refuse to assist him" (Hoebel 1978: 28). A youth's most practical strategy is therefore to flatter his parents and appeal to their generosity—a strategy that necessarily portrays parental help as generous, as an overfulfillment of their obligations. Children are inevitably cast as underfulfilling their obligation to obey because children who request parental help put themselves in a situation where parents may scold them for having been disrespectful or disobedient in the past.

Because parents are expected to help their socially defined children marry, parents appear most selfless and most generous in situations where marriages threaten to dissolve, for then both young people appear to be in the wrong. As Llewellyn and Hoebel's description of Cheyenne divorce reveals, a woman who has run "home to mother" is presumed guilty. Why else would she be put "through a cross-examination to determine her grounds for divorce" (Llewellyn & Hoebel 1941: 181)? Her husband is also presumed guilty. Why else would his wife have run "home to mother"? Because a wife who has returned to her natal kin is presumed to have behaved badly, her kin are under no obligation to listen to her story and offer her refuge, nor do her husband's kin have an obligation to listen to his story and help him recover his wife. If a man's and woman's senior kin help them settle their quarrel (and they usually do), then they must be acting out of selfless generosity.

Llewellyn and Hoebel do not mention that abandoned Cheyenne husbands asked their senior kin for help in recovering wives who had run away to natal kin, but this occurs in most equal bridewealth societies. When abandoned husbands ask for the return of their wives, the central issue is not what a son-in-law should do—for his obligations are, in theory, already defined—but whether his in-laws will forgive him. An abandoned husband, especially a young husband, is seldom in a position to negotiate with his in-laws. He has to defend himself against his wife's accusations and beg forgiveness.

An abandoned husband's ability to obtain pardon usually depends on his ability to enlist the support of his own senior kin. Women's kin usually refuse to listen to abandoned husbands; they are too busy accusing them of wrongdoing. But women's kin cannot long refuse to listen to a man's senior kinsmen. They have done no wrong, and they usually bring along a particularly respected elder to help argue their case.

Most negotiations concerning the return of a wife thus take place between the senior kin of a separated couple, not between a man and his in-laws or between a man and his wife. As a result, elders are considered responsible for the marriages of juniors. In equal bridewealth societies, young men appear to rely on their elders to obtain brides for them. Most commonly, it is a groom's elders who first persuade a woman's kin to give their daughter in marriage, and who later persuade the woman's angry kin to forgive their erring son-in-law. Youths and maidens may choose their mates, but elders validate marriages. In Cheyenne society, young couples might elope, but their elders met in their absence to exchange marriage-validating gifts (Llewellyn & Hoebel 1941: 172).

Finally, marriage negotiations establish the sexes as unequal. Culturally defined men initiate marriages; culturally defined women are given as wives. This inequality is most clearly revealed when unhappy wives run "home to mother." Unhappy wives in equal bridewealth societies, unlike their brideservice counterparts, have the option to return to natal kin. A woman who chooses to do so, however, must justify having left her husband if she is to enlist her kin's support against her husband and his kin. She does this by defending herself and accusing her husband of wrongdoing. Women who want their kin to shelter them from their husbands are unlikely to blame their kin for having given them away in marriage. In fact, in begging their kin to take them back, women tacitly acknowledge the right of their kin to give them away.

In this section on marriage I have briefly discussed how the ability of women's kin to keep them from their husbands structures the arguments people advance during marriage negotiations. These arguments define the affinal bond as determining each side's rights and obligations; the "parent-child" bond as one in which parents generously provide more support than their obligations require; and the gender difference that establishes women as being more giveable. In the next section I explore how these commonsense understandings are confirmed in everyday life. In particular, I examine the cultural idiom of "respect."

Production and Circulation

In equal bridewealth societies, rights and obligations inhere in specific long-standing relationships between people, of which socially defined kinship bonds are the most important type. Just as men do not earn their wives, so people do not earn most of the privileges they enjoy. Within household production units, those who are defined as children cannot earn the support their socially defined parents generously provide, nor can the people in one household buy the brides or ritual knowledge they request from another. Barter occurs in equal bridewealth societies, but most goods and services are exchanged as gifts.

In this book, I will not offer another analysis of "the gift" (see Mauss 1967; Gregory 1982), or of "primitive exchange" (see Sahlins 1972). Rather, I examine ongoing and recurring conversations to ascertain the meaning of work and gifts in equal bridewealth societies. People everywhere work and give things to others, but the meanings attached to labor and gifts vary according to the powers available to those present in situations where the meanings are defined. In equal bridewealth societies, labor and gifts take their meaning from the specific long-standing relationship between giver and recipient. Labor and gifts are perceived either as fulfilling existing obligations, or as earning the respect accorded to people who do or give more than existing obligations require. I begin this section by examining the contexts in which people presume the existence of, and thus define, specific long-standing status relationships.

The Meaning of Work

Children—sons and daughters—are the main category of people whose labor is appropriated by others—their "parents." In equal bridewealth societies, unlike brideservice societies, adolescent and adult children do not have either their labor or its products. Children, as a socially defined category, are obliged to obey their parents. Parents thus have the labor and products of their children.

In Cheyenne society, for example, young people were trained from birth to "be quiet and respectful in the presence of elders" (Hoebel 1978: 98). They showed their respect by obeying elders' commands, as Grinnell reveals in his description of the instructions given to a boy when he was about 12 years of age. "He was told that when older people spoke to him, he must listen and must do as they told him. If anyone directed him to go after horses, he should start at once. . . . [Horses] were his especial charge, and he must watch them, never lose them, and see that they had water always. He was told that when he grew older it was his duty to hunt and support his mother and sisters" (1923, 1: 117–18).

Cheyenne and Comanche child-rearing practices were strikingly different, and this difference reflects, I think, a crucial difference between equal bridewealth and brideservice societies.[7] The Cheyenne "child was carefully trained, and from early childhood. Its training began before it walked, and continued throughout its child life" (Grinnell 1923, 1: 103). Comanche parents thought children were a nuisance and did not bother to train them until age 10 or 11, when they were presumed capable of learning adult tasks (Gladwin 1948). Cheyenne children worked for their households. Girls worked for their mothers, both before and after marriage; teenage and preteen boys herded the household horses; and older bachelors hunted for their mothers. Comanche boys, in contrast, were not assigned "menial" tasks (Wallace & Hoebel 1952: 127), and older bachelors probably delivered their meat directly to the parents of girls they hoped to marry. Cheyenne children did not have either their labor or its products. Comanche children did.[8]

In equal bridewealth societies, "respect" is the central value, comparable to "bravery" in bands. People who have neither their labor nor its products have nothing to give away, and so have nothing to exchange for the goods and services of others. But people who have nothing can earn others' respect. Grinnell writes that

the instructor of the [Cheyenne] child did not attempt to entice him to do right by presenting the hope of heaven, nor to frighten him from evil by the fear of hell; instead, he pointed out that the respect and approbation of one's fellow men were to be desired, while their condemnation and contempt were to be dreaded. The Indian lived in public. He was constantly under the eyes of the members of his tribe, and most of his doings were known to them. As he was eager for the approval of his fellows, and greedy of their praise, so public opinion promised the reward he hoped for and threatened the punishment he feared. (1923, 1: 103–4).

People who have respect have control over their lives and can shape the lives of others. Because they have both autonomy and power, they can determine the course of events. People who lack respect must rely on others to negotiate for them. Respect in equal bridewealth societies is comparable to capital in capitalist societies. The person who has respect can set productive processes in motion; the person who lacks it is condemned to participate in productive processes organized by others. As we will see at the end of this section, grooms in equal bridewealth societies are condemned to seek aid from seniors when marrying, not because they lack goods but because they lack respect.

Respect is of course valued in all human societies, but societies vary in their standards for awarding respect and in the consequences of having or lacking it. This section is primarily concerned with the role respect plays in defining the content of specific long-term relationships between people. Because respect is assessed in terms of the fulfillment of status obligations, discussions of how much respect to accord necessarily assume that specific long-term relationships involve already defined rights and obligations.

In particular, I focus on negotiations within household production units between socially defined parents and children; this is the context in which the most inegalitarian long-term status relationship is established. In the preceding section, I noted (1) that the arguments advanced during marriage negotiations define the reciprocal status obligations of affines and of parents and children, and (2) that the parent-child bond is defined abstractly as a balanced exchange of parental support for children's obedience, but in each concrete situation, parents have inevitably overfulfilled their obligation to support, and children have inevitably underfulfilled their obligation to obey.

In all human societies, parents provide food and care for offspring who are too young to care for themselves, and children are expected to obey their parents. In most societies, however, the obligation of sons and daughters to obey their parents does not constitute the most important form of labor appropriation, so the support provided by parents does not justify an inegalitarian relationship. In brideservice societies, parents seldom seem to mention how much they do or suffer for children. And, indeed, parents seem to do little for sons and daughters beyond what is required to ensure their health. In equal bridewealth societies, however, parental care is emphasized. In societies where seniors acquire power and prestige by collecting working juniors in their households, parents take advantage of the normal growth process to dramatize their claims. As a result, children receive many things from parents before they become aware of the gifts or are able to offer obedience in return. By the time they reach awareness, parents have already fulfilled their obligation to provide support, and the children have necessarily underfulfilled their obligation to obey.

The Cheyenne believed that spirit from fathers and substance from mothers were required to create a child and that an infant needed a cradle, a name, and pierced ears (see Grinnell 1923, 1:

102–8). These postbirth gifts and services were provided by members of other households, who received gifts in return from the child's parents—or from the child's substitute parents if the child's parents were dead or lacked the requisite objects to give. By the time Cheyenne children came to awareness, they had already received many gifts and services that they in no way deserved.

In equal bridewealth societies, continuing interaction between parents and their offspring establishes the socially defined parent-child bond as one in which parents show selfless generosity toward undeserving children. Because children are already under an obligation to obey their parents, children are never able to offer their parents anything that parents do not already have. The extra gifts, services, or indulgences that parents provide are thus always given without remuneration. Children, as recipients of such selfless generosity, are never able to do enough in return.

This understanding of the parent-child bond is most evident in situations where sons and daughters make requests of parents. The situation where the most is at stake is that in which a deserted husband requests the help of his parents in negotiating for the return of his wife. A similar conversation is conducted in innumerable, less consequential situations. Adolescents and young adults inevitably have to make some requests of parents (for food, free time, and special treats). But children are also cast as needing things or services that can be obtained only from members of other households, such as sponsorship for initiation, spiritual blessing, spouses, or special types of ritual knowledge. Young men and women who would acquire these things need the help of their parents because no unmarried person has access to the valuables needed for presenting to sponsors, teachers, healers, or in-laws.

There are two senses in which sons and daughters in equal bridewealth societies cannot earn the goods and services they obtain from parents (and therefore are understood as being able to earn only respect). The first has just been discussed: children who already owe obedience have nothing to give parents that parents do not already have. The second is that parents cannot, in the end, refuse their children's requests for aid. In societies where people get ahead by collecting dependents in their households, parents must grant children's requests if they possibly can, to forestall children's turning to other, more generous relatives. The labor of children who go to live with a more generous relative is lost to their parents. As a result, parents tend to grant the requests of bad children as frequently as they do those of good children. There are thus no goods and services that bad children are denied, and therefore no goods and services that good children can be perceived as earning through their own efforts.

Bad children, however, are probably the objects of more "condemnation and contempt" than good children (which, of course, is what defines them as bad). Parents may be reluctant to deny their children's requests, but they can use such requests as an occasion for berating them if they have not shown proper respect—i.e. have not listened to their parents and done what they were told. As a result, respect, defined as the opposite of "condemnation and contempt," is construed as something that a child can earn. And respect is accorded depending on how well a son or daughter is perceived to have fulfilled his or her status obligations to obey. Discussions of how much respect a child deserves assume, and thus define, the dyadic status relationship between parents and children as one in which a child's obligation is to do as he or she is told.

Although, in theory, children should be able to fulfill their obligation to obey, and thereby earn respect, in practice, children inevitably fail to fulfill their status obligations. In equal bridewealth societies, the parent-child bond is based on an exchange of goods for labor. Parents are able to provide children with the goods they need for presenting to members of other households only because children's labor makes possible the products that parents have.

In Cheyenne society, for example, a man's ability to provide his sons with horses for giving to in-laws depended on his ability to obtain herding labor from his sons. A man without socially defined sons to care for his horses could not maintain a herd. Similarly, only a woman with free time could produce the beaded moccasins or quilled objects that the Cheyenne considered appropriate for presenting to teachers of ritual knowledge and providers of blessing. A woman without socially defined daughters to cook and perform routine chores could not produce such labor-intensive items.

In equal bridewealth societies, parents must obtain labor from children if they are to achieve respect and influence. The amount of work parents require, and from which sex, varies from society to society, but in all of them, married adults who fail to obtain labor from children—either because they do not acquire socially defined children or because they do not discipline the ones they have—

suffer relative to their peers. Parents in equal bridewealth societies must use children's requests for aid as occasions for exhorting them to be more obedient and hardworking. As a result, children are inevitably cast as persons who have not fulfilled their status obligations. They do not deserve respect.

Because children are defined within their households as lacking respect, they cannot negotiate for themselves with outsiders. No outsider will listen to them. Children therefore need parents to intercede for them. The objects that a young person presents to a member of another household when requesting ritual knowledge, blessing, or a spouse represent proof of that child's worthiness. First, the gifts testify to the child's parents' willingness to support the child. Second, because the child has no prior obligations to members of a different household, the gifts establish the child as someone who is giving more than required by status obligations, and thus is deserving of respect.

In equal bridewealth societies, most of the goods and services exchanged with members of other households are given as gifts, in the sense that people who enter into such exchanges do not haggle over the value of the articles or services transferred. People may haggle over value when bartering with members of other ethnic groups, but within their own society, people haggle (if it can be called that) primarily over the content of status obligations. The object of both giver and recipient is not to obtain as many goods and services as possible; rather both want their obligations understood in such a way that the gifts given or services rendered appear generous, or at least adequate, as judged by the specific long-term relationship between giver and recipient.

Exchanges between members of different households, like exchanges between members of the same household, foster discussions of reciprocal status obligations, not discussions of price or value. And status obligations are always cast as existing prior to the present transaction, because it is only by treating status obligations as already defined that people can present themselves as giving more than, or at least as much as, they are obliged to give. Equal bridewealth societies thus provide many contexts in which people can recognize that long-term status relationships are clearly defined and have inherent obligations. But they provide almost no contexts in which people can perceive goods or services as being discrete and having inherent values. As Gluckman observes, tribal property law defines the mutual obligations of people who are related to one another in long-standing ways (1968: 75). Tribal property law does not define goods and services as having inherent values that exist prior to the establishment of, or apart from, particular social relationships.

The Content of Status Obligations

The precise rights and obligations that people perceive as defined by particular long-standing relationships vary from one equal bridewealth society to another, but the most unequal relationship is always that between the socially defined parent and child. The parent-child bond is inevitably construed as one in which sons and daughters owe obedience to parents because they support them. However well balanced or natural such an exchange may seem, the relationship is neither balanced nor natural in equal bridewealth societies. Adult and adolescent children work for parents whose support consists of goods and services that children need only because the needs are socially determined. In this section I will examine (1) the social determination of needs; and (2) the power relations that enable parents to obtain compliance from the children they support.

In equal bridewealth societies, children need parental support because the amount of prestige a person can expect to enjoy upon reaching elderhood is dependent on the amount of support that person received from elders in earlier years. Equal bridewealth societies vary in the extent of inequality among elders. In some societies, almost all elders enjoy prestige, simply by virtue of their age; in others, respected Big Men or ritual leaders stand in marked contrast to despised "rubbish men" or "spongers." The nineteenth-century Cheyenne appear to have been one of the more inegalitarian societies. Cheyenne "peace chiefs" held ritual offices and were renowned for their generosity; Cheyenne "poor" men were despised for "sponging" upon the "rich" (see Llewellyn & Hoebel 1941: 33, 233). The Cheyenne dramatized this difference between successful and unsuccessful male elders in the ceremony they held to install new chiefs. "When the choosing of successors was over and the four days and nights of ritual in the chief's lodge were done, there was much gift-giving and celebration throughout the camp. The poor profited handsomely, because it was an esteemed gesture to give horses and robes, or whatever else of value to any person, especially the poor" (Llewellyn & Hoebel 1941: 76). The ceremony that publicly proclaimed the success of some men simultaneously proclaimed the failure of others.

In equal bridewealth societies, the prestige and power a male elder enjoys are related to the size of the household he heads. The correlation is never perfect, however; there are always some respected elders whose households have dwindled, and some heads of large households who are criticized for their selfishness and overbearing ways. In societies where generosity is the prime requisite for high status, the amount of goods a man has to give away is largely determined by the number of workers in his household.

In Cheyenne society, where generosity was the prime requirement for becoming a chief (Hoebel 1978: 43), a man who would join the Council of Forty-Four Chiefs had to have horses and robes for giving away. No man, of course, could produce these things for himself. He could not simultaneously herd horses, hunt bison, and conduct ceremonies, nor could he make robes, since that was women's work. As a result, the number of horses and robes available to a potential chief was a function of the number of herders, hunters, and women whose products he could appropriate.

Ethnographers of equal bridewealth societies usually focus on the differentiation among male elders, but in many (if not all) such societies, female elders are also differentiated in prestige and power. And when women enjoy conspicuous privileges, their privileges, like those of men, tend to be related to the number of workers in their households. John Moore describes a traditional division of labor among the women in a Cheyenne household: "the younger women do the drudgery, the middle-aged women cook and manage, while the older women sew and do beadwork" (1974a: 274). An older woman's ability to "sew and do beadwork" (and thus to produce the objects that, when given to others, would command respect) depended on having younger women around to do the drudgery, cooking, and managing of the household.

Although both male and female elders in equal bridewealth societies benefit by having many working children in their households, men and women differ in their ways of acquiring children. Men acquire children by accumulating women. Women acquire children by furthering the careers of the children they rear, particularly sons. The interests of older spouses tend to coincide. The interests of young spouses tend to be opposed. As a result, marriages are unstable in their early years.

Marriages in all societies tend to be unstable in their early years. It seems obvious that young spouses need time to adjust to one another and to their new responsibilities. But however universal newlyweds' marital problems may be, the meaning and consequences of their problems are socially determined and are therefore variable. In equal bridewealth societies, husbands who lose wives, and mothers whose children die or leave them, are condemned to "sponge upon" others and thus to incur the contempt of their peers.

To understand why the interests of young husbands and wives are inevitably opposed, we must examine the social determination of women's interests. Women, as already noted, benefit by furthering the careers of their children, particularly sons. Women are often emotionally close to daughters, but sons give a woman access to the male world. A mother in a patrilineal and/or patrilocal society would naturally want to further the careers of her sons. They, and their future wives, constitute her work force. But even in matrilineal and/or matrilocal societies (such as the Cheyenne), women benefit by furthering sons' careers. A Cheyenne mother's work force may have consisted of her daughters and their husbands, but a mother whose sons commanded respect retained the loyalty of her daughters because she could provide them with potent allies against their husbands.

Because of women's interest in furthering their sons' careers, the interests of mothers and sons tend to coincide. The difference between brideservice and equal bridewealth forms of social organizations is revealed by behavioral differences of Comanche and Cheyenne children. In both societies, children played "camp," but Comanche boys chose girls to be their "wives" (Wallace & Hoebel 1952: 128), whereas Cheyenne boys chose girls to be their "mothers" (Grinnell 1923, 1: 110). In brideservice societies, a man needs a wife if he is to be the equal of married men. In equal bridewealth societies, a man's future is determined largely by the cleverness and abilities of his mother.

The coincidence of interests of mothers and sons, and the divergence of interests of young wives and husbands, are two sides of the same coin. A woman gains benefits for her sons by playing off her husband against her brothers. A man furthers his career by collecting both wives and sisters. The interests of young parents are thus inevitably opposed. The resources and labor that a young husband might wish to utilize for furthering his own career or the careers of his sister's children, or for marrying another wife, are inevitably lost to his first wife and her children. And a mother's attempts to obtain benefits for her children utilize the resources and labor that her husband might wish to use for other purposes.

Marriage in equal bridewealth societies is thus a very different relationship from marriage in brideservice societies. In brideservice societies, husbands do not take from wives anything that wives can use in other ways. In equal bridewealth societies, however, a woman benefits by obtaining all the resources she possibly can for her children, including resources she may have to extract from her husband by threatening to turn to her brother instead. A man benefits by diverting some of the family resources to supporting people other than his wife's children.

This analysis of women's interests has been intended to provide the background for a discussion of the meaning of marriage-validating gifts, and to explain why young men work for seniors. In equal bridewealth societies, young men work, not because they need marriage-validating gifts but because they need respect. In those societies where marriage negotiations are initiated by the presentation of gifts from the groom's family to the bride's, people may tell ethnographers that bachelors work for their senior kinsmen because they need marriage-validating goods, or that recently married men work for their parents because they have to reimburse them for courtship and wedding expenses. Neither of these reasons is accurate, however. Young men work, not to obtain goods but to fulfill status obligations, and thereby to obtain respect.

Young men do not derive any benefit from *not* asking their senior relatives to provide marriage-validating goods. If, as natives and ethnographers suggest, young men work because they need goods, then we would expect to find that bachelors who manage in one way or another to obtain marriage-validating goods by themselves would not work for seniors. Yet they continue to do so.

Nor do we find that young men are prevented from acquiring needed valuables, as we might expect if the entire system of unequal labor obligations were based on young men's need for marriage-validating goods. In most equal bridewealth societies, it is difficult, but not impossible, for a young man to obtain the customary goods on his own. But youths who acquire such valuables do not then initiate their own marriage negotiations; they do not use the goods as a pretext to deny their senior kin the opportunity of negotiating their marriages for them.

This point is illustrated by the story of Beaver Claws, a Cheyenne bachelor who captured 70 horses during a raid. On returning to camp, he drove all of them directly to the lodge of his prospective bride's parents, for "to send as marriage gifts for a girl horses just taken from the enemy was the highest compliment that could be paid to the girl and to her family" (Grinnell 1923, 1: 142–43). But after delivering the horses, Beaver Claws did not enter the lodge to ask the girl's parents to give her to him. Rather, he went home to ask his parents to arrange the marriage, which they did (Grinnell 1923, 1: 143). Beaver Claws did not use his horses as an excuse for depriving his kin of the opportunity to negotiate his marriage for him. He used the horses to gain respect.

The behavior of Beaver Claws would be incomprehensible if bachelors in equal bridewealth societies needed goods to acquire wives, but his behavior is perfectly comprehensible, because men need respect. In societies where women with children need the help of respected men to advance their children's careers, a man who has respect has something to offer his wife and all mothers of children. He can intercede for children in their negotiations with members of other households and thus ensure that others listen to children's requests.

When Cheyenne elders told boys that "the respect and approbation of one's fellow men were to be desired, while their condemnation and contempt were to be dreaded" (Grinnell 1923, 1: 103–4), they were speaking the truth. In equal bridewealth societies, where mothers benefit by advancing children's careers, respect has practical consequences, for it enables men to collect women. A man who commands more respect than his wife's brothers is likely to enjoy a stable marriage. A man who commands more respect than his sisters' husbands is likely to find that his sisters come to him for advice and help. And a man who commands more respect than his peers is likely to find it easier to acquire secondary wives; maidens, widows, divorcees, and their kinsmen will seek him out. In summary, men who have respect attract mothers and potential mothers to their households. Men who lack respect find that their own wives and sisters turn to other men for help in furthering their children's careers.

Although men need respect, not goods, men's need for respect is perceived as a need for goods. In equal bridewealth societies, the amount of respect a groom receives is related to the amount of goods his senior kin provide to validate his marriage. A groom whose kin provide fewer gifts, or gifts of lesser quality, than is customary is understood to lack respect, whereas a groom whose kin provide more gifts, or gifts of high quality, is understood to have respect. As a result, a groom's senior kin are able to determine how much respect he will be accorded, and their ability to shape his future is a function of their control of marriage-validating goods.

Because respect is determined not by the amount of marriage-validating goods provided but rather by the relationship between what is customarily given and what is actually given, the ability of the seniors to command young men's labor is not undermined if bachelors gain independent access to valuables. Bridewealth has a natural tendency to inflate; if valuables become more accessible, the amount of what is customarily given will increase. A mere increase in valuables, therefore, cannot alter the organization of inequality. As long as respect remains the determinant of men's possibilities, and respect is determined by the relationship between what is customarily given and what is actually given, seniors will continue to have power over junior men because, as the recipients of marriage-validating gifts, seniors will inevitably have more goods than bachelors and thus will be able to control the amount of respect any young man receives.

The inequality of the parent-child power relationship—the dyadic status relationship in which labor is appropriated—is thus organized by the divergence between women's and men's interests. Because women need the help of respected men to advance their children's careers, seniors' power over women peaks in the years when women's children are growing up. Mothers of children (i.e. wives) are regarded as worth acquiring by men (and by women in equal bridewealth societies where women may marry wives). And because men need respect if they are to attract and keep mothers of children, seniors' power over men peaks in the years when young men are courting or are attempting to recover runaway wives. As a result, young men (i.e. sons) are considered worth acquiring by both men and women.

Relations between socially defined parents and children have a predictable pattern in equal bridewealth societies. The parent-child bond is always defined as one in which children owe respect (i.e. obedience) to parents who support them, but parents' ability to obtain compliance varies throughout the life cycle. Young children usually perform chores, but the usefulness of their labor is limited.[9] Adolescents are often rebellious. They are usually capable of assuming full adult work loads, but if they are not yet eligible to marry, parents have little to offer them in return. To adolescents, the parent-child exchange of labor for support must appear most unequal. John Moore describes a modern Cheyenne pattern in which maturing sons quarrel with fathers, then leave the reservation for several years, but finally return home to ask elder kinsmen for help in obtaining spiritual power and ritual knowledge (1974a: 78–82). Hoebel, writing about the nineteenth-century Cheyenne, reports that maidens often quarreled with their mothers and sought refuge with fathers' sisters (1978: 34).

Societies vary in the duration and severity of adolescent rebelliousness, but rebellious young people must eventually return to the fold if they hope to marry and become household heads themselves. Parents' power thus waxes and reaches a peak during the years when young men become concerned with acquiring respect and wives, and young women become concerned with advancing the careers of their children. Once young adults become concerned with their own futures, they must request parental help, thus putting themselves in a position where parents can scold them for disobedience or reward them for obedience.

Parents' power wanes and reaches a low when their adult sons and daughters stop requesting parental aid. Once a man's wife no longer runs away, he no longer has to ask his parents for help in recovering her. And once a woman has launched her children's careers, she no longer has to beg her parents or brothers for help. Respected men welcome her requests. The parents of children old enough to perform adult tasks may still owe respect to their own aging parents, but aging parents usually have little to offer in return for their children's compliance.

The Meaning of Gifts

The inequality of the parent-child power relationship organizes the circulation of valuables and thus establishes the meaning people ascribe to exchanges of things. First, the parent-child power relationship establishes a correlation between the amount of goods a person gives away and the amount of respect that person receives: the amount of respect a person receives in everyday life appears to be directly related to the amount of gifts and services that person provides for others over and above the person's established status obligations. People thus come to perceive respect as a function of gift giving—although, as should be clear, both respect and gift giving are functions of parental power to obtain compliance from their socially defined children.

Second, the parent-child power relationship establishes a correlation between the type of exchange and type of dyadic status relationship. As a result, people come to perceive their ability to establish desired status relationships with others as a function of their ability to fulfill the obligations associated with the status they wish to assume. Everyday experience thus has the effect of reversing the relationship between status obligations and access to goods that I have been discussing. I have already noted that status obligations determine people's access to goods for giving away. But people living in an equal bridewealth society seldom discuss this fact. When they talk about gifts, they focus on the apparent role of gifts in determining the status relationship between giver and recipient.

The parent-child power relationship guarantees a high correlation between respect and gift giving at both ends of the scale. At the low end, children, who give nothing away, gain little respect. To the degree that young people obey parents and therefore have nothing of their own, they have to ask parents for help, and thus put themselves in a position where parents can scold them for disobedience. They visibly receive the "condemnation and contempt" that all people dread. To the degree that children have nothing to give away, no one makes requests of them, and so few people show them the respect that everyone desires.

At the high end of the scale, adults who have goods or ritual knowledge for giving to others visibly receive respect. Because they have things that others want, others make requests of them. And because people who make requests must show respect if they are to have any hope of receiving what they request, those who receive many requests visibly receive the "respect and approbation" that everyone desires. To the degree that people have things for giving away, they never have to make requests of others and consequently need not put themselves in a position where others can scold them.

People who give many things away are seldom openly treated with condemnation and contempt, whatever others may say about them behind their backs.

The parent-child power relationship thus guarantees that respect and gift giving correlate with the two overt inequalities in equal bridewealth societies. First, respect and gift giving correlate with the inequality between seniors and juniors. Because parents appropriate the labor and products of children, juniors lack goods and respect, whereas seniors are able to give away the goods, daughters, and ritual knowledge that juniors lack and need to request. Parents not only give away the goods their children's services make possible but also receive goods for future giving from juniors in other households who request wives or ritual knowledge.

Second, respect and gift giving correlate with the inequality between elders who head large households and those who head small households. Because elders who have many workers in their households are able to give away goods, daughters, and ritual knowledge, they receive many requests. As a result, they receive much respect and many gifts from respectful requesters. Elders who have few children working for them have little to give away and therefore do not receive many requests. They receive little respect and few gifts from others. Elders who have few working children may even have to request the help of other elders to provide their children with the goods or knowledge they need.

These two correlations are evident in Cheyenne society. Boys normally joined war parties at the age of about 14. Before joining, a youth needed ritual instruction. Hoebel writes that "with every important activity among the Cheyennes, a beginner [had to] be instructed by a medicine man and [had to] secure a ritualized right to undertake the mission" (1978: 77). He therefore needed appropriate gifts (such as horses and decorated clothing) to respectfully offer the medicine man—gifts for which he had to humbly beg his parents since he was unlikely to have acquired such things on his own. Medicine men who had joined several war parties, in contrast, had the war records that proved that they could instruct others. They received respect from requesting youths as well as gifts that they could either use or give away.

Young Cheyenne men who wanted ritual knowledge could also apprentice themselves to experienced priests, to whom they had to present gifts. The gift giving continued over many years, because

Cheyenne priests gradually revealed ever more esoteric secrets (J. Moore 1974a: 267–68). Therefore, it seems reasonable to conclude that only heads of the largest households gained access to the most esoteric ritual knowledge. At the top of the Cheyenne ritual hierarchy were five sacred chiefs. To be eligible for such high office, a man must "have pledged or acted as instructor in either the Arrow Renewal, Crazy Animal, or Sun Dance [ceremony] at least four times" (Hoebel 1978: 49). A man could not act as instructor to the pledger of a ceremony without having previously pledged the ceremony himself, and a man who pledged a ceremony had to provide the vast amount of goods needed to stage the ritual, support the participants, and honor the instructor.

Cheyenne girls also had a need for ritual knowledge and therefore needed goods to give to teachers. Quilling (decorating hide objects with porcupine quills) was a necessary skill for any woman who wanted to be able to make the quilled items that the Cheyenne considered appropriate gifts. It was also a sacred skill. A girl who wanted to learn it could not simply ask her mother or a girl friend for instruction. She had to seek out "some old woman who belonged to the [quilling] society" (Grinnell 1923, 1: 160) and present her with appropriate gifts. No girl could acquire quilling knowledge without help from her mother to provide the gifts, the hides and quills necessary to do the work, and cooked food for the ritual meal.

At the head of the women's quilling society were old women who had quilled 30 robes apiece or made a lodge alone (Grinnell 1923, 1: 165). Such a position must have been held only by women who headed large households, for only a woman with many socially defined daughters to do the cooking and drudgery would have had so much time to spend quilling. The few women who reached this exalted position probably did not have to work any longer. As revered teachers, they must have received many gifts and ritual meals from eager novices and their families.

In summary, respect was correlated with gift giving in Cheyenne society. Children who lacked both goods and ritual knowledge had to beg their parents for help in acquiring the gifts they needed to present to elderly teachers. Children thus put themselves in a position where parents could scold them for past disobedience. Young adults who had acquired enough ritual knowledge to join war parties or to be able to quill objects did not have to ask parents for help in acquiring gifts. They could avoid scoldings, but they received little respect because no one asked them for anything. Finally, elders were differentiated in prestige. The old men and women who were known as great teachers received many gifts from eager novices. The other elders retired into obscurity, as few novices sought them out.

This brief discussion of gift giving suggests an explanation for why horses appear to have been more equally distributed among the Cheyenne than among the Comanche. In contrast to Comanche horse owners, some of whom had herds of 1,000 or more, a Cheyenne family that enjoyed social prestige kept approximately 40 or 50 good riding horses (Hoebel 1978: 29). Cheyenne horse owners, unlike their Comanche counterparts, had many opportunities for giving horses away. A father gave horses to his children to help them acquire ritual knowledge and spouses. Adult men who had their own herds gave horses to the teachers who instructed them in esoteric knowledge. An elderly man aspiring to the status of sacred chief gave horses to the poor (i.e. to household heads with few horses). Cheyenne horses apparently passed from herd to herd in the process of validating specific long-term status relationships and the acquisition of ritual knowledge or prestige.

In equal bridewealth societies, gift giving correlates not only with respect but with the type of dyadic status relationship. Particular types of exchanges of things (or the significant absence of a return gift) come to represent particular types of mutual obligations. People often seem to distinguish three types of exchange that correlate with three types of specific long-standing connections.

First, exchanges in which only one side gives something establish a dyadic status relationship in which the receiver owes the giver unending gratitude and respect. In Cheyenne society, the most unequal dyadic status relationships were those between parent and child and between a chief and the poor person to whom the chief showed generosity. Children who received parental gifts without giving anything in return, and poor people who accepted the horses and robes given away by chiefs without reciprocating, simultaneously accepted a permanent obligation to obey and show respect for the giver.

Second, exchanges in which the initiator offers gifts to show respect for the person from whom something is being requested establish a dyadic status relationship in which each side owes finite obligations. The requester owes respect only so long as the other person reciprocates with the desired knowledge or bride. In equal bridewealth societies, the association between unending obligation and receiving without giving ensures that most people who need to make requests try to give at least something to the person to whom the request is directed. Only people who have nothing to give, such as children making requests of their parents and members of households without resources, let themselves be put in a position of receiving without giving. As a result, most exchanges between juniors in one household and seniors in another are exchanges in which the requesting junior offers gifts to show respect.

Third, balanced exchanges establish a dyadic status relationship in which the exchangers are equals. In Cheyenne society, the senior kin of bride and groom exchanged equal gifts, thus establishing their mutual equality. People who exchange equal gifts have no basis for making further claims to one another, although, of course, they can continue to exchange equal gifts to demonstrate their mutual respect.

In equal bridewealth societies, there is seldom a clear distinction between gifts and loans because it is often in the interest of each side to define the transaction differently. Givers benefit by defining the objects given as a gift, thus defining the receiver as someone who owes respect (i.e. obedience) in return. Receivers benefit by defining the objects received as a loan that will be repaid, thus defining the receiver as someone who owes only return goods. A receiver who successfully defines the transaction as a loan claims the ultimate equality of the receiver with the giver, whereas a giver who successfully defines the transaction as a gift establishes the giver as someone who is entitled to respect.

Throughout this section I have argued that a person's existing status privileges and obligations establish that person's ability to give things away. This conclusion explains the obvious correlation between types of gift exchange and types of dyadic status relationship. Children's obligation to obey their parents condemns them to continuing their dyadic status relationship with parents, in which children receive parental support without giving anything in return. Parents' right to appropriate children's labor and its products supplies parents with things for giving to children and to heads of other households. People in equal bridewealth societies, however, seldom notice or talk about the fact that a person's existing status rights and obligations determine that person's ability to give things away. It is assumed to be a fact of life. It goes without saying—literally.

Instead, people stress the role of gifts in initiating and maintaining dyadic status relationships. In all human societies, people act within their social worlds; they seldom contemplate the structure of social relations that makes meaningful action possible. In equal bridewealth societies, people who show respect or give gifts want the recipients to reciprocate. Parents who help children acquire ritual knowledge want obedience. Children who dutifully obey hope to receive parental support. Novices who present gifts to teachers want knowledge. A bachelor's kin who present gifts to the family of an eligible girl want a bride. Women's kin who give a bride want respect and obedience from their son-in-law. People in equal bridewealth societies thus have innumerable occasions for contemplating and talking about the role of gifts in initiating and maintaining dyadic status relationships.

There are, in contrast, almost no contexts in which people have reason to think or talk about the role of existing dyadic status relationships in determining their access to goods. Children and young adults who want their parents to help them acquire ritual knowledge or spouses, for example, are in no position to assert that their obligation to obey parents deprives them of the ability to acquire goods for themselves. And the fact that inequalities are structurally produced and reproduced guarantees that deprived persons have no particular others to blame. A child can hardly blame parents for having needed a cradle, a name, or pierced ears in infancy, and for needing ritual knowledge. Similarly, a young man can hardly single out one person to blame for his inability to acquire a wife simply by setting up house with a woman. In equal bridewealth societies, individuals gain very little, as individuals, by understanding the structural causes of their oppression. It is of no practical use for a young man who needs ritual knowledge to understand that he needs it only because his society grants people who have such knowledge the right to speak for others. He still needs the knowledge if he hopes to speak for himself and for others.

The understanding that gifts establish dyadic status relationships is also protected from falsification by people's sense of reality. People who acquire things usually have the good sense not to try to give them away to establish status relationships for which they are not eligible. Beaver Claws, the Cheyenne bachelor who captured 70 horses during a raid, did not try to use his horses as an excuse to negotiate his own marriage or to claim chiefly status. He did not offer horses to junior kinsmen who needed brides or ritual knowledge. Nor did he try to give horses to the poor. Rather, he drove all 70 horses to the lodge of his prospective in-laws to gain respect. He did not try to establish long-term relationships that would be inappropriate for his existing status as a bachelor.

In summary, peoples' everyday conversations suggest to them that those who fulfill the obligations expected of one side in a dyadic status relationship can expect the beneficiaries of their acts or gifts to fulfill the obligations of the other side. In a society where the rights and obligations of particular dyadic status relationships appear to be already defined, people perceive their ability to enter into such relationships as a function of their capacity to provide the appropriate gifts and fulfill the necessary obligations. This understanding is only partially correct for two reasons. First, people do not consider how would-be givers or actors acquire the gifts or become defined as eligible to provide services. Second, people ignore the fact that those who provide gifts can expect others to fulfill obligations only because dyadic status relationships with defined obligations are presumed to exist prior to any given transaction and because the giver occupies an appropriate structural position relative to the recipient. Gifts take their meaning from existing status relationships. But in people's everyday experience, gifts appear to determine the relationship between any two particular individuals.

Political Processes

It is in the realm of conflict that people's understanding of gift giving as the way to establish desirable status relationships with others becomes a self-fulfilling prophecy. In conflict situations, disputants and mediators discuss past gift exchanges between the disputants to determine their specific long-standing relationship, and thus to decide the status obligations of each with regard to the other. Gift giving is also a way of establishing new status relationships. In situations of conflict, past gift exchanges may be invoked to decide which person, from among those eligible to assume a particular status, will succeed in having that status claim validated.

Gift giving may not determine the content of status obligations, because such obligations are presumably already defined. But it serves to acknowledge or validate existing status relationships and to establish new ones. Gift giving is the way to get ahead in the world. Conflict establishes it as the basis of political power.

In analyzing equal bridewealth societies, as in analyzing bride-service societies, it does not make sense to treat law and values as separate domains. People everywhere have systems of meaning that influence their perception of conflict and their understanding of how to handle it. In brideservice societies, most conflicts are perceived as resulting from a challenge to some man's reputation for bravery. In equal bridewealth societies, most conflicts are perceived as resulting from a failure to fulfill status obligations established by past gift exchanges.

This section on political processes, like the analogous section in Chapter 1, is concerned with overt cultural values. In the second and third sections of this chapter, I tried to lay bare the unstated assumptions behind what people say and do. The analysis was straightforward. I focused on the power relations that structure ongoing conversations: the power relation between affines that rests on the ability of women's kin to reclaim married women from their husbands; and the power relation between seniors and juniors that establishes gift giving as the way to set up desirable long-term status relationships. The analysis in this section and the next will not be so straightforward. Overt cultural values can be understood in many different ways, no particular one of which can be considered to provide an explanation for their existence. In the remainder of this chapter, I discuss only some of the possible ways to interpret what people say and do.

The Causes of Conflict

Ethnographers often describe equal bridewealth societies as exhibiting the three characteristics some Western jurists regard as the hallmark of primitive legal systems: strict liability, self-help, and collective responsibility (see S. Moore 1978: 83). It is true that equal bridewealth societies appear to exhibit these characteristics. Ethnographers often describe instances of people attributing blame without determining the intentions of wrongdoers, angry plaintiffs resorting to self-help, and kin groups being held responsible for the wrongs of one member. But it would be incorrect to think of equal bridewealth peoples as having a primitive version of a Western legal system. It is as improper to judge their system wanting by Western standards as it would be to judge a Western system wanting by theirs. Equal bridewealth peoples have a different system of meaning. We have to explore that system if we are to understand what equal bridewealth peoples are doing when they make statements or engage in behaviors that Westerners classify as strict liability, self-help, or collective responsibility.

Ethnographers usually report that people in equal bridewealth societies perceive conflicts as arising from unpaid debts (e.g. Bohannan 1957; Gulliver 1963; J. Collier 1973).[10] Aggrieved parties claim they are owed something by the person who wronged them. In some societies, the language pertaining to debt is explicit; in others it is implicit. The Cheyenne do not appear to have referred explicitly to debts (see Llewellyn & Hoebel 1941: 232–36), but they did handle conflicts as if wrongs created an obligation on the part of wrongdoers to offer compensatory damages. Adulterers and wife-stealers, in particular, offered horses to the husbands they wronged (Llewellyn & Hoebel 1941: 201).

My analysis of production and circulation in equal bridewealth societies suggests an explanation for why people think of conflicts as arising from unpaid debts. In societies where people perceive their obligations to others as a function of what they gave to them, or received from them (whether the object was willingly given, extracted by force,[11] or stolen), people expect others to fulfill the obligations implied by past exchanges, or to nullify past exchanges and past relationships by returning equivalent gifts. This is one sense in which people in equal bridewealth societies have strict liability. Once a wrong has been committed, a debt exists regardless of the intentions of the wrongdoer. This is also one sense in which they have self-help, for the creditor is believed to be actively seeking compensation whether observed to be taking action or not.

In equal bridewealth societies, as in brideservice societies, the conflicts that appear to occur most frequently, or are most often discussed, are those concerning men's claims to women. Even the sexually repressed Cheyenne were able to recount many lurid tales of elopement, marital conflict, adultery, and wife stealing (see Llewellyn & Hoebel 1941). Among the Cheyenne, as among the Comanche, men's fights over women also appear to have been more likely to lead to violence than their fights over horses or other objects. In all equal bridewealth societies, a man's access to goods for giving away depends on his status as a husband with rights to direct the labor and appropriate the products of wives and children. Challenges to a man's rights to women are challenges to the basis of his status.

Although men in both brideservice and equal bridewealth societies fight primarily over women, their different systems of inequality lead them to perceive such conflicts differently. For men in brideservice societies, men's fights over women raise questions about a man's ability to maintain a status that announces "don't fool with me." Men in equal bridewealth societies perceive elopement, adultery, and wife stealing as thefts that create debts.

The tendency of equal bridewealth peoples to perceive conflicts as creating debts suggests an explanation for Hoebel's observation that Cheyenne chiefs and ordinary men reacted differently to being cuckolded. "Where ordinary men customarily accept[ed] damages when their wives [ran] off with another man, a tribal chief [refused] the pipe, horses and gifts sent by the [wife stealer]" (Hoebel 1978: 44). In societies where the meaning of a gift varies according to the status of the giver, thefts imply different relationships depending on the status of the person from whom the object was stolen. In Cheyenne society, chiefs gave things to the poor without expecting gifts in return. As a result, a chief who refused to accept compensation from the man who absconded with his wife could expect that everyone would interpret his action as another example of chiefly generosity. He would both validate his claim to chiefly status and gain a follower. An ordinary man who was not in a position to claim chiefly status could not derive any benefit from giving his wife away. It made sense for him to accept the compensation that terminated his relationship with the man who had absconded with his wife.[12]

The Handling of Conflict

In a society where conflicts are perceived as caused by nonpayment of debts, which establishes a particular long-term status relationship between wrongdoer and victim, people handle conflicts by deciding what each side owes the other. If conflicts arise from unpaid debts, then the best way to handle conflict is to abolish the debt, either by ensuring that it is repaid or by having the debtor agree to fulfill the obligations implied in the dyadic status relationship established when the debt was incurred. In this sense, conflict-management procedures make the commonsense perception of gift giving as establishing long-term status relationships a self-fulfilling prophecy.

"Debt" in equal bridewealth societies is equivalent to "cowardice" in brideservice societies. "Debt" is the negative of "respect" (realized as gift giving), just as "cowardice" is the negative of "bravery." Both gift giving and bravery are cultural idioms that people use as grounds for asserting claims to privileges that, in fact, have other bases. In brideservice societies, bravery does not earn a man a wife and the privileges of marriage, just as in equal bridewealth societies, gift giving does not determine the obligations inherent in specific long-term status relationships. But in both cases, the idioms express concepts that organize people's understanding of conflict and thus encode meanings that come to have real consequences for people's lives. In brideservice societies, the man who is perceived as demonstrating cowardice when another man attempts to steal his wife not only risks losing her but also risks seduction of any future wives. In equal bridewealth societies, the person who is perceived as owing something to another has, by cultural definition, received a gift that establishes a dyadic status relationship between debtor and creditor. The creditor, as donor of the gift, is expected to claim the rights implied by the relationship or to nullify the debt by taking something of equal value.

Debt and bravery are different idioms and therefore have different consequences for dispute management. Bravery is a personal attribute of individuals, whereas the valuables whose exchange establishes or terminates dyadic status relationships must be acquired. In brideservice societies, disputes have to be handled by the disputants themselves, although elders may try to suggest appropriate outcomes. In equal bridewealth societies, disputes have to be handled by people who have the valuables necessary for paying debts, even though such people may not be disputants. Llewellyn and Hoebel report that Cheyenne conflict-management procedures frequently involved "the sacrifice of wealth and gain of prestige by an interceding person—usually a chief" (1941: 125).

The different idioms of bravery and debt also imply different types of confrontation. If the bravery of disputants is at issue, then disputants must face one another to prove their willingness and ability to fight. In brideservice societies, disputants confront each other directly in physical contests that are marked by ritualized displays of male prowess. But if debts are at issue, then people must meet to determine what is owed. In equal bridewealth societies, negotiation of the amounts, based on discussion of past exchanges, is conducted in moots. Violence may occur before, after, or even during such negotiating sessions, however.

Finally, the different idioms imply different types of settlement. If bravery is at issue, a dispute between men cannot be considered settled until each disputant has publicly demonstrated his ability to maintain a status that announces "don't fool with me." As long as the bravery of one disputant remains in doubt, conflict is an ever-present threat, for that man must prove his capacity for inflicting violence. But if debts are at issue, disputes cannot be considered settled until all debts are paid. As long as one disputant feels that a debt is outstanding, conflict is an ever-present threat. Everyone expects a creditor to make attempts to collect the debt in one way or another.

Compensation for unpaid debts, or unsuccessful relationships, makes sense in equal bridewealth societies in a way that it does not in brideservice societies. If people perceive their ability to establish desirable status relationships with others as based on gift giving, then those who have had something taken from them, or whose relationships are not working out, may use compensatory valuables to establish new or more satisfactory relationships (e.g. an abandoned husband can thereby begin negotiations for another wife).

The understanding that conflicts are the result of incomplete exchanges organizes the meanings people ascribe to the actions of disputants. The idiom of debt suggests that conflicts may be immediately resolved by a debtor's agreement to repay the debt or fulfill the obligations implied in the status relationship established by the gift. A striking fact about equal bridewealth societies is that settlement procedures are often initiated by the offenders rather than by the victims of wrongdoing.

Llewellyn and Hoebel describe "the basic and ideal norm" for handling wife-absconding cases in Cheyenne society as one "according to which the husband made no move, but waited for the emissary, usually a tribal chief, to come from the aggressor bearing the pipe and, (a) bringing horses or other goods acceptable to a man, or, (b) asking the husband what he desired in way of settlement. Smoking the pipe meant acceptance; the matter was closed, and the status of the woman in question changed" (1941: 201). The restraint required of a Cheyenne cuckold contrasts markedly with the action required of a Comanche cuckold.[13] In Comanche society, as noted in the preceding chapter, the man whose wife had been stolen could not afford to be passive. Rather he "was under social obligation to take action against the offender. For a man not to do so was not looked upon as an act of social grace; indeed, such behavior was a social disgrace. A man so acting was stamped not as magnanimous, but as lily-livered" (Hoebel 1940: 50).

In equal bridewealth societies, it makes sense for an offender to initiate settlement procedures because, as someone who has taken (i.e. received) something from someone else, the offender's status obligations are in doubt. The offender's goods and/or person are, to some extent, at the disposal of the victim. A known offender in this state of social limbo cannot take advantage of existing relationships, or enter into new relationships, until the relationship between offender and victim is clarified. In both equal bridewealth and brideservice societies, the person whose ability to establish relations with others has been called into question is expected to initiate settlement procedures. In equal bridewealth societies, offenders/debtors are expected to initiate such procedures. In brideservice societies, the victims of wrongdoing, whose bravery has been cast into doubt, are expected to prove their capacity for inflicting violence.

Although the idiom of debt provides a reason for offenders to initiate settlement procedures, it also provides a rationale for expecting victims to make the first move. The idiom of debt, as already noted, identifies victims as creditors who are involved in a reciprocal status relationship whether they want to be or not. In Cheyenne society, it *was* "magnanimous" for a man whose wife had absconded with another man to wait patiently for the arrival of an emissary from the offender. It was "an act of social grace" to refrain from obvious attempts at self-help.

But an offended person in an equal bridewealth society need not—indeed, often should not—wait patiently. Because they are involved in a dyadic status relationship, victims who appear to be patiently waiting rather than openly seeking a settlement are often not credited with magnaminity but accused of malice (see J. Collier

1973). They are perceived as seeking vengeance, either by surreptitiously engaging in witchcraft or by waiting until the time is ripe. In many equal bridewealth societies, therefore, victims are expected to initiate settlement procedures to show that they wish to end, rather than to exacerbate, a dispute.

This tendency to perceive victims as seeking vengeance may explain why ethnographers of equal bridewealth societies seldom describe people as handling conflicts by dispersing or moving away, as ethnographers of brideservice societies often do. People in equal bridewealth societies may move away, but because conflicts are understood as provoked by incomplete exchanges, the exchanges appear to remain incomplete regardless of where people are. Groups that are too weak to fight their enemies may disperse, and individual disputants may flee to distant kin, but everyone assumes such people are merely biding their time until they have the strength to fight back—even if it takes a generation or more. Because old conflicts never die, equal bridewealth peoples are famous for their ability to dredge up ancient wrongs as justifications for present warfare.

In summary, the idiom of debt fosters a cultural representation of conflict as involving not the two stages of offense and punishment (as in capitalist society) but three: "breach of norm," "counteraction," and "correction" (see Bohannan 1957: 211). In a society where wrongs create debts, the most reasonable justification available to someone who has harmed another person is that the wrongful act was a counteraction to a previous wrong by the victim. A wife who leaves her husband must state her grounds when asking her kin for asylum; she usually justifies leaving her husband with an assertion that he beat her or failed to fulfill some husbandly obligation. The accused husband usually tries to justify his actions with an accusation that his wife failed to fulfill some wifely obligation, such as not having his food ready on time or committing adultery. The person who takes something from another usually tries to justify the theft as the collection of an outstanding debt. The person who hits another justifies that behavior as prompted by anger because of the victim's failure (or the failure of a member of the victim's kin group) to fulfill status obligations.

As a result, people in equal bridewealth societies live in a world where mere punishment can never settle a dispute, for punishment is likely to be interpreted as an offense that demands a counteraction. One person's collection of a debt is another person's theft. Only a third stage, correction, can break the presumably endless cycle of wrongs and counterwrongs—of killings and vengeance killings.

Given the possibility of this endless cycle, a correction will be perceived as effective only when both sides appear to agree on the settlement terms. Since any unilateral action can be interpreted either as a direct breach of norms or as a counteraction that is not justified because the action being counteracted was itself a counteraction for a previous breach, any act that appears to be unilateral cannot count as settling a dispute.

This stage of correction would seem to explain why ethnographers report that disputes in equal bridewealth societies are commonly handled by elders rather than by disputants. Elders have the valuables needed for compensating victims; they can also help to achieve the balance of power between the two sides that is necessary in this stage if a successful settlement is to be negotiated. As long as one side is more powerful than the other, settlement terms can appear to have been unilaterally imposed by the more powerful side, and therefore can be perceived as demanding a future counteraction from the presently powerless party. As a result, a powerless person cannot negotiate directly with a powerful person. A beaten wife cannot negotiate with her husband, nor can an abandoned husband negotiate with his in-laws. The more powerful person would refuse to listen to the supposed wrongdoer; moreover, any settlement they reached could be regarded as imposed by force. A beaten wife, therefore, must run off to her natal family, and an abandoned husband must solicit the aid of his senior kin in negotiating with his in-laws unless he, himself, happens to be a respected elder. The Cheyenne man who absconded with another man's wife was not able to face the offended husband himself (particularly if he was younger and less respected than the husband). He had to send a respected chief.

The belief that correction is the only way of settling disputes explains why equal bridewealth peoples are so frequently portrayed as resorting to self-help and as recognizing collective responsibility. Attempts at self-help, as noted, are always interpreted as intensifying a dispute, but they are also a practical way for a person who feels wronged to pressure the wrongdoer to cooperate in negotiating settlement terms, or to involve others who will exert pressure on the wrongdoer to negotiate. By committing the wrong of leaving her husband, a beaten wife forces him to negotiate with her kin. By stealing something from an offender's senior kin, a victim is not only opting for a safer strategy (for the offender's kin are less likely to be on guard than the offender) but is also involving people who may have more leverage with the offender than the original victim. In equal bridewealth societies, it makes sense for A, who has been wronged by B, to steal from C to enlist C's support in confronting B, whether A, B, and C be individuals, kin groups, or larger political entities.

The understanding of conflict as involving the three stages of breach of norm, counteraction, and correction suggests a reason why ethnographers frequently describe people in equal bridewealth societies as handling conflicts by mediation and negotiation, not by arbitration and adjudication. Big Men and respected elders may act as arbitrators and adjudicators. They may use their power to impose the settlement terms they specify. But such imposed settlements can always be interpreted as worsening, not settling, disputes. In societies where disputants who are forced to accept solutions are assumed to harbor thoughts of vengeance, political leaders who use their power to impose solutions run the risk of being blamed for further conflicts. Therefore, a leader who might use his power in this way is avoided as a troublemaker (see Bohannan 1957). The ideal leader does not impose settlements but acts as a mediator. He suggests solutions, and he attempts to balance the sides by arguing for the underdog (see J. Collier 1973).

Ethnographers frequently describe negotiations as ending with reconciliation rituals, in which disputants demonstrate their agreement on settlement terms by drinking or eating together or by shaking hands. These reconciliation rituals publicly establish settlements as corrections rather than as offenses or counteroffenses that will be countered in turn. Llewellyn and Hoebel, for example, were impressed by Cheyenne concern with obtaining unanimous consent to decisions and "rehabilitating" (obtaining the public consent of) offenders (1941: 336).

Leadership and the Construction of Subordination

The understanding of conflicts as arising from unpaid debts allows Big Men considerable scope for leadership. They control the valuables needed to cancel debts, and they can ensure maintenance of a balance between opposing sides by speaking for powerless offenders and/or victims. By intervening in the disputes of others, they can shape the course of events. Big Men have the power to determine the fates of followers.

Ethnographers who portray equal bridewealth peoples as recognizing collective responsibility often suggest that membership in a kin group through birth or adoption determines liability. I wish to assert instead that equal bridewealth peoples appear to recognize collective responsibility because assumption of liability defines kin group membership. Equal bridewealth peoples, particularly those described as having unilineal descent systems, may talk as if a person's kin group membership were an unambiguous fact about that person. But kin group membership is *the* object of contention in equal bridewealth societies. Because the most unequal relationship is between socially defined parents and children, kin group membership is the object of constant negotiation by individuals seeking to claim parental rights over others or to deny others' parental rights to them.

Conflicts in equal bridewealth societies are public occasions for negotiating and redefining kin group membership. When a wrong is committed by an offender who lacks the valuables needed to pay compensation, everyone watches to see who will assume responsibility. In most instances, already recognized relationships will be reaffirmed. The parents of a wrongdoer will usually assume responsibility for paying the necessary compensation and by so doing will reaffirm their parental status vis-à-vis the wrongdoer. If a wrongdoer's parents are unable or unwilling to pay, another relative or elder may step in, thus claiming the offender as a son or daughter who owes obedience. An offender whose parents are dead and who is able to assume responsibility for paying the compensation may thereby escape being defined as the child of any living relative.

Conflicts also provide public occasions for Big Men and would-be Big Men to claim, or display their claims to, particular followers. Just as everyone watches to see who will assume responsibility for an offender's debt, so everyone watches to see which Big Man or would-be Big Man will speak for an offender's side. By speaking for another person, a political leader publicly displays his status as patron of the person spoken for, and therefore his right to expect obedience and political support from that person.

Middleton and Tait observe that in "tribes without rulers,"

people handle homicides by members of their own "jural community" (whose boundaries are defined in terms of the moral obligation to settle disputes peacefully) by payment of compensation, whereas they handle homicides by members of other jural communities by committing vengeance killings (1958: 9). I believe that there is less difference between "law" and "war" than Middleton and Tait imply. In equal bridewealth societies—which usually lack defined boundaries—all conflicts are interpreted within the framework of breach of norm, counteraction, and correction just discussed. Disputes between kin, between the followers of a Big Man, or between the followers of allied Big Men may provoke violent counteractions, but they usually do not because leaders step in to preserve their groups. The members of these groups appear to recognize a moral obligation to settle disputes peacefully because this is precisely the justification that Big Men offer for intervening in the disputes of others. Homicides involving the followers of rival or enemy Big Men, or of groups of Big Men, are usually handled by vengeance killings, although leaders may eventually meet to negotiate compensatory payments for all the accumulated deaths.

The Cheyenne may seem an exception to the "tribes without rulers" model just discussed, for Llewellyn and Hoebel describe the Cheyenne Council of Forty-Four Peace Chiefs as a high court that handled homicide cases by banishing murderers from the tribe (1941: 136). Llewellyn and Hoebel assume the applicability of Western jurisprudence, which casts kin group vengeance as the antithesis of law, however. Since in Llewellyn and Hoebel's view, the Cheyenne had law, they could not have kin group vengeance. Yet their book does provide enough information to suggest that the Council of Forty-Four Chiefs was not a high court,[14] but rather a group of allied Big Men who intervened individually or as a group in within-tribe homicides to prevent kin group vengeance and facilitate the negotiation of compensatory payments (see Llewellyn & Hoebel 1941, pp. 12–13, case 4).[15] The Cheyenne handled homicides by members of other jural communities, such the Crow, with vengeance killings.

Although leaders enjoy considerable power, ethnographers of equal bridewealth societies often focus on the limits of this power (e.g. J. Collier 1973). Many social mechanisms seem to protect the weak from the strong. In particular, the dependence of leaders on the support of their followers ensures that almost all oppressed people can find someone who is willing to stand up for them against their oppressors. A follower who feels that a Big Man is demanding too much can offer allegiance to another Big Man. A young person who feels oppressed by a household head can seek out a more supportive relative to serve as a parent, such as a father's sister or mother's brother. A woman who resents her husband's demands can turn to her brothers.

In addition, there is no cultural justification for the powerful to impose their will on the weak. As already noted, the Big Man who tries to act as a judge is regarded as prolonging rather than settling a conflict. And the required rituals of reconciliation provide protection for the weak who are being pressured to accept onerous status obligations or to renounce desired status prerogatives. Because a conflict is not considered settled until the actual victim and offender publicly indicate their acceptance of settlement terms, the powerful people who speak for socially insignificant disputants must keep negotiating until they agree.

Although the powerful lack cultural justifications for imposing their will, and reconciliation rituals provide the weak with some protection from the strong who speak for them in their disputes with others, neither consideration alters the fundamental power imbalance between juniors and seniors. In societies where the power of the weak comes from being able to play off seniors or Big Men against one another, the refusal of one senior or Big Man to support a junior puts the junior at the mercy of another senior or Big Man. A woman whose brothers refuse to take her in is at the mercy of her husband, just as a woman whose husband renounces her is at the mercy of her brothers. A man whose kinsmen refuse to help him marry is at the mercy of his prospective wife's kin. And a person who loses the support of the local Big Man is at the mercy of whatever political leader will accept that person.

Rey, discussing "the lineage mode of production," writes that "the different strategies available to a junior are largely illusory, and anyway limited in number" (1975: 53). Rey attributes juniors' lack of options to the fact that elders form a group. He thus implies that juniors' subordination results from collusion between seniors. My analysis suggests that this collusion is not conscious or deliberate. Rather, it is a consequence of dispute-handling procedures. The respected elders who act to balance disputing parties probably see themselves as wholehearted supporters of those they represent.

But in representing them, elders assume juniors' inability to represent themselves. Elders also assume the existence of inegalitarian dyadic status relationships. The senior kin of a married woman who has left her husband, for example, probably perceive themselves as acting for her, but in accusing her husband of misbehavior, seniors presume both the ability of a woman's kin to give her away and a marital relationship in which the wife can leave her husband only if he mistreats her.

Rey also describes "a much more final means of control" exercised by seniors over juniors: their ability to "transform a junior into a junior for life . . . by giving him to another elder as a slave" (1975: 53–54). In equal bridewealth societies, when a senior renounces a junior and consequently puts that junior at the mercy of another elder, the junior does become a "slave," for a slave in equal bridewealth societies is a person without recognized kin who is therefore at the mercy of alien masters. Children thus belong to their kin groups in the dual sense described by Kopytoff and Miers: they are members of a kin group, and they are "also part of its wealth, to be disposed of in its best interests" (1977: 10). In marital disputes, in particular, these two aspects of belonging are inextricably linked. The juniors who invoke group membership when soliciting aid from senior kin simultaneously put themselves in a position where their senior kin can give them away.

Women are, of course, more giveable, but men can also be given away because, should an abandoned husband's kin refuse to support him, they in effect give him to his in-laws. The husband who is not supported by his kin must either lose his wife (thereby remaining a junior) or keep his wife at the price of complete submission to in-laws (thereby becoming a slave). Dispute-handling procedures thus provide contexts for equating both men and women with valuables; however, women are usually given away *in exchange for* valuables, whereas men are commonly given away *in lieu of* valuables—i.e. when their kin refuse to provide the valuables men need for marrying or for paying compensation to victims (see Rey 1975: 54).

Because men and women are equated with valuables, equal bridewealth peoples often speak of one person owning another in the same way that a person owns a thing—or at least they make statements that ethnographers translate with the English verb "to own." The Cheyenne are not reported to have had elaborate concepts of rights to people of the kind found in many African societies (see Kopytoff & Miers 1977). Nevertheless, they made statements that ethnographers translate with words connoting ownership. Eggan quotes a Cheyenne girl telling the brother who had a right to dispose of her in marriage, "I am your property—I belong to you" (1955: 59). Llewellyn and Hoebel describe an incident in which Cheyenne warriors who were imprisoned by whites refused to let their chief accept the personal freedom the whites offered him. The warriors told their captors: "This man cannot go out; he owns us and can do what he likes with us" (1941: 106).

This equation of people with valuables is crucial to an understanding of why respect—rather than the accumulation of things—is the goal of individuals in equal bridewealth societies. In the end, it is by having respect that people become eligible to negotiate for themselves and others; it is because they lack respect that people are put in the position of needing others to negotiate for them. Disputants, for example, commonly ask the most respected of their kinsmen to negotiate for them, thus granting those kinsmen the power to decide what will become of them. Most people refuse to listen to those who lack respect (juniors and offenders), thus marking them as individuals who need respected people to speak for them. A person who has lost the respect of everyone falls into the category of slave, for slaves have been renounced by their kin. The consistently disobedient youth is sold into slavery (see Rey 1975: 54), left unrehabilitated after banishment (see Llewellyn & Hoebel 1941: 6–9; 174–75), or given to in-laws by kinsmen who refuse to provide marriage-validating goods. As I have already suggested, in this sense respect in equal bridewealth societies is equivalent to capital in capitalist societies. Those who have respect can organize productive processes; those who lack it are condemned to participate in the productive processes organized by others.

I have implied that the idiom of respect applies equally to men and women, but in reality it does not. Because women do not negotiate their own marriages, and because they are never asked to publicly negotiate settlements for dependent men (although women do privately intercede for sons with senior men), women often appear to be perpetually in need of a man to negotiate for them. The apparent correlation between being dependent and being female suggests an equivalence between dependent junior men and women of all ages. This equivalence naturalizes inequalities by grounding them in biological differences of sex and age.

But as I have been arguing, inequalities are socially created; they do not simply reflect differences in sex and age. In equal bridewealth societies, senior men can be dependent, if they lack children and are condemned to live in the households of other men. And senior women can be quite independent. One angry Cheyenne chief found out how independent women can be when he tried to give away two of his three wives. All three women ridiculed him and told him to give away the third as well (Llewellyn & Hoebel 1941: 186)—an act that would, of course, have left him without a household to head.

Folk Models of Social Structure and Human Agency

Equal bridewealth societies, in contrast to brideservice societies, appear to have well-developed bodies of norms. It is easy to understand why. Their perception of conflict as arising from unpaid debts requires people to discuss who owes what to whom and why. Because disputes are handled by exchanging the valuables that establish or terminate particular relationships, negotiators have to determine what the existing relationship is before they can decide what has to be given. In the process of talking about disputes, people tend to develop (1) explicit ideas concerning the rights and obligations of individuals involved in particular long-standing relationships, (2) norms concerning the transactions appropriate for establishing or terminating particular relationships, and (3) rules specifying the liabilities wrongdoers incur for committing particular offenses. Not all societies have the well-developed "conventional compensations for damage, adultery, loss of limb, and so forth" that Evans-Pritchard describes the Nuer as having (1940: 162). In some, disagreement over norms seems endemic. But in all equal bridewealth societies, people tend to speak of norms as if the ones they expound are generally accepted.

The norms do not dictate settlement terms, however. Equal bridewealth peoples invoke norms to support the positions they advance when bargaining with opponents, but their societies lack judges with the power to impose settlement terms. As a result, the settlements usually reflect, not norms, but the relative bargaining power of the two sides (see Gulliver 1963: 300).

Ethnographers may describe particular equal bridewealth peoples as anarchic, or orderly, or both, depending on which society the ethnographer is using for implicit or explicit comparison. To ethnographers who subscribe to the theory that social order results from the application of rules by impartial judges who have the power to enforce their decisions, equal bridewealth societies appear anarchic in comparison with societies that have true courts and judges, both because their norms do not dictate settlement terms and because their leaders lack cultural justifications for acting as judges or arbitrators. People in equal bridewealth societies handle conflicts on a case-by-case basis. Because each action may produce a counteraction, only a correction that is appropriate to the particular situation can restore balance and order.

But when equal bridewealth societies are compared with brideservice societies, equal bridewealth peoples appear quite orderly. Hoebel, for example, writes that "the Cheyenne law system was sedate and effective, calm and mature, when measured against the adolescence of Comanche behavior" (1954: 130). The Cheyenne, like other peoples appropriate for analysis with an equal bridewealth model, constantly referred to norms when handling disputes, not to the personal prowess or whims of offender and victim.

Because people in equal bridewealth societies invoke norms when discussing conflicts, they often perceive conflict as resulting from norm violations, and thus conclude that conflict would not exist if everyone did what they were supposed to do. In short, conflict-management procedures allow them to develop the notion of a rule-governed world. Equal bridewealth peoples vary in the degree to which people adhere to this notion, but some societies have developed elaborate cosmologies. Hoebel observes that "above all, the Cheyennes revealed a feeling for the social purpose of law" (1954: 130). They apparently thought that rule violations upset the balance of the universe, thus requiring a correction of such imbalances to restore social and cosmic order. The Cheyenne "universe [was] essentially a mechanical system which [was] good in essence, but which [had to] be properly understood and used to keep it producing what humans [needed] and [wanted]" (Hoebel 1978: 89). Hoebel compares Cheyenne rituals to "tune-up jobs" and to "major overhauls of a machine that has got out of adjustment or suffered a major breakdown in one of its parts" (1978: 90).

The notion of a mechanical, rule-governed universe suggests another explanation for the authority leaders enjoy. In such societies, people who know the rules that govern the universe have a cultural justification for telling others how they should behave, and what they should do if things go wrong. Knowledge is power.

Yet to have knowledge is not always to have power, because only a person who already has power will be credited with having knowledge. In equal bridewealth societies where knowledge is valued, having knowledge is equivalent to having women to give away in a brideservice society. Both possessions allow the possessor to perform the acts that appear to restore order and make social life possible. But only people who already have power can appear to have knowledge or to have women to give away. In neither type of society can a person who lacks power be perceived as having the necessary knowledge or women. Just as young men in brideservice societies can never be perceived as having women to give away, so young people in equal bridewealth societies can never be credited with having knowledge of how to run the universe, however much they might know. In most equal bridewealth societies where knowledge is valued, such as the Cheyenne, it is understood to be secret. Teachers reveal it gradually to novices who show them respect (i.e. offer them proper gifts). As a result, only elderly people who have given away many valuables are credited with having knowledge (although many people, including women and youths, may know as much as these elders).[16]

Having knowledge in equal bridewealth societies and giving women in brideservice societies are both idioms that people who live in such societies use to understand the basis of social order. The two idioms have very different consequences for women, however. In Chapter 1, I noted that the cultural logic of brideservice societies casts men who give women as making cooperative social life possible; it casts women who refuse to cooperate as destroyers of the fragile relationships on which survival depends. Cultural logic thus provides a justification for men to beat, kill, or mutilate unfaithful wives and uncooperative kinswomen. The idiom of having knowledge offers no such justification. Women in equal bridewealth societies are sometimes beaten, killed, or mutilated, but the man who carries out the act is liable to be accused of wrongdoing. Inflicting violence on a woman can, at most, be counted as a counteraction for a previous wrong, not as a correction that restores cosmic order. In Cheyenne society, killing a woman was considered murder (Llewellyn & Hoebel 1941: 138). In Comanche society, in contrast, it was "the privilege of the husband to kill his wife" (Hoebel 1940: 73).

Nor does the idiom of having knowledge distinguish between the sexes. Women as well as men can have knowledge. But the types of knowledge possessed by the two sexes are usually different and asymmetrical, as we will see in the last section of this chapter. In most equal bridewealth societies, women's knowledge is primarily concerned with rules for preventing pollution and mishap. Men's knowledge is primarily concerned with obtaining benefits and restoring an unbalanced universe to proper functioning.

In equal bridewealth societies, peoples' understanding of conflict and their notions of social order ensure that those who need to justify their behavior do so by claiming to be either counteracting a previous wrong or fulfilling an acknowledged status obligation. There is no obvious social context in which it makes sense for people to describe their actions as resulting from their inner feelings, but there are many contexts in which people talk about their status obligations vis-à-vis particular others. People thus come to think of their own actions and those of others as determined by the social relationships in which they are involved. I have no direct evidence that the Cheyenne understood human action to be determined by existing relationships, rather than by inner feelings or personal desires, but most Cheyenne stories of murder, beatings, elopements, and other violations reported by Llewellyn and Hoebel (1941) either refer to past wrongs committed by the victim or leave the question of motivation unexplored.[17] The lack of psychological explanation is particularly striking, given Hoebel's theoretical interest in personality and culture (see 1978: 95–104).

Because equal bridewealth peoples think of all human action as a response to the past actions of others, those seeking to understand and predict action tend to focus on the agent's relations to others. People thus come to think of themselves and others not as integrated personalities or as individuals with unique abilities and desires, as people do in capitalist societies, but rather as webs of relationships. In societies where relationships provide the context for understanding and predicting action, people appear to be their specific relationships with particular others. To know a person, in the sense of being able to understand and predict what that person will do, it is more important to know the history of the person's relationships with others than to know the person's capacities and desires. Yet because all relationships can never be known (for who can know all of another person's past or present actions, or even one's own?) behavior is never entirely predictable.

Practical Action

Because individual's actions are unpredictable, and because there is no concept of a superordinate authority to impose order, equal bridewealth peoples, like brideservice peoples, perceive social order as problematic, forever subject to disruption by conflict and violence. Equal bridewealth societies differ greatly in the amount of violence people are observed to express, however. The Jalé of New Guinea appear to be very violent (Koch 1974); the Arusha of Tanzania apparently deplore any resort to violent self-help (Gulliver 1963).

Although equal bridewealth peoples, like brideservice peoples, restrain themselves to avoid upsetting what they perceive as a delicate social balance, they have fewer methods open to them. Avoidance of conflicts by moving away, or by forgetting one's anger, are not strategies that equal bridewealth peoples can use. Because they understand conflicts as provoked by unpaid debts, they perceive conflicts as persisting wherever the parties involved may go or whatever they may do as individuals. As a result, equal bridewealth peoples concentrate on forestalling conflicts before they arise. They walk softly for fear of angering others (see Colson 1974). And more important, they try to anticipate what others will do.

Ethnographers often write that gossip is a major means of social control in equal bridewealth societies. Grinnell, for example, reports that "the [Cheyenne] Indian lived in public. He was constantly under the eyes of the members of his tribe, and most of his doings were known to them" (1923, 1: 103–4). The implication is that fear of public censure was an important force ensuring Cheyenne compliance with social norms. Social control is an unintended consequence of gossip, however. It is not the reason why people gossip.

People gossip because, in societies where actions are understood as counteractions to past actions, knowledge of past actions appears essential for predicting, and managing, the future. To predict how someone is likely to act, one must know the history of that person's past and present relationships. People thus seek out all the scurrilous information they can obtain and eagerly pass it on to allies.[18] And to the degree that people act on such information, gossip harms its victim.

People also seem obsessively to watch those around them. Because all actions can be understood as counteractions to past actions, all actions are open to being interpreted as confirming, modifying, or denying a particular relationship. No act, however insignificant it may appear, is without potential social consequences. Gluckman, in writing about African "tribal societies," notes:

This is why . . . persons watch, apparently greedily, what their kinsmen do with their goods; and why bitter disputes can arise over amounts which appear negligible to us—such as being overlooked in the distribution of a small pot of beer. It is not the beer that counts: the invitation to drink is a symbol of recognition of kinship. The African has to eke out his distribution of his products with great skill, lest he offend some kinsman or -woman. (1968: 74)[19]

For people who are constantly aware of the scrutiny of their fellows, hoarding obviously makes no sense. Rather, it makes sense to give things away, to affirm existing relationships or establish desirable new ones. Although equal bridewealth peoples give away almost everything that is not immediately needed or part of standard household equipment, they do not appear improvident, as brideservice peoples do. Because equal bridewealth peoples can use gifts to establish and maintain desirable relationships, they try to manufacture or acquire as many potential gifts as possible.

Both women and men engage in gift exchanges. Exchanges among men, or organized by men, may command more public attention, but in many equal bridewealth societies, exchanges among women are equally important because they also affect the women's children and thus, in the end, affect men as well. Only a few anthropologists have focused on women's exchanges (e.g. Weiner 1976), but ethnographers of many societies provide evidence suggesting the importance of women's everyday exchanges in establishing and maintaining the kinship bonds that organize the major appropriations of labor.

Llewellyn and Hoebel, for example, report two stories told by a Cheyenne woman who gave gifts to the children of her brothers (one real and one fictive), thereby publicly validating her status as "father's sister" to their children and simultaneously gaining "brothers" for herself and "mother's brothers" for her children

(1941: 247–51). The role of father's sister offered advantages to a Cheyenne woman because maidens unhappy with their mothers might take refuge with a father's sister, thus supplementing her labor force. I have already noted that women needed brothers if they were to bargain effectively with their husbands. Calf Woman, in discussing her fictive brother's family with Llewellyn and Hoebel, said "I knew they would always take care of me" (1941: 251).

The importance of "mother's brothers" for a Cheyenne woman's children, particularly sons, can be inferred from John Moore's observation that youths usually learned ritual knowledge from agnatically related males and joined the soldier societies of their fathers, but a man whose father was dead "joined the society of his 'protector,' who was usually a MoFa, or MoBr or MoSiHu" (1974a: 72). Mother's brothers were the closest competitors of fathers for a youth's loyalty and labor. A woman who maintained ties with influential brothers, and who astutely played off her husband against them, must have been able to provide her sons with many advantages not available to youths with less astute mothers.

Mothers in equal bridewealth societies are also important sources of information for ambitious sons. Because actions are understood as counteractions to past actions, young people face the problem that many of the actions credited with determining present-day relationships—and thus determining the significance of current acts—were taken before they were born or could have knowledge of them. Young people thus need information about the past, which can be obtained only from seniors. Young men do, of course, obtain considerable information from their fathers, but fathers are inevitably perceived as concerned with advancing their own careers, a goal that may bring them in conflict with sons. Only mothers, who, because they are women, cannot compete with sons, can be considered wholehearted allies. It is little wonder, then, that the mother-son bond is strong in most equal bridewealth societies. Aging mothers are frequently their mature sons' most trusted advisers—even in societies where harsh initiation rituals dramatize the separation of youths from their mothers.

Cultural Representations

Hoebel begins the first edition of his short monograph on Cheyenne society and culture with an account of their most important ceremony, the Renewal of the Sacred Arrows, which he describes as embodying all the dominant themes of Cheyenne culture. "It [emphasized] the dependence of human beings (the Cheyennes) upon the beneficent help of the supernatural world." "It [guaranteed] the authority of the tribal chiefs" and of old men in general. "It [stamped] the domination of males over females in ultimate determination of tribal matters, since men alone [could] actively participate in the rite." And it dramatized the unity of the Cheyenne tribe in contrast to other ethnic groups (Hoebel 1978: 18).

Hoebel's choice of starting point reflects the tendency of equal bridewealth peoples to describe their social world as governed by rules rather than by the personal whim and prowess that brideservice peoples say govern their world. When equal bridewealth peoples talk about the rules by which they think people should live, they may discuss their kinship system, religious system, or other system of values. But they seldom mention personal prowess or represent their way of life as determined by technology or ecology. Rather, they stress peoples' social and cultural obligations.

The differences in the beliefs, rituals, and cosmologies of equal bridewealth peoples are often more apparent than their commonalities. In some societies, initiation rituals embody dominant cultural themes. The most important ceremony in other societies may be the mortuary ritual or (as for the Cheyenne) rites celebrating agricultural renewal or fertility. Some peoples portray kinship as *the* ordering principle of social life, whereas others emphasize local contiguity, age grades, ritual expertise, or relations of exchange and enmity. These differences have real consequences for peoples' lives, but we cannot adequately grasp the distinctive meanings of any people unless we understand the concerns they share with other societies appropriate for analysis with an equal bridewealth model. As I suggest throughout this book, the ideas that people elaborate in rituals are those they invoke in negotiating the inequalities of everyday life. By recognizing that equal bridewealth peoples have common themes that are anchored in common social processes, we can better appreciate the uniqueness of each cultural elaboration.

The Cheyenne beliefs that humans were dependent on rule-giving deities, and that juniors were dependent on rule-knowing seniors, can be understood as variants of the cult of the ancestors common to equal bridewealth peoples, which identifies those who come after as dependent on, and indebted to, those who came before (see Meillassoux 1972: 99–100). The Cheyenne exclusion of women from active participation in their most important ceremony can be explained by their belief (also held by other equal bridewealth peoples) that potent femininity was dangerous to fragile masculinity and social order. Conceptions of human dependency and conceptions of gender are, of course, inseparable aspects of the same concept of personhood, but I will consider each in turn.

Human Dependency

Everyday social interaction offers people in equal bridewealth societies innumerable opportunities to talk about and meditate on young peoples' dependence on those who came before. Young people have many occasions in which to request seniors' aid— when they seek to acquire a wife, obtain shelter from an abusive husband, or gain ritual knowledge, for example. Elders also have many occasions to remind young people that they need spouses and ritual knowledge if they are to play adult roles. In equal bridewealth societies, in contrast to brideservice societies, people have many occasions to discuss their belief that humans come into the world lacking what they need to survive and prosper.

The Cheyenne conception of humans as dependent "upon the beneficent help of the supernatural world" (Hoebel 1978: 18) contrasts strikingly with the Comanche conception of humans as independent and self-reliant. As noted in the previous chapter, Wallace and Hoebel describe the Comanche warrior who sought supernatural aid as "confident of himself as a man. . . . He saw no call to demean himself in lamentation and self-pity" (1952: 157). A Cheyenne priest told John Moore, however, that "we men are nothing by ourselves. We have no claws or horns and we are not swift and powerful like a bear or an eagle. We only exist because we are the children of Maheo [the high God] and he pities us. It is Maheo that gives us everything we need to live. But he only helps us when we sacrifice ourselves and try to understand him" (1974a: 177). In Comanche society, men approached the gods with self-confidence. In Cheyenne society, men approached the gods with a deep sense of human need.

Although the Cheyenne apparently distinguished between spirits and humans (they did not practice ancestor worship), there is reason to believe that they drew their understanding of the relationship between spirits and humans from their experiences of the parent-child bond. Both spirits and living elders, for example, had the same critical resource: knowledge of how to make the universe run properly. "The great attributes of the spirits lie [not in having created the universe, but] rather, in their *knowledge*. They know how to make the universe run properly and how to get the most out of it. Their role, therefore, is that of instructor of men. They are the great teachers" (Hoebel 1978: 89, italics his). Senior men who had acquired ritual knowledge adopted the same role with regard to juniors that spirits adopted with regard to humans—"that of instructor."

If we assume that the Cheyenne modeled the spirit-human bond on that between parents and children, then we can interpret their religious beliefs as cultural representations of parental and filial roles. Their understanding of the spirits, for example, exemplifies the ideal parent in an equal bridewealth society. "Most spirit beings [were] beneficent; they [wanted] things to be pleasant and satisfying. They [were] generous in their blessings upon mankind. They [were] not niggardly and withholding by nature. They [were] not vindictive, punishing, cruel, or fearsome; although there [were] things to be feared, neither Cheyenne religion nor world view [rested] on fear of the 'Gods' " (Hoebel 1978: 89).

Although beneficent, the Cheyenne spirits (like parents in equal bridewealth societies) had to be asked to provide their blessings; they would willingly share their knowledge with mankind "if mankind [sought] and [listened] respectfully" (Hoebel 1978: 89). The spirits could also be moved by pity. "Since fathers are always moved by the tears and sufferings of their sons, so [was] Maheo moved by the tears and sufferings of Cheyennes. Weeping and bleeding [were] therefore the means by which Cheyennes [evoked] a response from Maheo" (J. Moore 1974a: 252).

In equal bridewealth societies, parents do appear to be moved by the tears and sufferings of their children. Because parents use children's requests for aid as opportunities to scold them for past misdeeds, requesting children are often reduced to tears. And because parents must grant children's requests to ensure that their dependents will continue to live with and work for them, parents usually grant the requests of children who cry. As a result, many equal bridewealth peoples believe that crying is the way to evoke a positive response from superior beings—parents and deities. Hoebel, writing about the nineteenth-century Cheyenne Sun Dance in the present tense, states,

self-torture is practiced by a number of northern Plains tribes as a form of religious sacrifice, but none carry it to the degree practiced by the Cheyennes. A few of the dancers in the Sun Dance Lodge may indulge in it, but most of the sufferers perform their acts of self-sacrifice outside the lodge. The sacrifice is made as the result of a voluntary, individual vow in the hopes of obtaining the "pity" of supernatural spirits, and thus achieving good fortune. The act also brings great public approval and is a conspicuous means of gaining social prestige. (Hoebel 1978: 23)

Parents in equal bridewealth societies may be moved by pity, but they also require work from children. Hoebel thus suggests that Cheyenne fathers were not always moved by the tears and sufferings of their sons: "Crying babies [were] not scolded, slapped, or threatened. They [were] simply taken out on the cradleboard away from the camp and into the brush where they [were] hung on a bush. There the squalling infant [was] left alone until it [cried] itself out. A few such experiences indelibly [taught] it that bawling brings not reward but complete and total rejection and the loss of all social contacts" (1978: 97).

The Cheyenne held contradictory beliefs not only about fathers' reactions to children's tears but also about the efficacy of ritual actions. On the one hand, the Cheyenne appear to have believed that human action compelled spirit acquiescence, a concept John Moore refers to as "the idea of certitude." He reports that "a common expression for Cheyennes when they speak of religious matters is: 'Since he brought the pipe, the priest couldn't refuse him.' Maheo, too, is said to be obligated to replenish the earth because the Sun Dance is performed" (1974a: 252). And Hoebel writes that "Cheyenne rituals [were] compulsive actions. . . . The acts [were] effective forces in themselves; they [worked] directly upon the mechanical system of the universe" (1978: 89).

On the other hand, the Cheyenne appear to have believed that the spirits helped humans only because they were beneficent. Spirits were not obligated to help humans. They did so only because humans approached them respectfully or because they felt pity.

In equal bridewealth societies, people's conception of the universe as mechanistic is probably advanced by elders who claim to have the knowledge needed to run it. And because these elders have social power, their activities probably produce desired results, thus confirming their possession of requisite knowledge. Elders also probably benefit from denying the efficacy of juniors' actions. It is in the elders' self-interest to emphasize that their granting of juniors' requests reflects their beneficence. It is not in their self-interest to portray juniors' acts as effective forces in themselves. And juniors' lack of real social power probably makes their acts ineffective, thus confirming juniors' lack of, and need for, the knowledge needed to run the mechanistic universe properly.

Ultimately, for the Cheyenne, knowledge and human dependency were linked through what Hoebel calls their "implicit energy concept." They thought of "the total energy charge of any object, and of the world itself, . . . as limited. As it [was] expended through activity, it [was] dissipated and diminished. Thus plants [withered], animals [became] scarce, the earth [ran] down. Renewal through regeneration [was] necessary, if the people [were] to survive" (1978: 90). The Cheyenne believed that humans had no energy source of their own. Humans merely expended, and thus dissipated, the energy given to them by the spirits (Hoebel 1978: 90). Energy therefore had to be continually acquired from the spirits by senior men, whose knowledge enabled them to do so. All energy passed from spirits to senior men, and from knowledgeable men to those who were unable to communicate with the spirits by themselves—women and children. The Cheyenne equated knowledge with life itself. A priest told John Moore that "we are the children of Maheo and we are ignorant like children. This is why so many babies die in the first few years. They do not know Maheo. But if a man grows up respecting Maheo, sacrificing himself and pledging ceremonies, why then he can live a long time" (1974a: 177). The Cheyenne reverence for knowledge, equation of knowledge with life, and restriction of knowledge (of how to run the universe) to males are common to many equal bridewealth peoples.

Gender Conceptions

It is appropriate to begin a discussion of the gender conceptions of equal bridewealth peoples with femininity because femininity is the conceptual basis of masculinity. The Cheyenne, for example, associated women with the Deep Earth, which they defined as the source and substance of all life. To bring forth life, however, Earth had to be fertilized by the life-giving rain provided by spirits in the High Sky (J. Moore 1974a). Deep Earth thus existed prior to High Sky, for fertilizing rain was meaningless without a Deep Earth capable of bringing forth life.

We can easily understand why equal bridewealth peoples celebrate women's capacity to bear children. In such societies, children are the source of all power. Men need sons and daughters to become household heads; women need children to work for them and so that they will have bargaining power relative to their husbands and natal kin. The most important thing about a woman is her fertility. A woman who bears many healthy children builds her own and her male sponsor's economic and political support group. A woman who is barren represents misfortune for her husband, her natal kin, and herself. In equal bridewealth societies, women appear to be "the means of reproduction" whose control constitutes the basis of all social power (see Meillassoux 1972).

Women's capacity to bear children is *the* contested resource. Both women and men claim to control it. Both thus have reason to talk about femininity as a potent force in need of their control. As a result, equal bridewealth peoples tend to perceive femininity as both good and evil. Femininity under control is the source of all life. Femininity out of control is the cause of social chaos.

Masculinity is a fragile force; it is forever trying to impose order on chaos by controlling femininity and is forever threatened with the possibility of failure. The Cheyenne associated masculinity with the High Sky, whose spirits were the source of energy. Just as the spirits provided the rain that enabled the Deep Earth to bring forth life, so men provided the semen that enabled women to do so. And just as the rain provided by the spirits sank into the Deep Earth never to reappear, so semen disappeared forever in women (J. Moore 1974a). As energy was "expended through activity," it was "dissipated and diminished. Thus plants [withered], animals [became] scarce, the earth [ran] down" (Hoebel 1978: 90), and children died. Masculinity had to be continually replenished if life was to continue and order was to be maintained. Men in equal bridewealth societies, like men in brideservice societies, understand masculinity as a force to be acquired. But men in equal bridewealth societies, unlike men in brideservice societies, tend to worry about losing masculinity, not merely about acquiring it.

It is easy to understand why equal bridewealth peoples perceive masculinity as necessary for life and order. In such societies, men get ahead by laying claim to women's products, particularly women's children. Men thus have many contexts in which to talk about what they give women, and particularly to portray men as givers of life. Men must also talk about what women have that men want, however. Therefore, men must credit women with doing/ having something. People in equal bridewealth societies, in contrast to those in brideservice societies, seldom portray men as totally responsible for producing children. In many brideservice societies, people believe that fetuses are made entirely of sperm. In equal bridewealth societies, however, women are usually credited with contributing an infant's blood and flesh; men provide the spirit or bone that gives them life and structure.

It is also easy to understand why masculinity is perceived as fragile, forever subject to being overwhelmed by potent femininity. Men's claims to women's products must be continually reasserted because women continually contest them. In equal bridewealth societies, unlike brideservice societies, men try to take from women things (and children) that women can use in other ways. When men are not actively claiming women's products (and sometimes when they are), women use their products in ways that women want. As a result, men's life-giving energy does appear to dissipate, or to have no long-term consequences. In men's daily experience, women do drain men of life-giving energy, so men must keep acquiring male energy if they are to keep imposing order on chaotic femininity.

Rituals

The major rituals in equal bridewealth societies tend to be those devoted to renewing masculine energy, either in male initiation rites or in societal rituals to revitalize the universe. Although equal bridewealth peoples commonly celebrate women as the Mothers and Source of All Life, the major societal rituals do not focus on women's fertility. Equal bridewealth peoples seldom worry about women's ability to provide the blood and flesh from which babies are made. Instead, they worry that women are voracious (for semen) or that they will overproduce blood and flesh without form. In short, they worry that male energy will not be sufficient to keep the vast feminine potential from destroying everything. Consequently, the major rituals focus on renewing male energy. Women are usually excluded from these rituals because their femininity is perceived as posing a threat to the masculinity that is to be renewed. Male initiation rituals, for example usually dramatize the separation of boys from their mothers, for boys must be separated from potent femininity if they are to acquire the fragile force of masculinity—that is, to become men.

Since femininity poses such a threat to fragile masculinity, men in equal bridewealth societies often limit their contacts with women. Hoebel writes that the Cheyenne believed that "sexual energy [was] a limited quotient which [had to] be spent sparingly" (1978: 90). Although he mentions "sexual energy" without specifying gender, Hoebel is clearly referring to men, for his next sentence is: "Therefore, the man of strong character and good family [vowed] at the birth of his first child (especially if it [was] a boy) not to have another child for either seven or fourteen years." By abstaining from sexual intercourse, a Cheyenne father could devote all of his spiritual energy to raising his one child. Hoebel believes that women accepted this imposed chastity, for according to Cheyenne belief, a mother's failure to do so would kill her child (1978: 90).

In many equal bridewealth societies, women have their own organizations and rituals. Both the male fear of femininity and the consequent male avoidance of women encourage women to establish separate organizations. Moreover, the societywide celebration of women's capacity to bear children provides women with a set of concepts to elaborate in rituals. Women *are* the Mothers and Source of All Life. Femininity *is* a force to be celebrated.

Equal bridewealth societies vary in the extent to which women establish women's organizations and rituals. Ethnographers of some of these societies portray women as disorganized, degraded, and exploited (e.g. Keesing 1985).[20] Ethnographers of other societies portray women and men as occupying "separate but equal" spheres, with male control of cosmic forces balanced by women's control of human reproduction (e.g. Schlegel 1977b). Cheyenne women appear to have been among the most powerful. Grinnell writes that Cheyenne women were "rulers of the camp" (1923, 1:

128) and that they appear to have had their own ritual hierarchy in the quilling society (1923, 1: 159–69).

Women also have many social opportunities to elaborate the virtues of femininity. In their roles as mothers who direct children's labor, women are frequently faced with having to justify their authority. Just as men tend to develop elaborate ideas of what men give women to justify claiming women's products and children, so women tend to develop elaborate ideas of what mothers give children in the process of justifying a mother's demands for obedience.

The common gender conceptions of equal bridewealth societies also provide women an opportunity to portray femininity as more important and more socially valuable than masculinity. Women's capacity to bear children is the basis of all that is socially important. Women can thus credit themselves with being responsible for social continuity and reproduction, casting men as mere transient actors whose projects have no lasting effects (see Weiner 1976). Social processes confirm this understanding. Men build their careers by asserting claims to women. They therefore appear concerned with building individual (albeit short-lived) social groups. Women, in contrast, make society possible.

Although women may celebrate their capacity to bring forth life, and may portray femininity as existing prior to, and more important than, masculinity, women, like men, tend to understand femininity as dangerous. The most unequal inequality in equal bridewealth societies is not that between men and women, but between seniors and juniors. Senior women, like senior men, have many opportunities to stress the dangers of uncontrolled femininity, for junior women's barrenness, adulteries, laziness, or refusals to marry disrupt the carefully constructed households of senior women as much as they disrupt the carefully constructed exchange relations of men.

Social processes usually cast women, rather than men, as disrupters of social life. Because women are associated with apparently natural reproduction and social continuity, their efforts to manipulate close kinspeople for their own advantage appear extremely unnatural in contrast to men's efforts to manipulate others—particularly female kin—in building their individual careers, for that is what they are expected to do. It thus seems significant that in the Cheyenne suicide cases reported by Llewellyn and Hoebel (1941), only women were accused of murder when a close relative committed suicide. A man whose wife hanged herself when he brought home a second wife was not accused of murder; people thought the wife was foolish (1941: 159).

Social processes also usually cast ambitious women as manipulative but ambitious men as virtuous. In Cheyenne society, the man who actively sought brides, war magic, and ritual knowledge was honored. A women was not expected to actively seek husbands or extradomestic exchange partners, however. Of relevance here are the contrasting descriptions of Stump Horn (a man) and Calf Woman: "Put together Stump Horn's stories of himself, and you find a somewhat naive and unselfish acceptance of the given pattern of the gentleman. Put together Calf Woman's stories about herself, and you see an enterpriser, skillfully using all available social devices to her own ends—which at times included the working out of grudges" (Llewellyn & Hoebel 1941: 264). Llewellyn and Hoebel contrast Stump Horn and Calf Woman in pointing out that every society has both rules and rules for getting around the rules. My analysis suggests that their description also reveals patterned differences in the cultural evaluations of men's and women's strategies for becoming heads of large households. Cheyenne society probably included many enterprising males and naive females, but it seems significant that Stump Horn, who had a "swarm of relatives and friends . . . 'camping on him' " (Llewellyn & Hoebel 1941: 33),[21] was credited with acquiring that swarm simply by following "the given pattern of the gentleman," whereas Calf Woman, whose husband became a chief, was perceived as an "enterpriser" who used "all available social devices to her own ends."

Because women as well as men understand femininity as dangerous, women's rituals, like those of men, usually focus on controlling potent femininity, even though women, of course, celebrate their power. Girls' puberty rituals are usually joyous celebrations, but they are also occasions for teaching girls how to control their newly acquired power to bring forth—and destroy—life. Menstrual blood is often portrayed as deeply polluting. In those societies, such as the Cheyenne, where babies are believed to be made of congealed menstrual blood (animated by male spirit), flowing menstrual blood represents failed conception—the awesomely destructive power of femininity gone wrong. Girls are therefore taught how to protect themselves, their children, and their men from women's capacity to pollute and to kill.

Many equal bridewealth peoples divide potent femininity into two opposed aspects: dangerous sexuality and beneficent motherhood. Female sexuality is perceived as a force that needs to be controlled if women are to utilize their beneficent capacity to bring forth life. In some societies, such as the Cheyenne, women, like the Deep Earth, are believed to soak up the limited supply of life-animating rain/semen. Consequently, it makes sense for these people to think that women's sexual activity needs to be restrained so that the limited supplies of rain/semen can be conserved for their appropriate life-animating purpose. Women who take too much of the life-animating fluid not only deplete men's supplies, but also endanger their fetuses and growing children. Social processes confirm this understanding of female sexuality as inimical to successful motherhood. Young women's adulteries, and even their sexual enticements to their husbands, disrupt the carefully constructed households of seniors. Furthermore, under premodern health conditions, parturition is dangerous to women and many babies die in their first year.

Many equal bridewealth peoples symbolically "bind up" female sexuality to protect human life. This binding up metaphor suggests an explanation for the famed Cheyenne chastity belts described by ethnographers. At puberty, each Cheyenne girl was outfitted with a chastity belt—"a thin rope placed about the waist, knotted in front over the abdomen, with the free ends passing down between the thighs to the back, thence down around the legs to the knees" (Llewellyn & Hoebel 1941: 176). Girls wore these belts constantly until married, and whenever alone after marriage. The belts were installed by senior women, and senior women also prosecuted any man who disturbed a woman's chastity belt (Llewellyn & Hoebel 1941: 177).[22]

In equal bridewealth societies, sexual antagonism appears to be centered in the husband-wife relationship. In people's everyday experience, that relationship is strained by the need of each spouse to appropriate the products and labor of the other to attain personal ends. Men must appropriate women's labor products, and keep their own products from their wives, if they are to have gifts for presenting to elders, in-laws, and teachers of ritual knowledge. Similarly, women need to keep their own products and obtain products and labor from husbands to advance their children's careers. Only when young couples become heads of households with dependents to work for them do the interests of husband and wife coincide.

At the same time, gender conceptions cast sexual intercourse as a contest of powers. Men are perceived as dominant because they control life-animating spirit; women are perceived as dominant because they forcefully appropriate men's powers. The contest of wills between husband and wife over each other's labor and products may be lived as a contest of powers in bed. Sexual intercourse in marriage—or in general—may come to be perceived, and experienced, as an aggressive act with winners and losers.

This manifestation of sexual antagonism as a fight between married partners differs from the manifestations of sexual antagonism usually found in brideservice societies. As noted in the preceding chapter, brideservice peoples tend to think of an opposition not between men and women but between the harmonious male world and the conflict-ridden heterosexual world. Women, in general, threaten the harmonious world of men, and sexual antagonism takes the form of all women against all men—often in playful contests (see Collier & Rosaldo 1981: 321). Gang rape occurs in both types of societies, but it seems to be mentioned more frequently by ethnographers of brideservice societies, where men unite to punish a woman whose misbehavior threatens their solidarity. The Cheyenne considered initiation of gang rape "a right of the husband." He put his wife "on the prairie" and arranged for her rape by his cousins or soldier band (Llewellyn & Hoebel 1941: 202).[23]

Many equal bridewealth peoples have developed the concept of a dualistic universe, in which all social and natural phenomena are ordered by the opposition between femininity and masculinity. It is easy to understand why dualistic cosmologies might appeal to people who perceive masculinity and femininity as opposed forces. Equal bridewealth peoples have many contexts in which to elaborate the gender opposition. Senior men, in particular, often have both cause and context for developing elaborate notions of how the universe is ordered. They claim to teach younger men how to run the universe; therefore, they must develop notions of how the universe runs. Senior men also enjoy the leisure time that allows them to think and to conduct ceremonies. In most cases, they elaborate an opposition between masculinity and an already given femininity. In their dualistic cosmologies, senior men most frequently map the male/female opposition onto superior/inferior and—with some degree of success—onto every significant opposition in the culture, such as senior/junior, culture/

nature, day/night, high/low, dry/wet, public/domestic, affinal/consanguineal, autonomous/dependent, domesticated/wild, and selflessness/selfishness.[24]

The most powerful connection elaborated in the dualistic cosmologies of senior men is the mapping of male/female onto superior/inferior in such a way that young men are equated with women. The Cheyenne believed that male was to female as senior men were to youths. John Moore writes that in the cosmology elaborated by (male) priests, "sexual roles" were the most prominent theme; "patterns of respect and authority among men" were "next in importance" (1974a: 144). As already noted, the Cheyenne equated masculinity with High Sky and femininity with Deep Earth. The spirits in the High Sky were ranked on the basis of their height; the highest spirits controlled more knowledge than the lower ones (1974a: 169). Cheyenne youths, like Cheyenne women, began without knowledge and were taught how to contact lower spirits before being taught the rituals necessary for contacting higher spirits.

In many cultures, the opposition between male and female is mapped onto the opposition between superior and inferior men, thus equating inferior men with females and vice versa. But not all cultures define masculinity and femininity in the same way. In both brideservice and equal bridewealth societies, youths—as archetypal inferiors—are equated with women and contrasted with superior senior men. But the two types of societies have different concepts of femininity. The available evidence suggests that in societies appropriate for analysis with a brideservice model, where the concept of femininity is not elaborated, youths have a desire to acquire masculine potency, not a need to discard feminine traits. In equal bridewealth societies, where the concept of femininity is elaborated, youths apparently feel themselves burdened with a femininity they must discard or destroy if they are to become men. Male initiation rituals in many equal bridewealth societies are aimed at purging femininity from growing boys.

The mapping by people in many equal bridewealth societies of the male/female opposition onto the superior/inferior opposition is far from perfect, as should be obvious. The mapping is always contradicted by daily experience. Senior women, unlike junior men, can be, and often are, quite powerful. The attempt to posit cosmic dualism by mapping masculine and feminine onto all other

significant cultural oppositions is also inherently doomed to failure. All the oppositions simply do not map onto one another.

Paradoxically, it is this failure of oppositions to map onto one
another that invests cosmic dualism with the influence it enjoys.
Efforts to posit cosmic dualism appear to be revelations of an order
underlying complex and chaotic experience. But they are also, necessarily, mystifications. All cultural oppositions can be mapped
onto one another only if people ignore such facts as the power
enjoyed by senior women. The failure of oppositions to map onto
one another guarantees the vitality of cosmic dualism because it
ensures that such mapping will be continually repeated in the face
of recalcitrant reality. If the oppositions did map onto one another,
then no one would have an incentive to keep rediscovering their
congruence.

Equal bridewealth peoples, like brideservice peoples, have a rich
and contradictory vocabulary for negotiating social inequality. Just
as brideservice peoples may talk about marriages either as prescribed or as achieved by male prowess, so people in equal bridewealth societies may say that self-torture evokes both pity and
contempt, that ritual actions compel and do not compel godly
compliance, and that the male/female oppositions does and does
not map onto other significant oppositions.

Marriage Revisited

In equal bridewealth societies, marriage is the moment when the
oppositions of gender and age are realized. The conversations of
people engaged in making and breaking marriages define the content of the three paradigmatic long-term status relationships of
woman's kin—woman's husband, husband-wife, and parent-child.
To understand marriage is to understand how inequality is organized in equal bridewealth societies. To understand marriage is to
understand the socially defined categories of woman's husband,
wife, and child.

Marriage and its opposites, fornication and adultery, are mutually defining. Young men and women can sleep together, and even
set up housekeeping and have children, but their union is perceived
as establishing a relationship of debt (in the form of either labor or
valuables) between the young man and his wife's kin. Until a union
is validated by the seniors' exchange of appropriate gifts, the young
man and his possessions belong to his wife's kin. Similarly, a mar-

ried woman may sleep with or abscond with her lover, but their act establishes a debt between the lover and the woman's husband.

This relationship of debt between the man who lives with or sleeps with a woman and the woman's kin (or former husband) establishes the socially defined category of woman's husband. A woman's husband is a person who owes a finite debt to his (or, in those societies where women may acquire wives, her) in-laws. The debt relationship also establishes the socially defined category of wife. A wife is a person whose actions create debts for others— someone who cannot give herself (or himself, in those societies where boys may be given as wives). The debt between a woman's husband and the woman's kin establishes the socially defined category of child. A child is a person who can be given away or redeemed by parents. Females are usually given away in return for valuables, whereas males are usually redeemed by the payment of valuables. But parents may also redeem females by repaying their husbands and give away males in return for valuables.

To understand marriage is also to understand conceptions of gender, for marriage is a relationship shared by socially defined men and women. My brief overview of gender conceptions suggests that the men and women whose skilled performances produce and reproduce an equal bridewealth society perceive themselves as having opposed and dangerous potentialities, whose conjunction in sexual intercourse can create or destroy life. It thus makes sense for junior women to submit to the marriages arranged for them by senior kin. To become successful mothers, they need the help of senior women who know how to control the destructive aspects of femininity responsible for infertility and how to develop the beneficent aspects that can ensure successful childbirth and the growth of healthy children. It also makes sense for young men to beg seniors' help in marrying. Senior men control the knowledge that allows young men to limit their contact with powerful femininity and to channel its potential so that women provide them with children and the products of their labor. Young people therefore allow, even urge, seniors to validate their marriages through exchanges of equal, or standard, bridewealth.

3

The Unequal Bridewealth Model

The unequal bridewealth model proposed in this chapter is most appropriate for analyzing ranked, acephalous societies. It is not appropriate for analyzing the hierarchical, centralized societies with recognized positions that are commonly called chiefdoms (see Service 1962).

Preliminary Description of the Type

No anthropologist, to my knowledge, has suggested that ranked, acephalous societies should be regarded as a type separate from, and comparable to, bands, tribes, or chiefdoms. Rather, ethnographers usually portray groups appropriate for analysis with the unequal bridewealth model as transitional social formations—as egalitarian societies on the way to becoming chiefdoms (see Mishkin 1940; Meillassoux 1981: 73; Service 1975), or as chiefdoms in the process of disintegrating under the impact of capitalism and colonialism. Ethnographers seldom portray such groups as societies. Leach (1954), for example, describes the *Gumsa* Kachin of Highland Burma not as a society, but as an unstable point in a historical oscillation between the egalitarian political system of the *Gumlao* Kachin and the hierarchical, feudal system of the valley-dwelling Shan. However, there are enough ethnographic descriptions of similar, supposedly transitional social formations to suggest that a systemic model might be worth developing.[1] But because no anthropologist has proposed that such groups form a recognized type of society, the unequal bridewealth model proposed in this chapter is the most tentative of the three models discussed in this book.

Unequal bridewealth peoples are not egalitarian. They have ranks—named, hereditary status groupings. Hoebel writes that the Kiowa had "a system of horizontal rating unique for the Plains" (1954: 170). According to Richardson, they "distinguished three semi-formalized named ranks into which one was born," plus a category of outcasts (1940: 15). Most societies seem to have equivalent divisions. They have a lowest, nonhereditary category, labeled "outcasts," "slaves," "debt bondsmen," or something similar, and they have a category of "commoners" who rank below "nobles" or "aristocrats." In some societies, such as the Kiowa, the highest rank is subdivided into "nobles" and "chiefs."[2]

People in unequal bridewealth societies tend to believe that no two people can be truly equal. Within kinship groups, full brothers are unequal, and between kinship groups, wife-givers outrank wife-takers. Among the Kiowa, for example, the ranks "were not sharply demarcated: there was a gradual shading of one into the other and there were gradations within each" (Mishkin 1940: 37). In theory, everyone's place on a ranking continuum extending from the lowest slave to the highest chief should be knowable. In fact, each person's rank is never precisely known and therefore is the subject of lifelong negotiation. The unending negotiation of rank is the most apparent feature of unequal bridewealth societies. It is little wonder that ethnographers portray such societies as unstable and transitional.

Labor appears to be divided by rank. People in high-ranking families are free to pursue culturally valued activities because they have slaves, outcasts, or debt bondsmen to perform necessary, but unprestigious, tasks for them. Mishkin writes that among the Kiowa, captives and "poor" men "were compelled to specialize in the prosaic activities, hunting, camp duties, etc." (1940: 62). High-ranking men, freed from the performance of such tasks, were able to leave camp for long periods. They specialized in warfare and thus readily acquired the war honors and captured horses that Kiowa regarded as the basis of male prestige.

The main economic units of unequal bridewealth societies are larger than households and are usually composed of people who have specific kinship or affinal links with the leader. Among the Kiowa, the economic unit was not the extended family of parents and married children, as it was for the Cheyenne, but rather the entire *topotoga* or band (Mishkin 1940: 26), which "did not maintain common residence throughout the year" (Richardson 1940: 7–8). "The oldest brother was almost always head of the family" (Richardson 1940: 12), and the core of the band consisted of full brothers, their wives and children, and their half, classificatory, and pact brothers (Richardson 1940: 5–6). Kiowa bands also included such affines of these brothers as the husbands of full, half, and classificatory sisters (Richardson 1940: 5–6). And Kiowa headmen attracted "energetic though poor" young men to their bands by giving them sisters or daughters (Richardson 1940: 6).

Ethnographers commonly report that marriages are validated with bridewealth and/or by an exchange of gifts whose number and quality vary according to standing of the bride. Those who write about bridewealth frequently report that high-ranking brides "cost" more than low-ranking ones, and those who write about gift exchanges often report that the marriages of high-ranking women involve more lavish gifts than the marriages of low-ranking ones.

Observers of Kiowa society differ in their descriptions of marriage, depending on whether they participated in the 1935 ethnology field-study group that included Richardson, Mishkin, and Donald Collier. Observers who were not part of that group report that men married with brideprice. Mayhall, for example, observes that among the Kiowa, "horses served for buying a wife" (1962: 110). Battey writes that during marriage negotiations, the bride's "value is extolled by her mother, while her father, anxious to drive as good a bargain as possible, fixes her price in ponies, blankets, or other articles of value" (1968: 328). Neither reports that high-ranking brides cost more than low-ranking ones, but it seems reasonable to assume that high-ranking fathers were more successful at driving good bargains than low-ranking men. This assumption is supported by Wharton's (1935) report of General Custer's 1868 encounter with an eloping Kiowa couple. The young people were afraid to return home because the bride's father, "Black Eagle, now the ex-officio first chief," . . . "demanded twenty horses for his favorite daughter" (1935: 146). Among the Kiowa, "a herd of twenty or thirty [horses] was considered a proper size" (Richardson 1940: 14).

Anthropologists who were part of the 1935 field-study group write that marriages were validated with exchanges of gifts between the two families. "The boy's family approaches the girl's family and if accepted initiates a gift exchange between the two families. Both sides help to establish the married couple in housekeeping, and maintain friendly relations through continued gift exchange" (D. Collier 1938: 11). Should a Kiowa couple elope—the most common method of contracting a marriage (Mishkin 1940: 27)—"the girl's family retaliates by raiding the property of the boy's family, later making gifts in return for what they have taken" (D. Collier 1938: 11). No member of the 1935 field-study group reports that the families of high-ranking couples validated their marriages by exchanging more lavish gifts than the kin of low-ranking couples, but as we will see in the next section, these anthropologists provide information for inferring that this was the case.

Ethnographers of unequal bridewealth societies commonly write that wife-givers outrank wife-takers. Among the Kiowa, a marriage established "a fixed and unalterable one-way relation called the 'downhill' relationship. H[usband] was downhill from WB [wife's brother] in that H might never refuse a request from WB. A man was also downhill among others to his father-in-law and his parallel fathers-in-law" (Richardson 1940: 66). In these societies, the obligation of wife-takers or wife-borrowers never to refuse a request from wife-givers organizes social inequality.

Leadership in such societies appears to be hereditary rather than achieved. Leaders are not self-made Big Men who gradually emerge from the common herd. Rather, they usually begin with the advantage of high rank. Not all sons of high-ranking families become chiefs, because in the end, leadership requires followership, but high-ranking families can provide sons with freedom to pursue prestige-giving activities, and with access to valuables for giving away. In Kiowa society, where "war record was the single most important determinant of status" (Richardson 1940: 14), high-ranking families "could afford to set their [male] offspring on the path of military careers" because they had low-ranking men to perform the necessary, but unrewarding, tasks of hunting and herding (Mishkin 1940: 62).

The lifestyle of high-ranking families usually differs from that of low-ranking families. As a result, the personalities of children born to high-ranking families appear to differ from those of children born to commoners or slaves. Among the Kiowa, "there were semi-formalized attitudes or modes of behavior associated with the semi-formalized statuses, i.e., the 'ranks' " (Richardson 1940: 120). Men of the highest rank were expected to be "mild, generous; gracious to women; respectful of the Medicines, i.e. the agencies of law and order; courteous to high and low alike; never making a scene unless resisted illegally . . . ; never [disturbing of] the peace; lofty, so that slight insults might pass by unnoticed; [and] very courageous." Second-rank men were "touchy, quick to defend honor; [and] rivalrous." Third-rank men were "submissive; . . . [and] immune to insult because [they had] little honor to defend" (Richardson 1940: 120). The outcasts, called *Dapom* or "no-accounts," were "the tribe's bad characters, poor because lazy, lacking ambition and respect for others and themselves" (Richardson 1940: 15).

In unequal bridewealth societies, as in the two other types of societies examined in this book, marriage organizes social inequality. In brideservice societies, men are obligated to give the best portion of their meat to their wife's parents; in equal bridewealth societies, children work for the parents who arrange their marriages; and in unequal bridewealth societies, wife-takers who lack valuables for giving to wife-givers work instead. Not all unequal bridewealth peoples are as explicit as the Kiowa about stating a man's obligation "never [to] refuse a request" from his wife's brother or father (Richardson 1940: 66), but most share the reality.

The obligation of wife-takers to comply with wife-givers' requests is theoretically the same for all men, but the implications of the obligation vary according to the wife-taker's access to valuables. Men who have valuables are able to comply with wife-givers' requests by providing gifts rather than labor. They thus retain control over their own labor and have the potential to acquire more gifts. Men who lack access to valuables must give labor instead. To the degree that such men lack control of their labor and its products, they remain unable to obtain gifts and so must continue to give labor, sometimes for life.

In societies appropriate for analysis with an unequal bridewealth model, a groom's labor obligations to his in-laws appear to be determined by the relationship between his bride's "value" and the amount the groom "pays."[3] Grooms who pay full worth, as measured by the relationship between the groom's gifts and the gifts returned reciprocally by the bride's family, enjoy a near-equality with in-laws that lasts as long as both sides continue exchanging nearly equal gifts. Grooms who cannot give as many gifts as the bride's family returns fall into "debt" and become subject to requests for political support and/or labor. At the bottom of the social scale are "poor" men who are "given" women by high-ranking families. Because such men have no hope of ever being able to provide as many gifts as the woman's family can return, they become debt bondsmen and continue in that capacity as long as they live with the woman. At the top of the social scale are high-ranking men who take secondary wives from low-ranking families. These men so outgive their in-laws that they become patrons of their lower-ranking wife's brothers.

Ethnographers commonly report that men marry women of equal or slightly higher rank. This pattern occurs because a man's rank is in fact determined by the kind of marriage(s) he contracts. Were a man to take wives only from families usually thought to be of lower rank than his own, people would assume he lacked the gifts necessary to marry a higher-ranking woman. As a result, a man must take at least one wife from a family of equal or higher rank if he is to engage in the kind of gift exchanges necessary for maintaining his own claim to rank. In particular, a man who hopes to establish the high value of his own socially defined sisters and daughters must marry at least one high-ranking woman so that he can display high rank by exchanging lavish gifts with her family.

Although marriage to women of equal or higher rank is the normative ideal, high-ranking men also take secondary wives of lower rank. Low-ranking families often give a sister or daughter in marriage to a high-ranking man in the hope of obtaining his patronage. High-ranking men thus tend to acquire several wives. Richardson writes that among the Kiowa, "polygyny was reserved only for those of high status" (1940: 12). And Mishkin's list of high-ranking men reveals that all Kiowa band headmen were polygynous (1940: 54–55).

The following paragraphs are intended as a preliminary discussion of how a marriage system of unequal bridewealth gives rise to what appear to be three hereditary ranks plus a category of outcasts or slaves. High-ranking families are sets of full siblings who have access to many goods for giving away. The brothers are able to marry high-ranking wives, and to give many gifts to the husbands of their full sisters, thus validating their high rank. As a result of the polygynous marriages of their father, and their own polygynous marriages to lower-ranking women, the brothers have low-ranking wives, and half sisters or daughters by low-ranking wives, for "lending" to lower-ranking men, or for "giving" to poor men in return for lifelong labor. The brothers' access to goods—made possible by the freeing of their own labor for prestigious activities, the resources of many socially defined sister's husbands, and the labor of debt bondsmen—enables them to help other men marry and thus to acquire classificatory and pact brothers, whose sisters may then become available for giving to other men. High-ranking men thus acquire many socially defined sisters' husbands of varying ranks and labor obligations, as well as junior half, classificatory, and pact brothers who are dependent on them for access to goods for giving to their wife's kin. Rank appears to be hereditary because high-ranking men, who are able to draw on the labor and products of many others, are able to provide their children by high-ranking wives with the valuables those children need to validate their own high rank in turn.

The two middle ranks are composed of men who validate their marriages by means of gift exchanges and therefore have proper marriages. Men of upper middle rank are those whose families can provide enough gifts to enable them to meet most in-laws' requests; consequently, they can live virilocally, far from their wife's kin and their requests for support and labor. Men of lower middle rank are those whose families provide fewer gifts. If such men are unable to satisfy wife-givers' requests for gifts, they may have to submit to wife-givers' demands that they live uxorilocally, in which case the wife's kin may ask them to lend a hand with chores. The three upper ranks appear to be hereditary because a young man's access to gifts for giving to his wife's kin is a function of his parent's access to goods.

At the bottom of the social scale are men who, for one reason or another, lack kin to provide marriage-validating gifts for them.[4] These men have been orphaned, disowned by their families, or separated from their kin because they have been kept in captivity. They must accept "gifts" of women from wealthy families or remain wifeless. They become debt bondsmen for life, working for their benefactors.

In unequal bridewealth societies, as in equal bridewealth societies, people of the highest rank give away more things than they receive. Goods thus appear to be quite equally distributed throughout the society. Mishkin describes Kiowa band headmen as "not the richest men in the tribe; they seldom owned more than 50 to 60 horses" (1940: 42). Richardson reports that "a herd of twenty or thirty [horses] was considered a proper size" (1940: 14)—in contrast to the 40 or 50 good riding horses considered proper for a Cheyenne family (Hoebel 1978: 29), and the thousand or more animals collected by some Comanche men (see Hoebel 1940: 123). But if goods are equally distributed in unequal bridewealth societies, labor obligations are not, and it is this unequal distribution of labor that explains the ability of high-ranking families to give away more than they receive.

This preliminary discussion offers some insights into how inequality is organized in societies appropriate for analysis with an unequal bridewealth model, but, like the other preliminary discussions, it is ultimately problematic. The central problem is well illustrated by an example from ethnographies of the Kiowa. In writing about how men became political leaders, Richardson reports that "one important formal mechanism to induce persons to join one's family was to give one's daughter or sister to some energetic though poor young man" (1940: 6). But it is clear that women were not passive pawns in male marriage exchanges. Mishkin reports that elopement was the most common form of marriage (1940: 27); Richardson writes that "trespass upon a husband's exclusive sexual rights to his wife was by far the most frequent source of grievance" (1940: 80). She also writes that "no woman would consort with a man of low rank unless he were most attractive" (1940: 21). In what way, then, could political leaders "give" a sister or daughter to "some energetic though poor young man," since not all poor men could have been irresistibly attractive? This is the central problem raised by my preliminary discussion.

The discussion also leaves unexplored the sense in which wife-givers outrank wife-takers. If, as I have been arguing, social inequality is organized by the obligation of wife-takers never to refuse a request from wife-givers, then how do we interpret this obligation? When Richardson writes that a Kiowa man "might never refuse a request" from his wife's kin, what does she mean? Once again, the problem is to understand the construction of commonsense understandings. In this chapter, therefore, I examine the idiom of rank, which is the unequal bridewealth counterpart of the brideservice idiom of bravery and the equal bridewealth idiom of respect. As in previous chapters, I begin with an analysis of marriage negotiations.

Marriage

Marriage exchanges in unequal bridewealth societies are a public statement of rank—the ranking of a bride and groom and their kin groups relative to one another and to the rest of society. The exchanges also validate a marriage, but whereas everyone involved in a marriage exchange in an equal bridewealth society is concerned with the amount of respect a groom enjoys, everyone in an unequal bridewealth society speculates on the ranking of the couple and their families.

People in most societies appropriate for analysis with an unequal bridewealth model seem to engage in frequent exchanges with affines, although not all ethnographers portray these two-way exchanges as the accepted procedure for validating marriages.[5] Exchanges between a man and his wife's kin usually continue for the duration of a specific sexual union. They serve both to indicate its status and to display the ranking of the two kin groups.

The status of a union and the ranking of the partners are, in fact, two sides of the same coin. Ethnographers of many unequal bridewealth societies report that at any given time, the status of many or most sexual unions is ambiguous. Leach writes that "many Kachin families are in a sort of ambiguous social status, neither married nor unmarried" (1954: 75). Similarly, Gibbs writes that among the Kpelle of Liberia, "the several forms of union mean that a man can have genuine doubt as to whether or not a woman is really married and therefore legitimately open to his attentions" (1965: 214). Ethnographers of Kiowa society have not reported that unions were ambiguous (probably because most of them were writing before kinship theorists began treating marriage as a process rather than an event), but they provide evidence to indicate that this was the case. Donald Collier observes that, for Kiowa couples, "residence with one or the other family [was] often not permanent. Frequently young married couples [visited] back and forth between their respective families" (1938: 12). This observation suggests that for the Kiowa, as for other unequal bridewealth peoples, marriage was a process in which people negotiated the residence, ranking, and hence relationship of a bride and groom.

Sexual unions in unequal bridewealth societies are ambiguous because exchanges between affines are the principal public means for negotiating relative rank. Wife-givers establish their superiority over wife-takers by giving them more goods than they can return, and wife-takers establish their equality with, or superiority over, wife-givers by doing the same thing. Given the expectation that men will marry women of equal or higher rank, men in the process of establishing a sexual union can hope to accomplish little more than demonstrating their equality with in-laws. But as time passes and fortunes change, the balance between affines may shift in such a way that one side can decisively outgive the other and, by so doing, reduce the other to debt-clientage.

The affinal relationship permits collusion as well as competition. High-ranking families may engage in carefully balanced exchanges, giving each other enough valuables of sufficient quality to demonstrate their superiority over other families, but avoiding costly, and possibly destructive, competition. And low-ranking families may collude to keep their exchanges below a level that would force either side to borrow from distant kin.

The Meaning of Marriage Gifts

Ethnographers of Kiowa society provide enough information on the negotiation of marriages to illustrate the sense in which marriage in unequal bridewealth societies validates rank. The best description of Kiowa marriage that I have found is the one by Donald Collier:

Marriage is of four kinds, two types by family arrangement and two by elopement. In the *first*, which will be called regularly arranged marriage, the boy's family approaches the girl's family and if accepted initiates a gift exchange between the two families. Both sides help to establish the married couple in housekeeping, and maintain friendly relations through continued gift exchange. In the *second* type the girl's family picks out a deserving young man and gives her to him. There is no initial gift exchange between the two families, although later there usually is. The boy lives with his parents-in-law and works for them. This form of marriage is often preferred for his daughter by a wealthy man who wants assistance in herding his many horses and providing for his large family. In the *third* form a boy and a girl elope and go to the tipi of his father or some other of his relatives. The girl's family retaliates by raiding the property of the boy's family, later making gifts in return for what they have taken. The *fourth* form is the elopement of a married woman. The deserted husband retaliates by shooting horses of the man who has stolen his wife, and occasionally by doing physical injury to the fleeing couple. The first and third forms of marriage are the most frequent (1938: 11–12, italics mine)

There was also a fifth form of marriage: the marriage of an already married man to secondary (lower-ranking) wives. Collier may not have distinguished this form because such marriages were probably validated in all of the ways he lists except the second.

Although ethnographers of Kiowa society have not written that marriage exchanges and property destructions were displays of rank, they do provide evidence that such exchanges determined the residence of newlyweds and thus a groom's obligations to his affines. In unequal bridewealth societies, as we will see in the next section, residence is the primary determinant of rank. Men who live near their wife's kin rank below men who are able to live far from wife-givers.

Ethnographers of Kiowa society report that newlyweds tended to settle with the band of the higher-ranking family (Richardson 1940: 12; D. Collier 1938: 12). Mishkin writes that "the relative wealth and rank of the two families, parties to the marriage, might be determinative" of a couple's band membership, with "the poor being attracted to the *topotoga* [band] of the rich" (1940: 27). He also suggests that families competed for the residence of newlyweds: "ideally, every male brought his wife to live in his *topotoga* and every female brought her husband back to her band to increase its size and political supremacy" (1940: 27).

It is easy to understand why each family hoped to attract the newlyweds to their band. In a society where a man might never refuse a request from his wife's brothers and fathers (Richardson 1940: 66), a bride's kin benefited by acquiring a coresident sister's or daughter's husband who might never refuse their requests for aid. Similarly, the groom's kin benefited by keeping him nearby so that he could help them and support them politically.

Because each family hoped to attract the newlyweds to their band, the Kiowa probably expected each family to provide as many wedding gifts as possible to display the superior "wealth and rank" that reportedly determined a couple's band membership. People probably considered the number and quality of gifts exchanged at a wedding as an important, if not the most important, public statement of each family's rank.

As a result, the Kiowa probably evidenced a pattern common to unequal bridewealth societies and noted by Leach for the Kachin of Highland Burma: "Kachin formal theory is that bride price is adjusted to the standing of the *bride*. . . . [But] in every case the scale of the bride price, as measured by the number of cattle, corresponds to the ranking status of the bridegroom" (1954: 151, italics his). If Kiowa families hoping to attract newlyweds to their bands tried to outgive each other, then the number of gifts a groom's family needed if they were to outgive the bride's family would appear to vary according to the bride's family's access to goods for giving away. Kiowa brides would thus appear to vary in price according to the wealth and rank of their families.

The amount a groom's family gave would, in turn, establish the rank of the groom, whether or not they backed him to fullest extent of their resources. If a groom's family provided as many gifts as they could muster, then that amount would constitute a public declaration of their wealth and rank. If the groom's family did not support him to the fullest extent, the amount of gifts would still determine the rank of the groom as an individual. If his family provided some gifts, but not enough to attract the newlyweds to their band, then the groom had to live uxorilocally and be subject to requests for labor from his wife's kin. If the groom's family refused to provide any gifts at all, they condemned him to serve as a debt bondsman for the duration of his relationship with the woman.

Because residence probably correlated with rank, Donald Collier's observation that Kiowa newlyweds frequently visited back and forth between their two families (1938: 12) reveals that Kiowa unions were as ambiguous as the unions of the Kachin and Kpelle. As long as couples had not settled with one band or the other, the ranking of their families remained ambiguous, as did the groom's obligations to his in-laws. Further evidence concerning the ambiguity of Kiowa marriages is provided by ethnographers' observations that exchanges between affines affected the status of particular unions. Richardson (1940: 72) and Donald Collier (1938: 90) both report that a man who refused the request of a wife's brother might have his wife taken from him; Collier reports that a man who made too many requests of his sister's husband might find his sister returned to him (1938: 90).[6]

The Negotiation of Marriage

In unequal bridewealth societies, as in the other two types of societies discussed in this book, the meaning of marriage transactions is most clearly revealed in situations where marriages are on the verge of dissolution. In unequal bridewealth societies a woman's kin can not only offer to shelter her from her husband when she runs home to mother, but can threaten to take a wife away from her husband. The ability to issue this threat, as we will see in the next section, is based on the fact that a woman's kin have the ability to refuse her shelter.

Ethnographers of Kiowa society clearly state that a woman's kin can threaten to take her away from her husband. Richardson writes that "a certain amount of beating by H[usband] was permitted as legitimate by W[ife]'s kin, but if W were beaten too hard, too much or without good reason, W's kin stepped in and took her away from H. If W were wantonly killed by H, her kin sought to avenge her death. This coercive threat of taking W away acted as a real restraint to a miscreant H, for it would always cost him and his kin considerable property to get her back, if at all" (1940: 65). Kiowa parents, unlike their Cheyenne counterparts, did not simply cross-examine an unhappy sister or daughter to determine her reasons for leaving her husband. Rather, they portrayed themselves as actively intervening to take a woman away from her husband. The crucial phase in the quote from Richardson is the last one, for it reveals that among the Kiowa, discussions of divorce centered not on a woman's grounds for leaving her husband, as they did among the Cheyenne, but on how much her husband would pay to get her back. And such discussions necessarily presumed the ability of a woman's kin to give her back—i.e., to refuse a woman shelter if her husband paid enough.

The reasons why women's kin in unequal bridewealth societies can refuse women shelter are complex and will be elaborated in this chapter. The principal reason can be stated briefly here: it makes sense for them to do so if her husband is willing to pay enough. In societies, such as the Kiowa, where commonsense understandings cast a man as never being able to refuse a request from his wife's brother, every man has (in theory) both "wife's brothers" whose requests he can never refuse and "sister's husbands" who can never refuse his requests. The ability of a man to satisfy the requests of his wife's brothers rests, to some extent, on his ability to extract valuables or labor from his sister's husbands. As a result, it is often advantageous for a man to return his sister to her husband (i.e., to refuse his sister shelter) if her husband offers to pay enough. Unlike men in equal bridewealth societies, who benefit by maintaining claims to sisters whose children they may collect as dependents, men in unequal bridewealth societies benefit by having cooperative or subservient sister's husbands who will help them satisfy their own wife's brother's requests.

In unequal bridewealth societies, the ability of women's kin to refuse women shelter structures the claims people make when negotiating marriages, and so structures the commonsense assumptions that underlie the organization of social inequality. Specifically, the negotiations establish that (1) wife-takers cannot refuse wife-givers' requests and still be wife-takers, (2) wife-givers and wife-takers are internally homogeneous groups of kinsmen who negotiate collectively with one another, and (3) women can be given away by their socially defined brothers.

The Kiowa provide a particularly good example of how the ability of women's kin to refuse women shelter structures the claims people make during conversations surrounding marriage in such a way that wife-takers have to comply with wife givers' requests if they are to acquire and keep wives. In Kiowa society, the fact that a woman's kin had the ability to refuse her shelter put them in the position of having to decide whether to refuse shelter in any particular case. The conversations thus centered on whether a woman's kin should give her back to her husband, that is whether an abandoned husband could provide them with enough gifts or labor to make it worthwhile for them to return her (i.e., how much it was going to cost a husband to get his wife back, if at all [Richardson 1940: 65]).

The conversations surrounding marriage in Kiowa society were very different from marriage conversations among the Cheyenne. In Cheyenne society, where women's kin had the ability to keep a woman from her husband, their conversations centered on whether they should do so; they cross-examined the woman to determine her grounds for divorce. An abandoned Cheyenne husband had to defend himself against his wife's accusations and beg pardon of his in-laws if her accusations seemed justified. An abandoned Kiowa husband did not have to talk about his behavior; he talked about how much he could offer his in-laws.

Because men in unequal bridewealth societies have to offer gifts to recover wives, and because they obtain those gifts from their kin, the conversations that occur when marriages threaten to dissolve emphasize the similarity, not the differences, between a husband and his kin. In equal bridewealth societies, as noted in Chapter 2, a man's kin are helpful to him in recovering his runaway wife to the degree that they emphasize their difference from him. A man's senior kin deserve respect. They are the opposite of their disgraced son, whose wife is accusing him of doing terrible deeds. In divorce proceedings, respected seniors on both sides are cast as generously negotiating for irresponsible, quarreling juniors. The conversations of people in equal bridewealth societies thus foster an image of kinship groups as including juniors who cannot speak for themselves and seniors who speak for them. In unequal bridewealth societies, a man's kin are helpful to him to the degree that they take his side and put their resources at his disposal, thus emphasizing the cohesion of the kinship group. The divorce proceedings thus pit two internally homogeneous groups, wife-givers and wife-takers, against each other.

By emphasizing the similarity between a deserted husband and his kin, the conversations prompted by unsuccessful marriages in unequal bridewealth societies tend to minimize generational differences within wife-giving and wife-taking groups and therefore to foster the image of such groups as composed of socially defined brothers. Richardson appears to be recording a Kiowa perception when she describes "the basic economic and social group in Kiowa life" as "a group of brothers and their wives and children, including, under [certain circumstances], sisters and their spouses and children. Half-brothers, half-sisters, classificatory brothers, and even pact-brothers might be permanent members of this relatively stable unit" (1940: 5). Richardson's description contrasts with Eggan's portrayal of the basic Cheyenne unit as composed of parents and their adult and subadult children (1955: 61).

Richardson's description also reveals the complexity of the social category brother. She reports that the Kiowa distinguished at least four types: full brothers, half brothers, classificatory brothers, and pact brothers. As we will see later in this chapter, the sibling bond is the most crucial one for determining a person's life chances. It is therefore the bond most subject to manipulation. Just as people in equal bridewealth societies try to establish claims to sons and daughters who will owe them obedience, people in unequal bridewealth societies try to establish claims to siblings. Full siblings form the basic social group. Although ranked internally by age, outsiders usually perceive them as having the same rank unless one member is disowned. Because most sets of full siblings are small, however, the basic wife-giving/wife-taking groups are usually composed of sets of full siblings who are close cousins, with their children. These wife-giving/wife-taking groups may expand or diminish by taking in or losing members. Men get ahead by acquiring lower-ranking half, classificatory, or pact brothers whose sisters they may "give away." And men lose rank if their full siblings or close cousins turn to higher-ranking, more distant brothers for aid.

Unlike divorce discussions in equal bridewealth societies, where women's kin encourage women to explain their reasons for leaving their husbands, the conversations surrounding marriage in unequal bridewealth societies cast women as sisters who (in theory) have no say about what their brothers do with them. Richardson describes Kiowa women's kin "stepping in" to remove a woman from her husband (1940: 65). Whereas Llewellyn and Hoebel portray Cheyenne women as initiating divorce proceedings by going "home to mother" (1941: 81). Because conversations surrounding marriage in unequal bridewealth societies cast women as silent pawns in male marriage exchanges, these peoples have no language for talking about women's active role in choosing sexual partners and deciding whether to remain with them.

Production and Circulation

In discussing marriage transactions, I noted a correlation between rank, residence, and the status of particular sexual unions. In this section, I explore correlations between these features, labor obligations, and circulation patterns. In unequal bridewealth societies, work and gifts validate rank, just as in equal bridewealth societies they testify to the nature of specific, long-standing relationships between people. I begin this section by analyzing the relationship between the apparent division of labor by rank and the obligations of wife-takers to wife-givers. Then I consider the power inequities underlying unequal work obligations. Finally, I examine circulation patterns to show how the distribution of valuables within extended sibling sets determines the ranking of full siblings, both within the extended set and relative to outsiders. Rank is the idiom by which people in unequal bridewealth societies understand and establish relationships with others. And rank, I will suggest, is realized in sharing patterns among siblings. Ethnographers of unequal bridewealth societies commonly write that labor is divided by rank. Mishkin, as already noted, writes of Kiowa men that "the wealthy class could afford to set their offspring on the path of military careers while the poor, for the most part, were compelled to specialize in the prosaic activities, hunting, camp duties, etc." (1940: 62).[7] Other ethnographers echo his observation that male labor was divided by rank—that high-ranking men specialized in the prestigious activities of warfare and raiding, whereas low-ranking men performed the necessary, but unprestigious, tasks of hunting and herding.

The division of labor in unequal bridewealth societies is thus different from that in equal bridewealth societies. In equal bridewealth societies, as noted in Chapter 2, labor appears to be divided by age. Seniors of both sexes are free to spend their time sponsoring rituals or acquiring the objects whose gift to others brings respect. Juniors of both sexes perform drudgery, but most of them can hope ultimately to become leisured seniors. In unequal bridewealth societies, some people enjoy leisure throughout their lives, even in early childhood; others may be condemned to perform drudgery as long as they live.

The Meaning of Work

Ethnographers of unequal bridewealth societies observe that labor is divided by rank, but few ask what rank is. Most seem to treat rank as given—as something that individuals have, based on wealth, genealogy, achievements, or all three. But rank is far from obvious. The question of what it is needs to be answered. I begin my discussion of the social processes that give rise to the appearance of ranking, not by assuming the existence of rank, but by analyzing ethnographers' concrete observations about who works for whom and why. I focus on male labor. Women will be considered in the next subsection.

Since high-ranking men do not perform the tasks necessary to sustain life, they must be able to direct other men's labor and control its products. Ethnographic descriptions suggest that this control resides in the wife-giver/wife-taker relationship: wife-takers have to obey their wife-givers. As already noted, Richardson reports that a Kiowa man "might never refuse a request from" his wife's brother, wife's father, or wife's parallel fathers (1940: 66).[8] She also writes that "the poorer class constituted a desirable labor group, and there was considerable competition among the different *topadok'i* [band headmen] for these followers. One important formal mechanism to induce persons to join one's family was to give one's daughter or sister to some energetic though poor young man" (1940: 6). An analysis of the organization of work in unequal bridewealth societies must therefore focus on the processes by which the obligations of wife-takers give rise to an apparent division of labor by rank. I begin by examining the nature and organization of production units.

The production units of unequal bridewealth societies are difficult to describe in simple terms because they are larger than households but bear no resemblance to manors or factories. Ethnographers of Kiowa society suggest that the entire band was an integrated economic unit (Richardson 1940: 7; Mishkin 1940: 27). Richardson observes that band chiefs were required to have "competence in economic organization" (1940: 102). She also reports that the peace "pipe was not used within the close kindred, and rarely within the [band] for in Kiowa terms these could not by any stretch of the imagination be split into 'two independent groups' " (1940: 11). Since use of the peace pipe implied the possibility of paying compensatory damages to victims of wrongdoing, its nonuse within the band suggests that, by definition, the band was a single economic unit.

Evidence that a Kiowa chief could command the products of households other than his own also suggests the economic integration of Kiowa bands. Mayhall describes the arrival of two regiments of dragoons from Fort Gibson at a Kiowa camp in 1834: "[The Kiowa] chief ordered the women to supply the dragoons with food. [The dragoons'] rations had all been eaten twelve hours before, and they were delighted to see the women bring in 'backloads' of dried buffalo meat and green corn, which they threw down amongst them" (1962: 65). Grinnell describes the ceremony marking conclusion of the Great Peace of 1840 between the Cheyenne and their former enemies, the Kiowa, Comanche, and Apache. At the ceremony, Sa tank', a Kiowa chief, gave 250 horses to the Cheyenne, many more than had any other Kiowa (1915: 64–65). The 250 horses take on special significance in the context of

Richardson's statement that "a herd of twenty or thirty was considered a proper size" (1940: 14), and Mishkin's observation that
Kiowa band chiefs "were not the richest men in the tribe; they seldom owned more than 50 to 60 horses" (1940: 42). If Sa tank' gave
250 horses, he must have given away horses that came from other
peoples' herds. His extravagant act is in striking contrast to the
reported behavior of the Cheyenne chief, High-Backed Wolf,
who, instead of giving many guns himself, called out to his men
that each should bring his own presents (Grinnell 1915: 65–66). A
Cheyenne chief could apparently organize large giveaways, but he
could not himself give away the products of people who were not
members of his household. A Kiowa chief apparently could.

The complex production units of unequal bridewealth societies
are made up of several households; each household head has a
particular kinship bond with the leader. Ethnographers of Kiowa
society provide evidence that enables us to piece together a tentative explanation of how band chiefs acquired rights to the labor
and products of band members. Richardson writes that a Kiowa
band "was by legal fiction considered a kin group" (1940: 6). She
also notes that "the oldest brother was almost always the head of
the family" (1940: 12) and that Kiowa brothers usually herded their
horses together (1940: 25). The Kiowa had a "strong sense of private ownership," but this sense "ran counter to the general feeling
that possessions and commodities, though not communally owned
really, were for the free use of all the kindred" (1940: 125). A Kiowa
band chief, therefore, had some access to the possessions of his
full, half, classificatory, and pact brothers. The requirement that a
man never refuse a request from his wife's brother also afforded the
band chief some control over the labor and products of his coresident sisters' husbands. And a chief had almost complete control
over the labor and products of those "energetic though poor"
young men whom he had attracted to his band with "gifts" of
sisters or daughters.

In unequal bridewealth societies, production units are made up
of kin whose labor obligations and privileges vary according to
their rank, residence, and type of kinship bond they have with the
group leader. Among the Kiowa, for example, a leader and his full
brothers who lived with him were of the highest rank. They apparently enjoyed the prerogative of directing others' labor. They thus
had time to devote to rustling horses and accumulating war hon-

ors. Some of their half, classificatory, and pact brothers were of second rank. They had few coresident sisters' husbands to command but, because they lived virilocally, they at least escaped their wife's brothers' requests for labor. Those coresident sisters' and daughters' husbands who validated marriages with gift exchanges must have been of third rank. They probably enjoyed some economic independence, but nevertheless had to endure living near their wife's kin, whose requests could never be refused. Finally, men "disowned by their own relatives" who "made out as parasitic hangers-on to outstanding men of high rank" (Hoebel 1954: 171) had nothing to call their own. They were the "poor" youths who accepted gifts of women and thus had to devote all their time to carrying out sponsors' commands.

In summary, residence in unequal bridewealth societies is the key to the relationship between wife-takers' obligations and the apparent division of labor by rank. High-ranking men live far from their wife's kin; low-ranking men live near their wife's kin. This observation raises the question of why some men consent to live uxorilocally. Ethnographers of Kiowa society write that newlyweds tended to settle with the band of the higher-ranking family. But Mishkin's observation that elopement was the most common method of concluding a marriage (1940: 27) and Donald Collier's observation that Kiowa couples frequently visited back and forth between their respective kin (1938: 12) indicate that Kiowa grooms at least tried to resist settling near the bride's kin. Given that young men apparently resist, why do some of them capitulate?

The answer is that grooms who consent are of low rank. Although low rank is actually a lack of access to women on favorable terms (see next subsection), people in unequal bridewealth societies perceive low rank as a lack of access to the valuables used to validate marriages and to meet the continuing requests of wife-givers.

In these societies, men cannot refuse requests from their wife's kin because they may lose their wives if they do. A Kiowa informant told Richardson that "a WF (wife's father) always takes W[ife] away when H[usband] refuses a request, even if it is the first time he has refused. But such refusals are rare. In most cases where there is refusal H thinks he has a strong hold on W and can get away with a refusal without losing her" (1940: 72). The first sentence of this quotation implies that in the ordinary course of events, the Kiowa perceived a man's ability to live far from his wife's kin as depending on his ability to satisfy his in-laws' requests by giving them valuables, particularly horses. As long as a man could give valuables he did not need to fear having his wife taken from him. He could live virilocally and control his own labor. But if a man lacked access to valuables, he might have to refuse a request. And if his wife's kin took her from him in retaliation, he would probably follow her back to her band, and, to secure the continuation of his marriage, he might have to settle near her kin and never refuse their requests for labor (see D. Collier 1938: 49). The Kiowa, therefore, must have perceived low rank (having to comply with others' requests for labor) as following from a lack of access to valuables.

The Content of Affinal Obligations

Although men who lack valuables in unequal bridewealth societies have to work for their wife-givers, they do so not because they they are unable to provide gifts (although this is usually true) but because women do not want to stay married to men who lack valuables. These men consequently depend on wife-givers to help them keep their wives.

In unequal bridewealth societies, as in brideservice and equal bridewealth societies, the men who work hardest, and whose labor and products are most directly appropriated by others, are men who need the help of those others to acquire and keep wives. In unequal bridewealth societies, in contrast to the other two types, marital instability correlates not with age but with rank. High-ranking men have no difficulty acquiring and keeping wives; "women seem to love them more," a Kiowa informant told Mishkin (1940: 53). Low-ranking men have difficulty marrying. Richardson reports that "no [Kiowa] woman would consort with a man of low rank unless he were most attractive" (1940: 121). As a result, high-ranking men never have to work for wife-givers, even when they are young. Low-ranking men never escape having to work for wife-givers, even when they are old.

It is, of course, impossible to know if women really love high-ranking men more than low-ranking ones, as claimed by Mishkin's Kiowa informant, or even to know what particular peoples mean by the word translated as "love." But it is easy to understand why women prefer to marry high-ranking men. Such men have more to offer their wives. As directors of others' labor, high-ranking men can provide helpers for their wives. And, because they have many valuables, high-ranking men can help a woman's sons and daughters to marry well.

If women prefer to marry high-ranking men, why do some women stay with or return to low-ranking husbands? As already noted, women in unequal bridewealth societies play an active role in deciding which man to marry or to stay with. In Kiowa society, elopement was "the most common form of marriage" (Mishkin 1940: 27), and married women frequently absconded with lovers (Richardson 1940: 80). This active role in choosing lovers and husbands explains why a woman's kin might be able to persuade her to leave a husband who refuses their requests. No woman wants to consort with a man who lacks valuables. But it is difficult to understand why a woman might return to a husband who had agreed to live near her kin, since his consent constituted a public declaration of his low rank. It is also unclear why a woman would let herself be "given" to a poor youth who agreed to become a debt bondsman. In what sense, then, are wife-givers able to return wives to men who agree to live uxorilocally? And, even more problematic, in what sense are high-ranking men able to "give" women to low-ranking men in return for labor?

The key to understanding the organization of inequality in unequal bridewealth societies lies in the answer to the question of why some women let high-ranking men give them to poor men in return for labor. Such women either lack supportive male kin or have low-ranking brothers who collude with the high-ranking men who give them away. This answer, however, is not immediately obvious. We obtain it by examining the social construction of women's interests—the ranking of wives within polygynous households and the ranking of full, half, classificatory, and pact brothers within extended sibling sets.

In unequal bridewealth societies, not all the wives of a high-ranking polygynous man are equal. Some wives enjoy many privileges. Others derive few benefits. Donald Collier reports that the wives of a polygynous Kiowa man competed "to be the favorite wife. The wives [tried] to gain their husband's favor by doing things for him. They [made] him fine clothes, [prepared] him special meals and [waited] on him" (1938: 88). Although "being the favorite wife [did] not imply authority over the others, but merely special attention from the husband" (1938: 88), "special attention" was probably important to a woman. A high-ranking Kiowa husband might distribute various favors, such as captive women to work for his wives[9] and opportunities for their sons to join raiding parties; he might also give lavish gifts to their daughters' husbands.

It seems reasonable to conclude that despite their competition, Kiowa co-wives were ranked according to the ranking of their brothers, as established by the number and quality of gifts they provided for the husband. In unequal bridewealth societies, the polygynous man deserted by a wife whose brothers desperately need valuables for giving to their own wives' brothers can expect to obtain the return of his wife with the offer of a few gifts. But if a man is deserted by a wife whose brothers do not need his valuables, then he might have to offer "considerable property to get her back, if at all" (Richardson 1940: 65). In unequal bridewealth societies, a husband who distributes his favors according to his affections rather than according to the ranking of his wife's brothers is likely to find himself with few wives.

If a wife's rank in a polygynous man's household is determined by the rank of her brothers, then the opportunities open to her are ultimately determined by her brothers' need for valuables. A woman whose brothers need her husband's valuables is at the mercy of whatever husband she happens to live with, whereas a woman whose brothers do not need her husband's valuables knows that if her husband does not treat her with the respect she feels due a woman of her rank, she can leave him and he will have to provide many valuables to secure her return. In unequal bridewealth societies, the brother-sister bond is crucial. A Kiowa informant told Richardson that "a woman can always get another husband, but she has only one brother" (1940: 65).

In a society where a woman's ability to obtain benefits from her husband is a function of the ranking of her brothers, women with high-ranking brothers can obtain many benefits for their children, whereas women with low-ranking brothers can obtain few, even if they are married to high-ranking men. This explains why many unequal bridewealth societies consider a women's brideprice as the primary determinant of her children's status (see Hoebel 1954: 53). A mother's rank is frequently more important than that of the father in determining the status of their children, although the children's rank is sometimes perceived as intermediate between the two.

The ranking of wives within polygynous households explains why some women might be willing to return to husbands who agree to live uxorilocally. A woman whose brothers need her husband's gifts or labor to maintain their own marriages knows she will have only an intermediate rank wherever she lives. She might thus prefer living near supportive natal kin to being an intermediate wife in the household of a polygynous, high-ranking man.

But the ranking of co-wives within polygynous households does not explain why a woman would let her high-ranking kinsmen "give" her to a poor man in return for the man's labor. Such gifts of women are the basis of inequality in unequal bridewealth societies, for it is by giving women to poor men that a high-ranking man acquires the debt bondsmen whose labor allows him to outgive everyone else. In some unequal bridewealth societies (e.g. the Kpelle), high-ranking men "lend" their low-ranking wives to slaves or debt bondsmen. In others (e.g. the Kiowa), high-ranking men "gave" sisters and daughters.

It is easy to understand how a high-ranking man might "lend" one of his low-ranking wives to a debt bondsman without incurring problems. The woman is not a member of his wife-giving/wife-taking group, so her sorry fate does not reflect on the ranking of his sibling set. He can also secure the cooperation of his low-ranking wife's kin by offering them gifts and political patronage. But it is hard to understand how a man might "give" away a sister or daughter. Such a woman is, by definition, a member of his own wife-giving/wife-taking group. She is his own sister or the sister of his sons. The reason, I suggest, is that the sisters and daughters high-ranking men give away are not their full sisters or the daughters of high-ranking wives, but are rather daughters of low-ranking women.

In unequal bridewealth societies, all women are dependent on their brothers, but women who are daughters of high-ranking fathers and low-ranking mothers must have a special relationship to their half and full brothers. Such women are probably unlike daughters of more equal unions in that they cannot count on their brothers—either half or full—to support them in quarrels with their husbands.

Most men probably have to shelter unhappily married sisters, at least temporarily, to avoid having others believe that their refusal to do so reflects a need for the sisters' husbands' gifts. Brothers may be reluctant to alienate a sister's husband, and they may return a sister to her husband in exchange for a few valuables, but they have to at least offer an unhappy sister shelter and negotiate with her husband if they are to maintain their family's status. High-ranking men who exchange lavish gifts with the kin of their full sisters' husbands are in a position to refuse a low-ranking half sister's request for aid without having others question their access to valuables, however. As a result, high-ranking men can make their aid to low-ranking half sisters contingent on the half sisters' cooperation.

The full brothers of a woman born to a low-ranking mother and a high-ranking father can probably be easily induced to cooperate with their high-ranking half brothers against the interests of their full sisters. Richardson's description of Kiowa bands as including the half, classificatory, and pact brothers of the headman (1940: 5) suggests that high-ranking Kiowa men regularly provided the horses and valuables their half brothers (by their lower-ranking mother's co-wives) needed to give to their wife's kin so that they could live virilocally. In contrast to most Kiowa men, therefore, sons of high-ranking fathers and low-ranking mothers did not need to obtain their sisters' cooperation to ensure them access to horses for giving to in-laws. Such men had more to gain from cooperating with their high-ranking half brothers.

In unequal bridewealth societies where high-ranking men "give" sisters and daughters to poor men in return for labor, as in those societies where high-ranking men "lend" low-ranking wives to debt bondsmen, some women are subordinated to high-ranking men who can give or lend them without having their own rank questioned. These women also have full brothers who benefit from co-operating with the high-ranking men who give them away. In all unequal bridewealth societies, therefore, some women are faced with a choice between two less than ideal options: earning the support of their high-ranking husbands or half-brothers, or facing the world without supportive male kin.

The Meaning of Gifts

In unequal bridewealth societies, a woman's fate depends on the rank of her brothers. But what social processes determine the ranking of men? The answer can be obtained by analyzing the ranking of wife-giving/wife-taking groups relative to one another—a ranking that is organized by the circulation of valuables.

The ranking of wife-giving/wife-taking groups depends on the number and quality of gifts they exchange with affines, particularly the gifts they present to wife-takers. All men must present gifts to those from whom they receive wives. But because no man is obliged to give valuables to his sisters' and daughters' husbands (his wife-takers), gifts to them prove, more than gifts to wife's kin, that a man has access to valuables for giving away. Moreover, gifts to wife-takers are recoverable if needed.

Although ethnographers of Kiowa society stress a man's obligation never to refuse a request from his wife's kin, they provide evidence that men also gave gifts to wife-takers. Donald Collier, for example, writes that the families of a bride and groom maintained "friendly relations through continued gift exchange" (1938: 11). Ethnographers also provide evidence that gifts to wife-takers were more easily recovered than gifts to wife-givers. In Kiowa society, a man could ask his sister's husband for anything, but it was considered disgraceful for a man to make a request of his wife's brothers (see Richardson 1940: 66).

In unequal bridewealth societies, a man's gifts of valuables to his sisters' husbands actually put him in a position where he is likely to need fewer valuables for giving to his wife's kin. If gifts of valuables to sisters' husbands constitute a public demonstration of high rank, then men who give many such gifts enjoy such a rank. They have secure marriages and are able to attract many women. As a result, they seldom have to face the problem of trying to recover runaway wives. As men of demonstrated high rank, they can refuse wife-givers' requests without fear of having their wives taken from them.

A man who is unable to give valuables to his sister's husband is likely to have an insecure marriage. Because of his low rank, his wife will not be eager to stay with him, and he will have a hard time attracting other women. He will be afraid to refuse requests from his wife's kin, and he will have to conduct many negotiations with them to secure his wife's return. There is good reason to believe that high-ranking men who have many valuables for giving away have fewer occasions in which they are obliged to give them, whereas low-ranking men, whose wives "love" them less, have both fewer valuables to give and more occasions in which they must give them away. In unequal bridewealth societies, as in many other societies, much is given to those who have, whereas those who have little are obliged to part with that which they do have.

In unequal bridewealth societies, the ranking of socially defined brothers and sisters within wife-giving/wife-taking groups is mutually established. Men establish the ranks of sisters in their husbands' households by the number and quality of gifts they give to their sisters' husbands, even as those gifts establish the ranking of the brothers. Exchanges with affines, however, establish not only the ranking but also the composition of wife-giving/wife-taking groups.

In these societies, the minimal wife-giving/wife-taking units are sets of full siblings. Full brothers and sisters have the same rank, unless one brother or sister is disowned. But most sets of full siblings are too small to constitute effective units. As a result, the actual wife-giving/wife-taking units are minimal lineages or kindreds that include cousins as classificatory siblings, and that may also sponsor the marriages of half, and perhaps pact siblings. Such extended sibling relations are realized in sharing patterns within the group.

I have been arguing that among unequal bridewealth peoples, as among equal bridewealth and brideservice peoples, the organization of inequality within production units determines the meaning that people assign to gifts of valuables, rather than the reverse. And in all three types of societies, inequality within production units is organized by marital instability. Men who work for others do so because they need their help in acquiring and keeping wives. In unequal bridewealth societies, men who enjoy secure marriages retain control of their own labor and have others working for them. They are able to acquire many valuables for giving away. Men who have insecure marriages need valuables and have to work for their wife's brothers when they no longer have access to valuables.

At this point, however, I wish to suggest that although inequality organizes men's access to valuables, people perceive men's access to valuables, not marital instability, as organizing inequality. In equal bridewealth societies, labor obligations within production units establish a correlation between gift giving and status obligations; similarly, in unequal bridewealth societies, marital instability organizes the circulation of valuables in such a way that circulation patterns correlate with bonds between siblings, i.e. members of the same wife-taking/wife-giving group. As a result, unequal bridewealth peoples come to perceive sibling bonds as a function of circulation, rather than the reverse.

I have already mentioned that unequal bridewealth peoples define social mobility in terms of access to valuables. As long as a man is able to give valuables to his wife's brothers, he can secure their cooperation in persuading his wife to live virilocally. But when a man no longer has access to valuables, he has only his labor to offer his wife-givers. Women's dislike for marrying low-ranking men may doom such men to working for their wife's kin, but in any man's experience, this doom can be avoided as long as he has valuables to give instead. All men need wives, but only those without access to valuables have to work for their in-laws. Everyday experience, therefore, must suggest to people that it is a lack of access to valuables, not a need for wives, that puts some men in the position of having to work for others.

I also wish to suggest that men perceive their access to valuables in terms of their relations with siblings. Richardson writes that when a Kiowa wife had returned to her kin, "property alone was not enough to get [her] back; a man had to have kinsmen to be successful" (1940: 76). In unequal bridewealth societies, to have kinsmen is to have property. Men who have socially defined brothers have valuables. Men without brothers lack them.

As long as a man's full brothers (a category that may include close cousins) have valuables that they share with him, he does not have to beg valuables from others. And in societies where men cannot refuse requests from their wife's brothers, men who have the same full sisters' husbands in common have the same access to valuables. If one brother gives gifts to a full sister's husband, he is, in a sense, giving valuables to his full brothers. Similarly, when a brother requests valuables from a full sister's husband, he is, in a sense, taking valuables away from his full brothers. Full brothers appear to have the same kinds of claims to each other's valuables that they have to the valuables of their common full sisters' husbands. For a man to request valuables from his full brothers is almost equivalent to drawing on his own supply. As noted, Kiowa brothers usually herded their horses together (Richardson 1940: 125).

A man whose full brothers lack valuables or refuse to share them with him must turn to classificatory, half, or pact brothers. Such distant brothers will probably grant a petitioner's request if they can, just as parents in equal bridewealth societies grant children's requests if they can. But however generous a man's classificatory, half, and pact brothers might be, having to beg is an admission of low rank, and low rank is the cause of marital instability. In general, men who have to beg for valuables from distant brothers have unstable marriages and often end up working for their wife-givers, even though their classificatory, half, and pact brothers may never refuse any of their requests for valuables.

Begging distant brothers for valuables must also cause sets of full brothers to disband, for men who beg have insecure marriages, often necessitating that they live uxorilocally, far from their full brothers. Furthermore, begging distant brothers interferes with the sharing patterns of full brothers. A man who has to borrow from a distant brother probably has to repay him before being able to contribute any valuables he acquires to his full brothers' supply. As a result, the pool of valuables available to full siblings decreases, and other brothers also have to turn to half, classificatory, and pact brothers for aid.

In unequal bridewealth societies, the recognized ranks appear to correlate with residence and sharing patterns within sets of full siblings. Men from high-ranking sibling sets live near, and borrow valuables only from one another; they have valuables to share with lower-ranking half, classificatory, and pact brothers who live either with them or uxorilocally with their wife-givers. Men of second-ranking sibling sets can live near each other and share valuables, but they probably have too few valuables to share with distant brothers or kin. Members of third-ranking sibling sets have to live near their wife's kin, perhaps far from one another, and must continually fulfill wife-givers' requests. Such men have few valuables to share with each other and might even have to ask distant kin for aid. Finally, the lowest-rank men are those without recognized siblings.

If people in unequal bridewealth societies define social mobility in terms of access to valuables, and perceive access to valuables as a function of the sharing patterns of sibling sets, then people will logically focus on the implications of particular exchanges for sibling set solidarity. People have little reason to sit back and contemplate how marital instability organizes the distribution of valuables. But they have many occasions to wonder what a particular gift means for relations within a given set of siblings. People thus come to think of sharing patterns as determining relations within wife-giving/wife-taking groups. By borrowing only from full siblings to fulfill affinal obligations, a man may demonstrate high rank.[10] And by providing valuables for distant kin, a high-ranking man may acquire classificatory, half, or pact brothers (and thus acquire sisters whose husbands can never refuse requests). By refusing to share, a man can renounce kinship ties.

In unequal bridewealth societies, affinal exchanges appear to establish the wealth and ranking of the members of wife-giving and wife-taking groups. People who participate in such exchanges perceive themselves as claiming, validating, or modifying relationships with other members of their group. And everyone watching such exchanges considers the gifts indicative of the group's composition and of the relative wealth and ranking of the brothers involved.

In summary, unequal bridewealth peoples understand wealth and rank as being demonstrated by sharing patterns within sibling sets. There are many kinds of hierarchical societies, but people vary in their understanding of what constitutes high or low rank. In many agrarian societies with classes, status appears to be inherited within lineages; high status is evidenced by ownership of land or possession of a noble title. In capitalist societies, high status appears to depend on an individual's earning power or ownership of capital. In unequal bridewealth societies, the rank of members of sibling sets is apparently established in exchanges with their wife-givers and wife-takers. Whereas people in agrarian societies with classes define upward mobility in terms of acquisition of land or titles (and seldom think about the role of the state in making it possible for people to own such things), people in unequal bridewealth societies define upward mobility in terms of sibling set solidarity, established and maintained in affinal exchanges (and seldom think about the role of marital instability in determining the obligations of wife-takers).

Political Processes

My analysis of rank—a person's access to valuables for giving away, determined by sharing patterns within the sibling set— underlies my interpretation of political processes in societies appropriate for analysis with an unequal bridewealth model. Rank organizes people's understanding of their relationship with others, and thus defines those relationships.

People's everyday conversations lead them to assume that sharing patterns within sibling sets determine individuals' access to valuables, and thus their rank. This assumption becomes a self-fulfilling prophecy in the realm of conflict. When a conflict erupts, disputants must acquire valuables rapidly; their means of doing so provide evidence of sharing patterns within their sibling sets. Conflicts mobilize sibling sets to display their solidarity (or lack of it). They determine, at least for a moment, the ranking of particular individuals. Thus, conflict situations determine the kinds of relations the disputants and their kin may establish with others. The sharing of valuables among siblings is not simply an expression of their bond. It is a way of establishing, validating, or denying bonds with full, half, classificatory, and pact siblings. It is the way to get ahead in the world.

In analyzing unequal bridewealth societies as in analyzing brideservice and equal bridewealth societies, it makes no sense to separate law from values. All people have systems of meaning that shape their perception of conflict and their understanding of how to handle it. In unequal bridewealth societies, people perceive conflicts as challenges to a person's rank; they therefore settle conflicts by displays of rank (i.e. by demonstrations of sharing patterns within sibling sets). In brideservice societies, people perceive conflicts as challenges to a man's reputation for bravery; they handle conflicts through displays of personal prowess. In equal bridewealth societies, people perceive conflicts as a failure to fulfill status obligations; they settle conflicts by having disputants agree on the nature of the long-standing relationship between them.

The Causes of Conflict

In unequal bridewealth societies, challenges to a person's rank appear to be the cause of conflict. Hoebel observes that "most Kiowa delicts occurred among the up-and-coming *ondegupa* [second-rank men] and were almost always status challenges" (1954: 173). This is Hoebel's interpretation of Richardson's observation that "trespass upon a husband's exclusive sexual rights to his wife was by far the most frequent source of grievance" (1940: 80), and her statement that for men, "absconding was a recognized means of raising position" (1940: 123). In unequal bridewealth societies, rank provides the principal language for talking about the kinds of claims people can make to one another, and therefore for thinking and talking about conflict.

Although ethnographers of unequal bridewealth societies commonly describe rank as a property of individuals, determined by individual wealth and ability (see Richardson 1940: 12–13), ethnographies usually provide evidence that rank is not a property of individuals but rather realized in sharing patterns among siblings. Donald Collier writes that "It is not an overstatement to say that relationships between siblings, and particularly between brothers, are the most striking and pervasive in Kiowa culture" (1938: 72). He implies that sibling bonds were evidenced in exchanges of horses.

Toward each other brothers are very generous. They share their belongings and exchange gifts. A man would not even contemplate refusing any request of his brother and conversely he would be careful not to make a request that his brother would have to refuse. Refusal by a brother shames both parties and is one of the worst things that can happen to a man. Of eighteen cases of suicide recalled by informants five were attributed to shame, abuse, or neglect between brothers. In four of these five suicides a request was refused or one brother reproached the other for using one of his horses—the abused brother killed himself in shame. (1938: 57–58).[11]

Richardson's description of Kiowa horse ownership confirms the impression that the sharing of horses established or validated sibling bonds: "A strong sense of private ownership prevailed with individual rights recognized within the family. . . . However the strong sense of private ownership ran counter to the general feeling that possessions and commodities, though not communally owned really, were for the free use of all the kindred" (1940: 125). A Kiowa kindred was apparently defined as family members who had access to each other's horses; "private ownership" reflected the fact that horses had to be assigned to somebody if sharing patterns were to be assessed.

It seems reasonable to conclude that among the Kiowa, as among other unequal bridewealth peoples, conflicts were perceived as calling into question the nature of sibling bonds, and thus the access of siblings to the valuables that allowed them to establish or validate their relationships with others.

The Handling of Conflict

In societies where conflicts are understood as challenges to a person's rank and where rank is demonstrated by sharing patterns within sibling sets, people logically handle conflicts by having sibling sets demonstrate their sharing patterns, thus establishing the disputants' access to valuables, and hence their rank. Because conflicts are always about rank, people interpret all actions taken by disputants and their kin as statements about their rank. Disputants who are able to muster large quantities of valuables only from full siblings demonstrate their own and their full siblings' high rank. Those who are unable to do so reveal the low rank of their sibling set.

People in societies appropriate for analysis with an unequal bridewealth model handle conflicts differently from people in equal bridewealth societies. In both, people perceive their ability to establish relationships with others as a function of their access to valuables for giving away. But the two types of societies have different understandings of how valuables are acquired; consequently they have different ways of proving a person's access to valuables. In unequal bridewealth societies, a person's access to valuables is viewed as a function of sharing patterns within the sibling set. Conflicts thus focus everyone's attention on those sharing patterns; they encourage discussions about relations between siblings. In equal bridewealth societies, a person's access to valuables is viewed as a function of a person's obligations to others. Conflicts thus focus everyone's attention on disputants' status obligations; they encourage discussions about the obligations of each disputant toward the other.

After comparing the legal procedures of the nineteenth-century Comanche, Cheyenne, and Kiowa, Hoebel (1954) concludes that the Kiowa fall between the Comanche and the Cheyenne on a scale of legal development based on the extent to which disputes are handled by third parties rather than by aggrieved individuals and their kinship groups.[12] The Kiowa resembled the Comanche in handling disputes by confrontation rather than by negotiation. Both groups did so because they understood status as belonging inherently to people rather than being determined by relationships between people. To the Kiowa, rank was an attribute of siblings who progressed through life's stages together; to the Comanche, bravery was an attribute of individual men. Both therefore handled conflicts by staging confrontations that allowed disputants to demonstrate their intrinsic qualities. The Kiowa resembled the Cheyenne in recognizing peace chiefs who could intervene in the conflicts of others. Both groups did so because they established and validated relationships between people by means of gifts. Both therefore handled conflicts by arranging compensatory payments for victims of others' wrongdoing, using procedures that involved the intervention of people who had access to the necessary valuables.

Hoebel writes that although "in social structure the Kiowas were much more akin to their Cheyenne neighbors on the north than they were to their close Comanche allies to the south," the Kiowa and the Cheyenne used their social institutions very differently (1954: 169–70). Both the Kiowa and the Cheyenne had soldier societies (organizations of warriors), but Kiowa societies did not generate new law as Cheyenne societies did (1954: 171). And even though the Kiowa had chiefs and peace pipes as did the Cheyenne, Kiowa cuckolds did not patiently await the arrival of a chief, as their Cheyenne counterparts did; they reacted so violently to being cuckolded that terrified bystanders had to send for a chief posthaste (1954: 172).

Because Kiowa disputants were interested in establishing their personal access to horses (as demonstrated by the support they received from siblings), not in negotiating the relationship between themselves and their opponents, there was no reason for Kiowa soldiers, or any other Kiowa intermediaries, to think up creative solutions to reconcile disputants. In Cheyenne society, however, where people believed that only a "correction" could avoid a potentially endless cycle of breaches of norms and counteractions, intermediaries who invented solutions acceptable to both disputants were rewarded the respect that everyone desired.

Kiowa cuckolds also had good reason to react violently rather than to wait patiently for the arrival of a chief sent by the offender. In Kiowa society, as in Comanche society, wife stealing called into question the rank of the man whose wife had been stolen, not, as among the Cheyenne, the status obligations of the wife-stealer. A Kiowa cuckold, however, did not have to confront his cuckolder personally, as a Comanche cuckold did. In Kiowa society, sharing patterns within sibling sets, not personal bravery, determined rank. A Kiowa cuckold, therefore, had only to make a great deal of noise. "Proclaiming aloud one's intentions [to murder one's opponent] always brought out any defendant's kin"—accompanied by chiefs, peace pipes, and compensatory horses (Richardson 1940: 27).

In unequal bridewealth societies, as in equal bridewealth and brideservice societies, men's disputes over women are the most dramatic and memorable conflicts. In societies where social inequality is organized by kinship, rather than by class relations, men's claims to women are the basis of their social rights and obligations. Any challenge to those claims is a challenge to a man's status. But because marriages are differently validated in the three types of societies, men react to challenges in different ways. In unequal bridewealth societies, where rank is established by exchanges within sibling sets, elopement and adultery elicit displays of access to valuables by wife-giving/wife-taking groups.

Donald Collier, writing about the nineteenth-century Kiowa in the present tense, reports that

When a girl elopes, her mother, mother's sisters and other interested female relatives (often the father's sister) raid the boy's family and take property. His parents are not supposed to resist the raid. To do so is an insult to the girl and her relatives, and is done only if the boy's parents strongly disapprove of the girl and are determined to prevent the union from becoming permanent. In the case of an elopement of a girl her father plays the role of counselor, urging the women of the family not to act rashly. Sometimes he accompanies the raiding party, not to take part in the seizure of property but to prevent immoderate action on the part of the raiding women. His first concern is whether the boy will make a suitable husband for his daughter; then, whether the boy intends a permanent union; and finally, how best to establish and maintain cordial relations between the two families. To this end he will make sure that the gifts presented in return for the seized property are sufficiently generous. In contrast with the cautious attitude of the father, the women raiders seem to be interested only in retaliating for the 'theft' of the girl, and take no thought of the consequences.

The attitude of parents toward the elopement of a son with an unmarried girl is quite different. His elopement attests to his initiative and prowess; a successful elopement reflects honor upon a man. Provided the parents approve of the girl they receive the raiders with good humor and sometimes even urge them to take property. Occasionally horses are staked out beside the tipi for the convenience of the raiders. (1938: 52)

In Kiowa society, an elopement cast doubt on the ranking of the bride's full brothers. Donald Collier writes that for a girl to elope was considered a slight to her brothers.

[Brothers] generally . . . disapprove of an elopement marriage for their sister. When their sister elopes they feel that she is indirectly showing disrespect for them by not asking their advice about her marriage. Furthermore, they feel that an arranged marriage is more honorable, and that an elopement of the sister reflects unfavorably on her family. Ordinarily, while the brothers are not very pleased about their sister's elopement, they do nothing about it. But if they thoroughly disapprove of the lover, they will ask their mother to fetch the girl home and thus prevent the union from becoming permanent. (1938: 66–67)

In unequal bridewealth societies, elopement reflects unfavorably on a bride's family because no one knows whether the bride's brothers will be able to obtain valuables from the groom for giving to their own wife-givers.

This would seem to explain why Kiowa mothers sometimes chased eloping daughters, whereas Cheyenne mothers apparently did not. In both Kiowa and Cheyenne societies, the brothers of an eloping woman were insulted by her elopement, for they had the primary say regarding whom she should marry (see D. Collier 1938: 66; Llewellyn & Hoebel 1941: 172–73). But among Cheyenne, a man's access to horses depended on his status obligations, not the sharing patterns within his sibling set, as among the Kiowa. In Cheyenne society, therefore, an elopement cast doubt on an eloping groom's ability to make claims to others, not the abilities of the bride's brothers to make such claims. As a result, Cheyenne mothers (and brothers) did not chase after an eloping woman. They, like cuckolded Cheyenne husbands, waited for the groom's family to send an emissary. In Kiowa society, however, because a girl's elopement cast doubt on her brothers' access to her husband's horses, it made sense for a mother to chase an eloping daughter, particularly if the girl's chosen lover was not of a rank that would benefit her brothers.

The Kiowa mothers who raided the camps of eloped daughters' husbands were apparently representing their own and their sons' interests. A Kiowa mother, whatever her feelings about the theft of her daughter, benefited by seizing or destroying as much of a groom's family's property as possible. The more property she seized, within reason, the more property her husband had to return if he was to appear sufficiently generous (i.e. to support his claim to rank). And the more property a woman's husband returned, the more convincingly she proved her sons' access to horses, hence the higher their rank.

The father of an eloped girl, in contrast, had to balance the interests of her mother and brothers against those of his other wives and their children if he was polygynous, and, if not, against the interests of his brothers, whose help he would need in obtaining valuables for giving to the kin of his eloped daughter's husband. A Kiowa father had good reasons for adopting a cautious attitude toward seizing the property of his daughter's husband's kin, and for accompanying his wife and sisters "to prevent immoderate action on the part of the raiding women" (D. Collier 1938: 52).

In unequal bridewealth societies, "a successful elopement reflects honor upon a man" (D. Collier 1938: 52) because in societies where women love high-ranking men and refuse to consort with men of low rank, a man's rank can only be raised—never lowered—by eloping with a woman. The groom's kin have little to fear from a raid conducted by the bride's mother and aunts. However much the bride's relatives take, they have to return an equal or greater number of gifts to maintain their rank. Consequently, a Kiowa groom's family understandably received "the raiders with good humor" and urged them to take property. The more property a Kiowa bride's family seized, the more prestige accrued to the groom's mother and uterine siblings.[13]

The most dramatic and consequential conflicts in unequal bridewealth societies arise not over elopement but over adultery and wife stealing: stealing a wife is a more direct challenge to another man's status than eloping with an unmarried girl. By choosing her lover over her husband, a wife directly ranks the two men; if she is the wife of a high-ranking man, she confers great prestige on the man she absconds with.[14] Richardson observes that for Kiowa men, "judicious absconding" was a recognized "means of raising one's status" (1940: 86).

In Kiowa society, absconding was also more prestigious than eloping because it allowed an absconder to publicly demonstrate his lack of concern over property. In cases of wife stealing, abandoned husbands commonly retaliated by killing the horses of a lover and/or those of his kinsmen, not by seizing them with the intention of initiating a gift exchange. For a man to risk destruction of his property and that of his kin was therefore to claim high rank. Richardson writes that "this lack of concern over property, the pose being that 'they could always get more', was important in the status-raising and status-maintaining goal" (1940: 121). To steal the wife of a higher-ranking man was a very effective, if not the most effective, way for a Kiowa man to claim a higher rank.

The observation that unequal bridewealth peoples perceive adultery and wife stealing as challenges to the rank of the abandoned husband would seem to explain how the Kiowa handled such cases, as reported by ethnographers. Richardson suggests that an abandoned husband's reaction depended on his rank: "men of very high status did not prosecute abscondings and other grievances vigorously, if at all" (1940: 121); she notes that "in extreme cases, a very low plaintiff could not prosecute at all, except as a pitiful figure" (1940: 118–19).

Although very high-ranking Kiowa men did not always prosecute, the fact that very low-ranking men did not prosecute either must have put men whose access to horses was not indisputable in the position of having to prosecute or lose rank. Most Kiowa cuckolds reacted violently. Their characteristic response was to loudly proclaim their intention of killing their wife's lover and/or to shoot some horses belonging to the cuckolder and/or his kin. The violence of a cuckold's response apparently correlated with the seriousness of the threat to his claim to rank. Richardson reports that "the closer the status levels of the two men, the more violent the prosecution, provided they were not both on the topmost rung" (1940: 119).

Most Kiowa and Comanche cuckolds responded to adultery and wife stealing with violence, but Kiowa cuckolds did not have to take direct action against a wife's lover, as Comanche cuckolds did. A deserted Comanche husband had to confront his wife's lover or be judged a coward. But because the Kiowa assessed rank in terms of sharing patterns, not personal bravery, a Kiowa cuckold did not lose face by obtaining aid from his kin.

In actuality, Kiowa cuckolds always obtained aid from kin, for challenges to rank in Kiowa society were not challenges to individuals but to sibling sets. Brothers always prosecuted together—or, by not doing so, publicly repudiated their membership in the sibling set. Donald Collier writes that

in conflict situations a man receives his strongest support from his brothers. Not only do they come to his aid in disputes and fights, but they are held collectively responsible for his acts. When a man's wife is stolen it is customary to retaliate by raiding the paramour's property. The raid usually takes the form of shooting a number of horses. Now if the paramour's horses are not available, the horses of his immediate family and particularly of his brothers will do just as well. On such a raid the injured husband is usually accompanied by one or more of his brothers or male cousins. The brothers feel that the wife stealing is an insult both to the husband and to themselves and desire to see the insult avenged. When the husband happens to be absent at the time his brothers will carry out the retaliatory raid without his knowledge or consent. Should the husband desire to ignore his wife's infidelity he would find it difficult to restrain his brothers' thirst for retaliation. (1938: 60)

In Kiowa society, wife-stealing cases mobilized not only a deserted husband's male kin but also his female kin. Richardson writes that the women of a deserted husband's family "embarked on a property raid of their own. Ganging up, armed with butcher knives, the sisters and mothers descended on the household of C's [the correspondent's] mother or sisters, hacked, chopped and destroyed everything within sight, even to the point of injuring personally some of C's female relatives. Men did not participate in any way in this raid except to stop it. This kind of a property raid was the woman's sole means of legal action in any situation, be it rape, first elopements or absconding" (1940: 115–16). Because Kiowa women lacked direct access to horses for giving away, they could not defend claims to rank by giving things themselves. But they could display family rank by destroying the possessions of others. In elopement cases, women seized and destroyed property as a means of forcing their male kin to return many gifts. And in cases of adultery and wife stealing, women destroyed property to indicate the value of family wives.

Cases of wife stealing frequently mobilized the wife-stealer's kin group as well. Kiowa and Comanche men who stole other men's wives gained prestige by the act and therefore never refused to admit guilt. But because the Kiowa assessed rank in terms of sharing patterns rather than personal bravery, a Kiowa wife-stealer, unlike his Comanche counterpart, could allow his kin to act for him without losing face. Absconding couples in both societies usually joined raiding parties or otherwise put distance between themselves and the wronged husband, but a Kiowa absconder did not eventually have to face his victim alone. Richardson reports that a Kiowa wife-stealer might hide while his kin (or members of his soldier society) offered peace pipes and compensatory horses to the man whose wife he had stolen (1940: 23). Hoebel, in contrast, reports that he found no cases in which a Comanche wife-stealer marshaled his kin and friends to help him face the man he had wronged (1940: 60).

In unequal bridewealth societies, the settlement of wife-stealing cases depends not on the personal prowess of contestants, as it does in brideservice societies, but rather on the size and prestige of the opponents' kin groups. Richardson observes that "whenever [Kiowa] opponents were actively supported by their kindred, the greatest display of man power, with due regard to the status of the kinsmen, intimidated and conquered" (1940: 118). The non-involvement of a Kiowa man's kin group must have been as significant as their involvement; a man whose kin refused to help him was publicly proved to lack access to their horses.

Richardson sums up her analysis of Kiowa legal procedures as follows: "What was probably the crucial point determining the procedure followed in absconding cases, in horse quarrels, and to some extent in the crimes and quarrels we have previously mentioned, was the status, relative and absolute, of the two litigants" (1940: 117). I suggest the reverse conclusion: rank did not determine procedures; the procedures used determined the ranking of the disputants. Just as in brideservice societies, where the actions of men quarreling over a woman are taken as proof of their bravery, so in unequal bridewealth societies, the procedures followed by disputants are taken as public proof of their access to valuables.

Ethnographers frequently report that "fines" in unequal bridewealth societies are graded by rank. Some unequal bridewealth peoples have norms specifying that high-ranking offenders must pay more compensation than low-ranking ones and/or that high-ranking victims should receive more (see Leach 1965: 205; Barton 1919; Kroeber 1926). In her discussion of Kiowa absconding cases, Richardson states that "in general the amount of the compensation was proportional to the wealth of the defendant, except that plaintiffs of very high status took very little and those of very low status did not dare exact much" (1940: 114–15). She concludes that the higher an offender's rank, the more compensation his kin group paid. I suggest that the more compensation an offender's kin group paid, the higher they proved their rank to be.

Richardson does not discuss the relationship between a Kiowa cuckold's rank and the amount of compensation he received, but we might speculate that, except for very high ranking cuckolds who demanded few or no valuables, the amount of compensation a plaintiff received was proportional to his rank, with high-ranking plaintiffs receiving more than low-ranking ones. If most absconding cases were status challenges, and if defendants and their kin benefited by paying as high a compensation as possible, then it seems reasonable to assume that defendants who were able to convince the wives of high-ranking men to abscond with them also had access to many valuables. The amount of compensation paid in absconding cases would thus testify to the rank of both plaintiff and defendant.

Observers from a capitalist society might admire the apparent fairness of a legal system that requires high-ranking offenders to pay more for wrongdoing. My analysis, however, suggests that unequal bridewealth societies do not provide a model worthy of imitation. In capitalist societies, where high status is indicated by ownership of property, fining wealthy offenders more than poor ones promotes social equality. But in societies such as the Kiowa, where high rank is demonstrated by giving things away, the correlation between high rank and high fines strengthens, rather than undermines, the existing system of inequality.

Leadership and the Construction of Subordination

Ethnographers of unequal bridewealth societies commonly portray them as having real chiefs—or report that they would have real chiefs if people could agree among themselves as to which man holds the highest rank. The Kiowa, unlike the Comanche and the Cheyenne, did not make a distinction between inferior war chiefs, who directed raids against outsiders, and superior peace chiefs, who directed the activities of the whole group (Hoebel 1954: 170). To the Kiowa, war record was "the single most important determinant of status" (Richardson 1940: 14); the most famous chiefs were also the most famous warriors. Kiowa leadership was not situational; leaders were leaders in all activities affecting their groups.

Ethnographers of Kiowa society differ in their descriptions of leadership patterns. Mooney writes that the Kiowa had a high tribal chief who "must have exercised almost despotic powers" (1898: 233), whereas Richardson writes that band headmen never surrendered their individual authority to the "formal tribal head," the Taime-keeper. "There was no doubt that although chiefs accorded all honor to the religious authority of the Taime-keeper, they paid but lip service to his temporal authority. The Taime-keeper listened carefully to their advice at nightly smoke-meetings, and handed it out the next day as his own" (1940: 9). That these reports conflict probably reflects two different aspects of the Kiowa ranking system. In unequal bridewealth societies, where affines and siblings are ranked, no two people can be fully equal. In any social group, one person is expected to be superior. When different Kiowa bands camped together, for example, the most prestigious band head took "the lead in matters affecting the whole group" (D. Collier 1938: 109).

But the Kiowa tribe was also composed of economically independent bands, each of whose members had a specific kinship or patronage tie to the leader. The unity of these economically independent bands must therefore have varied with the degree of consensus as to the ranking of band headmen. Because of the apparent primacy of war record in determining rank, we can assume that the Kiowa appeared most unified to ethnographers when a single band headman had such an outstanding war record that no other man could match it. At those times, the Kiowa must have appeared to have a high chief who enjoyed "despotic powers." But when various headmen were contending for superiority, bickering between rival headmen probably split the tribe and revealed the unwillingness of band headmen to relinquish their authority.

As should be obvious, societies appropriate for analysis with an unequal bridewealth model offer more scope for leadership than do equal bridewealth societies. In both, leadership requires followership, but a marriage system based on unequal bridewealth offers would-be leaders two mechanisms for acquiring subordinates. Leaders can incorporate followers into their economic units not only by collecting wives, children, orphans, and strays in their households but also by acquiring varieties of siblings and affines. And the idea that no two people can be equal allows leaders to rank themselves.

These two mechanisms explain why ethnographers of some unequal bridewealth societies report the existence of "hereditary" chiefs who enjoy a privileged lifestyle and "rule" large territories. In areas with concentrated resources, some chiefs may be able to build large followings and subordinate many rivals. In areas where resources are dispersed, as among the Kiowa, groups usually remain small. Chiefs then appear to rule only close kin.

Ethnographers suggest that political leaders have considerable power to settle disputes within their local groups. Richardson, for example, writes that a Kiowa headman's responsibilities included "maintaining law and order without any 'police' assistance" (1940:

7). She reports that "Big Bow said to two of his men fighting, 'I have charge of this camp. I am responsible for your protection. You two be friends' " (1940: 20). Leaders have specific kinship and patronage ties with each group member that enable them to reward compliance or punish disobedience; they also have a vested interest in preserving peace among members of their production units: unhappy members may seek out rival chiefs. Given leaders' ability and incentive to rapidly settle conflicts within their groups, it is understandable that the Kiowa tended not to notice or remember the quarrels of "insignificant persons" (Richardson 1940: 121).

Leaders have no power to settle disputes between members of separate production units, however, particularly when the disputants are high-ranking people. When describing conflict-management procedures in unequal bridewealth societies, ethnographers commonly mention "go-betweens" who travel back and forth between disputing groups, trying to arrange compensatory payments (Barton 1919; Kroeber 1926). Hoebel writes of the Kiowa that "in all cases where violence seemed to threaten, a Ten Medicine Bundle Keeper appeared on the scene to intervene with his sacred pipe. He asked the aggrieved demonstrator not to take violent vengeance on the aggressor but to promise to accept a peaceful settlement with compensation. To refuse the request of a Ten Medicine Keeper with his pipe was very bad form and supernaturally dangerous. In most cases the request was heeded" (1954: 172). Hoebel stresses sacred pipe owners' lack of power to settle disputes. These men could forestall violence, but they could not act as arbitrators or judges. In unequal bridewealth societies, high-ranking men have the moral authority to urge peaceful solutions, but they have few rewards or sanctions to offer disputants who are not members of their own personal followings. Prestigious leaders can serve only as go-betweens in arranging compensation, payment of which allows the members of competing sibling sets to display their wealth and rank.

In both unequal and equal bridewealth societies, kinship organizes peoples' possibilities for autonomy, dependence, and power. Leaders' need for followers affords followers a measure of protection from any particular leader. In Kiowa society, "there was considerable competition among the different *topadok'i* [band headmen] for" members of the "poorer class" (Richardson 1940: 6). At the same time, being disowned by one's kin is the ultimate sanction. In Kiowa society, men who were disowned by their families—

that is, whose families refused to provide marriage-validating gifts—became "poor young men" who had to offer their labor in return for gifts of women from high-ranking men. Such men might change masters, but they had little chance of escaping servitude. Similarly, women whose brothers refused, or were unable, to help them were at the mercy of the husband they were living with. At the other end of the social scale, people whose sibling sets headed large kindreds enjoyed the privileges of high rank.

In both equal and unequal bridewealth societies, people depend on their kin, but the different organizations of inequality result in the establishment of different types of kinship groups. In equal bridewealth societies, those who lack power need socially defined parents to speak for them. In unequal bridewealth societies, people need brothers to support them in their relations with others. As a result, dependency is perceived differently in the two types of societies. To people in equal bridewealth societies, as noted in Chapter 2, dependency is the human condition. Each generation is dependent on those who came before (Meillassoux 1972: 99). To people in unequal bridewealth societies, dependency appears to result from individual failure.

Folk Models of Social Structure and Human Agency

In view of ethnographers' descriptions of hereditary ranks, it may seem surprising that unequal bridewealth peoples perceive dependency as resulting from individual failure. Those who recognize hereditary ranks would not be expected to assess rank on the basis of personal attributes and achievements. Yet unequal bridewealth peoples apparently emphasize individual accomplishments (or failures) in determining a man's rank. Richardson asserts that "war-record was the single most important determinant of status in Kiowa life" (1940: 14).

The explanation of this seeming inconsistency is that people are born into particular ranks, but an individual's success is determined by the person's own actions and those of full siblings. Richardson writes that although "the cards were stacked in favor of a [Kiowa] son's achieving at least the rank of his father," "the position [into which one was born] had to be maintained or validated, of course, by appropriate achievements. . . . There were many cases of people rising to eminence from poor and inauspicious beginnings, and some cases of 'losing caste' by dishonorable actions. Relatively great vertical mobility, one of the general characteristics of the Plains, was found, but it is significant that even in this individualistic culture, there were specific terms denoting absolute status" (1940: 15).[15] In unequal bridewealth societies, members of wife-giving/wife-taking groups who claim high rank must continually validate it by providing many gifts for full sisters' husbands and wife's brothers, and by fulfilling the behavioral requirements of that rank, such as accumulating war honors, as among the Kiowa, or sponsoring ceremonies, as among the Kachin (Leach 1965 and the Ifugao (Barton 1919). Individuals and groups that fail to fulfill the requirements of rank lose status relative to competitors.

In societies where rank must be continually validated by appropriate behaviors, people naturally focus on individual achievements when ranking near-equals. Richardson, writing about the Kiowa, states that "if any debate arose over the relative position of two [men] rather closely matched, it was usually settled by a recitation of the two coup counts." If coup counts did not settle the issue, they were followed by a recitation of "the number of captives and horses taken, and the horses given away" (Richardson 1940: 16). People in unequal bridewealth societies thus have many occasions in which to talk about the determination of rank by individual achievements and few occasions in which to discuss genealogies.

Individual achievements also provide the basis for would-be leaders' claims to speak for their wife-giving/wife-taking groups. Just as leaders in equal bridewealth societies justify their right to speak for followers by emphasizing their knowledge of the rules that govern the universe, leaders in unequal bridewealth societies justify their right to speak for their groups on the basis of their own accomplishments. Richardson suggests that war record was the major determinant of a Kiowa man's ability to speak for his siblings, as well as to attract and keep them.

A large family of kindred who "loved" a person, i.e. who backed him, was in itself a status point of major importance. In any intra-tribal situation where prestige might be involved, relatives rushed to protect an individual by backing him lest they all fall with his defeat. . . . However, the emphasis was not on the sheer size of the kindred. More important than the number was their status. Three great warriors outranked ten no-accounts, but one warrior probably could not outface ten commoners. Hence a great leader sought every means to raise the war record of his kinsmen and followers, for by the predatory nature of Kiowa warfare their rise was no loss to him. (1940: 13)

In unequal bridewealth societies, a man of high achievement can speak for himself and thus need not depend on others. In Kiowa society, a great warrior could prosecute his own disputes; consequently, he could avoid subordinating himself to any senior brother. Richardson writes: "There is some indication in general that the [cuckold's] kindred, although watching developments very closely, did not enter [the dispute] as long as their representative was competent to prosecute alone. They probably prided themselves on a member who could singlehandedly defend his honor well" (1940: 119).

Although people in unequal bridewealth societies must recognize that individuals' possibilities for achievement are determined by the wealth and cohesion of their sibling sets, people probably have few occasions for discussing this fact. They take it for granted. But people have many opportunities to speculate on why one sibling set outranks another, and thus to focus on the achievements of its members. As a result, people perceive their social world as one in which achievements determine a person's rank and rank determines an individual's ability to establish relationships with others. In unequal bridewealth societies, rank, as evidenced by individual achievements, appears to organize social interaction; in equal bridewealth societies, rules appear to organize social interaction; and in brideservice societies, personal power appears to do so.

There is ample evidence that the Kiowa understood rank as the basis on which people related to one another. In the beginning of this chapter, I noted that ethnographers portray male labor as divided by rank (Mishkin 1940: 62) and mentioned Richardson's description of the "semi-formalized attitudes or modes of behavior associated with the semi-formalized statuses" (1940: 20). According to Richardson, men of the highest rank were expected to be mild, generous, gracious, lofty, and courageous. Second-rank men were touchy, rivalrous, and defensive of their honor. Third-rank men were submissive and had little honor to defend (1940: 120). And "no-accounts" were lazy and lacking ambition (1940: 15).

The difference between the Kiowa folk model of social structure and that of the Cheyenne is exemplified by the different attitudes of the two groups toward the effect of compensatory payments on the woman's status in wife-stealing cases. Llewellyn and Hoebel write that among the Cheyenne, a husband's acceptance of compensation legally validated his wife's change of status (1941: 192). The Kiowa, by contrast, were not clear about the effect of the wife-stealer's payments on the woman's status. Richardson writes that the Kiowa felt that "compensation should in no way be regarded as payment for the wife," but she also notes "a general feeling that if compensation has been paid, [the wife] ought to go to [her lover]" (1940: 115).

In unequal bridewealth societies, compensatory payments testify to the ranking of disputants, not to the relationship between them. As a result, people who arrange compensatory payments for wife stealing and adultery focus on rank. They have no reason to discuss the status of the woman. In equal bridewealth societies, people think about their rights and their obligations to others in terms of specific long-standing relationships. Therefore, those who handle wife-stealing and adultery cases have good reason to discuss the relationship between compensatory payments and each disputant's relation to the woman in question.

The difference between the Kiowa folk model of social structure and that of the Comanche is exemplified in their different treatment of women suspected of adultery. In Chapter 1, I noted that the idiom of bravery provides a cultural justification for men to beat adulterous wives. Comanche women were frequently killed or maimed by their husbands and a Comanche woman's kin "showed no inclination to retaliate when a husband killed his wife" (Hoebel 1940: 73). In unequal bridewealth societies, the idiom of rank does not provide a cultural justification for a man to harm his wife. A man's rank is based on his past achievements and his relations with siblings, not his ability to maintain a status that announces "don't fool with me." A Kiowa wife, therefore, "usually went unprosecuted for infidelity. In spite of the fact that Kiowa in generalizing said the usual thing to do to an unfaithful wife was to cut her nose off, this occurred only three times" in 62 cases (Richardson 1940: 116). A Kiowa woman's kin also intervened to protect her from her husband's brutality. Richardson reports that when a Kiowa husband beat his wife for infidelity, "her kin usually hastened to protect her, as if even under these aggravating circumstances she ought to go unharmed" (1940: 116). And, unlike a Comanche woman's kin, the kin of a Kiowa woman were likely to extract blood vengeance from a murderous husband (1940: 76).

Unequal bridewealth peoples' understanding of rank as the basis of social order would seem to explain why they assess action in terms of a person's rank. To know a person's rank is to understand and be able to predict that person's actions. Richardson undoubtedly recalls the accounts of her Kiowa informants when she writes that "a man of a given rank tended to act in a way prescribed for his class" (1940: 120). In unequal bridewealth societies, people perceive rank as the cause of behavior, and behavior provides the most eloquent testimony of rank.

Practical Action

Richardson characterizes Kiowa society as "braggadocian" (1940: 19); Hoebel observes that United States "Army men who had to deal with the Kiowa called them insolent" (1954: 130). The everyday behavior of Kiowa men thus appears to contrast markedly with the reserve and dignity of Cheyenne men (Hoebel 1978: 95) and moderately with the "rough, tough, aggressive, and militant" stance of Comanche men (Hoebel 1954: 129).

The analysis of rank presented in this chapter suggests a reason why observers from capitalist societies describe the Kiowa as insolent braggarts. Unequal bridewealth peoples live in a world where rank determines a person's opportunities but is not fixed; it is forever being negotiated. In such a world, to brag about one's deeds and to respond insolently are practical behaviors.

In a society apparently composed of insolent braggarts, social order must seem fragile. Richardson suggests that the Kiowa worried about maintaining peace. She quotes a band head "who, hearing that a serious quarrel had been settled, said, 'That's good. We won't have to be uneasy now. We won't have to be prepared for trouble' " (1940: 19). Richardson also observes that the Kiowa were, in fact, usually prepared for trouble: "When a fight started, women yelled, 'Somebody stop it!' Even men without the authority of a *topadok'i* might step in to settle a quarrel" (1940: 19). The Kiowa thus appear to have shared the strategy common in brideservice societies of having outsiders intervene in quarrels to prevent disputants from killing each other.

But there is no evidence that the Kiowa used another strategy common to brideservice peoples, that of trying to avoid quarrels. If unequal bridewealth peoples are indeed given to insolence and bragging, then it seems unlikely that those who feel angry go off by themselves or deliberately try to avoid provoking others. Nor do unequal bridewealth peoples need to forget their anger. Unlike leaders in brideservice societies, who lack power to intervene in disputes, leaders in unequal bridewealth societies enjoy considerable power over their followers and can arrange compensatory payments for disputants who belong to different economic units.

Cultural Representations

Richardson and Mishkin begin their monographs on Kiowa law and stratification, respectively, with discussions of social structure: Richardson describes "the basic economic and social group" of Kiowa society as a set of "brothers" and their coresident "sister's husbands" (1940: 3); Mishkin describes wealth differences between families (1940: 18–19). Neither Richardson nor Mishkin is writing a general ethnography of Kiowa society, but like Wallace and Hoebel (1952) who begin their Comanche ethnography with a discussion of values, and Hoebel (1978) who begins his Cheyenne ethnography with a description of tribal ceremonies, they begin their monographs with discussions of what appears to have been the dominant cultural concern of the people they studied. The Kiowa were obsessed with asserting and contesting claims to rank: "There was almost no corner of the culture where status aspects were not important" (Richardson 1940: 117). The emphasis on social structure by Richardson and Mishkin reflects, I think, the tendency of people in unequal bridewealth societies to understand their world as being organized by social inequalities rather than by displays of personal prowess or divine rules.

My discussion of the cultural representations of unequal bridewealth peoples is not as complete as my discussions of brideservice and equal bridewealth peoples' cultural representations. I have not read ethnographies of enough unequal bridewealth peoples to have knowledge of the commonalities of their beliefs and rituals. And, unfortunately, not as much information is available about Kiowa religion and world view as about the beliefs of the Comanche and the Cheyenne.

The evidence I do have suggests that unequal bridewealth peoples, in general, are preoccupied with social inequality. Leach observes that all actions of the Kachin of Highland Burma, even the most necessary and routine, have a "ritual" component that "serves to express the individual's status as a social person in the structural system in which he finds himself for the time being" (1965: 10–11). Leach argues that ritual is a component of human action in all societies—and indeed it is. But only in some societies do people so continually assert their claims to status that ethnographers comment on the fact. Most people, in most societies, seem to take their world and their place in it for granted. In only a few societies, particularly those appropriate for analysis with an unequal bridewealth model, such as the Kachin and the Kiowa, do people seem to be consciously aware that they are continually negotiating, and thus creating, their social order.[16]

Leach describes the Kachin as having two inconsistent "systems" of social structure (1965: xii). The same conclusion can be drawn from Hoebel's observation that "the Kiowas never had a clear idea [of whether they preferred individualism or social well-being] and muddled along trying to serve both ends. When cultural goals are not clear-cut, it is not likely that social action will be either" (1954: 176). The Kachin, Leach suggests, do not merely compete with one another according to accepted rules of the game; they actually argue over which rules should apply. He writes that both "*Gumsa* and *Gumlao* use the same words to describe the categories of their own political system and that of their opponents but they make different assumptions about the relations between the categories in the two cases" (1965: xiii).

Although I have found no indication that the Kiowa recognized two inconsistent political systems with a common set of categories, the unequal bridewealth model does suggest that people in such societies may interpret a single gift of valuables in contradictory ways. A man who borrows a valuable from a distant brother may think of himself as intending to return its equivalent, and thus as being independent from and potentially equal to the lender, whereas the lender may interpret the loan as initiating a one-way flow that defines the recipient as a junior brother. Similarly, men are expected to marry women of equal or higher rank, but wife-givers who make too many requests of their wife-takers may be perceived by others as the lowly client of a wealthy patron. In such societies, a gift of valuables from a man to his wife's brother can be interpreted either as a gift from an inferior wife-taker to his superior wife-giver, or as a gift from a superior patron to a lowly client who has courted his favor by giving him a woman in marriage.[17]

If, as my analysis of unequal bridewealth peoples suggests, every action is open to contradictory interpretations and the status of a particular sexual union is never clear, then it is easy to understand why these peoples appear to be obsessed with asserting and contesting claims to rank. When norms are unclear and contradictory and the stakes are high, people consciously try to impose their preferred meaning on action. They must continually assert the interpretations they hope will prevail. The Kiowa must indeed have seemed braggadocian and insolent to ethnographers and army men. The Kachin community Leach studied must have appeared "unstable" and faction-ridden (1965: chap. 4). And many unequal bridewealth societies must appear to their ethnographers as transitional social formations, in the process of becoming ranked or unranked.

Unequal bridewealth peoples' obsession with social inequality suggests a reason why ethnographers of Kiowa society (D. Collier 1938; Mishkin 1940; Richardson 1940) did not begin their monographs with discussions of religion, as Hoebel (1978) did when writing about the Cheyenne. In societies where people constantly praise their own achievements and attributes, they have few occasions in which to talk or think about themselves as dependent on supernatural beings. Scott (1911) describes the Kiowa Sun Dance as a joyful occasion, notable among Plains Sun Dances for its lack of self-sacrifice. The braggadocian Kiowa, unlike the Cheyenne, had no reason to seek pity from the spirits.

Gender Conceptions

Ethnographers of unequal bridewealth societies seldom mention the concepts masculinity and femininity, thus suggesting that for these people rank is a more important aspect of personhood than gender. There is some evidence that Kiowa women, for example, thought of themselves as family members first and women second. The Kiowa women who prosecuted cases of elopement, adultery, and wife stealing appear to have been more concerned with the ranks of the male offender and female victim than they were with the violation of feminine interests (see Richardson 1940: 112). And Richardson's description of the rape of a Kiowa woman implies that the raped woman and her mother were more incensed by the presumptuousness of the low-ranking rapist in raping a high-ranking woman than they were by the act of rape (1940: 112).

Ethnographers' lack of attention to gender also suggests that women in unequal bridewealth societies, like their men, tend to think of rank in terms of individual attributes and achievements. Mishkin writes that high-ranking Kiowa women were ideally "virtuous, wealthy, and beautiful" (1940: 47). And he records a Kiowa version of the story of "The Princess and the Pea" in reverse, in which top-ranking women are described as "beautiful and accomplished," meticulous in cooking, and "snooty and particular," whereas a lowest-rank woman is an ugly creature without manners (1940: 50). In an appendix to his discussion of rank, Mishkin presents a list of the 21 "most famous women" in the tribe, with the bases of their claims to eminence (1940: 55–56). Of these 21, all but seven were of the highest rank.[18]

Because all 14 of the highest-ranking women on the list were married to men of equal rank, Mishkin concludes that "the rank of woman . . . reflects the rank of their fathers and secondarily of their husbands" (1940: 47). It seems more reasonable to assume, however, that women did not take the rank of their husbands, as happens in the Cinderella stories of stratified agrarian societies. My analysis suggests that a Kiowa woman born to a high-ranking mother and father could maintain her claim to high rank only if she married a high-ranking man. If she married a lower-ranking man, people might begin to question her own (and her brothers') high rank. In Kiowa society, high-ranking men were polygynous and had wives of various ranks. But a Kiowa woman had only one husband at a time.

The unequal bridewealth model developed here helps to explain why women in such societies are more concerned with rank than with gender, and why they think of rank in terms of individual attributes and achievements. They have more occasions in which to stress their rank than their gender. It is a mother's rank, not her mothering, that most affects her future and the futures of her children. And it is on the basis of rank, not feminine fertility, that women claim special privileges.

Nevertheless, people do have occasions in which to think about women as being different from men. Cases of elopement, adultery, and wife stealing provide contexts for elaborating somewhat contradictory images of women. On the one hand, people think of women as behaving rationally in choosing lovers; in Kiowa society, "no woman would consort with a man of low rank unless he were most attractive" (Richardson 1940: 121). But on the other hand, Kiowa "women were not considered entirely responsible for their actions nor competent. It was said, 'Women are foolish, and will believe any story which is told to gain their love' " (Richardson 1940: 116). Such contradictory views of women probably reflect different stages of elopement, adultery, and wife-stealing cases. When a woman first commits adultery or runs off with her lover, people try to understand why she chose her lover over her husband or the man preferred by her brothers. They tend to assume that the woman is rationally trying to better her lot. But abandoned husbands, and people analyzing a woman's action after property destructions and compensatory payments have established the ranking of her husband and lover, are in a different position. They have good reason to assume the fallibility and foolishness of women.

Rituals

The rituals and ritual organizations of unequal bridewealth societies are usually intended to promote well-being, but they also appear to provide people with forums for asserting and contesting claims to rank. The Kiowa Sun Dance, as already noted, was a happy event, not an occasion for invoking heavenly pity through self-mutilation (Scott 1911). However joyful such public rituals may be, people's obsession with negotiating rank differences suggests that ceremonies and festivals, whether overtly concerned with harvests, renewal, or fertility, are also occasions for contesting rank. Leach writes that in the Kachin village he studied, "major festivals were the occasions on which, according to orthodox *gumsa* practice, the formal status of the chief ought to have been made visibly manifest. What was actually made manifest was the intensity of the factional hostility [among rival claimants to the position of chief]" (1965: 72). It thus seems reasonable to conclude that the Kiowa Sun Dance, a gathering of the entire tribe, was an occasion for negotiating rival headmen's claims to preeminence.

Ritual organizations also dramatize rank differences. The Kiowa soldier societies differed from those of the Cheyenne in this respect. Llewellyn and Hoebel describe Cheyenne military societies as being of the ungraded type, open to all men of all ages (1941: 99). A Cheyenne man apparently joined one society for life, advancing within it as his war record improved. Kiowa military societies "were roughly graded according to age and achievement" (Mishkin 1940: 38). Men apparently changed societies as they gained renown. High-ranking youths never had to join the lowest-ranking society. They began their careers in more prestigious societies than did low-ranking youths (see Mishkin 1940: 38).

Kiowa women also had two societies concerned with curing and with furthering success in war. These societies, like the men's, ably distinguished high-ranking people from low-ranking ones; Donald Collier reports that a heavy initiation payment was required of women who were invited to join (1938: 16). The Cheyenne women's quilling society, in contrast, was apparently open to all women, and it graded them on a single scale of achievement.[19]

Because unequal bridewealth peoples understand social order as based on ranking differences between individuals, they, like brideservice and equal bridewealth peoples, have a rich but contradictory vocabulary for talking about social inequality. Rank is both hereditary and achieved. It is an attribute of both individuals and of sibling sets. It is both inherent and forever negotiable.

And like the idiom of bravery in brideservice societies and the idiom of respect in equal bridewealth societies, the idiom of rank masks the social relations that make it possible. Just as people in brideservice societies talk about men earning wives without discussing the role wives play in allowing men to appear independent, and just as people in equal bridewealth societies talk about what seniors do for juniors without mentioning that juniors produce the gifts seniors give to others, so people in unequal bridewealth societies talk about the achievements of high-ranking people but forget to acknowledge the drudgery performed by their low-ranking wife-takers. Indeed, the conversations of unequal bridewealth peoples define those on the bottom of the social scale as lazy. Low-ranking people become the subject of others' conversation only when they are not doing what others want them to do.

Marriage Revisited

I began my discussion of the unequal bridewealth model by asserting that marriage exchanges validate rank: marriage and rank are mutually defining. They are both negotiable and negotiated together. The status of a marriage is as stable as the status of the individuals involved.[20]

The men and women who form sexual unions appear to perceive themselves first and foremost as bearers of particular ranks. It is as bearers of particular ranks that women contemplate alternative unions, and the unions they form are interpreted as indications of their rank. And it is as bearers of particular ranks that men persuade women to marry them, or to stay with them once married.

As a result, women really do appear to love high-ranking men more than low-ranking men, as a Kiowa informant told Mishkin (1940: 53). Few women are willing to contract marriages that constitute declarations of low rank. Should a woman be foolish enough to fall for an attractive but low-ranking man, her mother and brothers would probably try to break up the match unless the man agreed to work for them. Thus low-ranking men do have difficulty finding and keeping wives, they must spend their lives working for those who can provide them with access to women. A high-ranking man, in contrast, can get any woman he wants, as a high-ranking Kiowa cuckold told Richardson (1940: 121). Therefore, he never has to work for others.

In summary, unequal bridewealth peoples, through their skilled performances, realize a world in which men who give things away attract women. By giving gifts rather than labor, they retain control over their own labor and can continue to produce gifts for others. Men who lack access to valuables for giving away have insecure marriages that condemn them to work for others. High-ranking men give more valuables to their wife's brothers than do low-ranking men, and high-ranking men who are polygynous give more valuables to the brothers of high-ranking wives than to the brothers of low-ranking wives. As a result, the scale of the brideprice does appear to reflect the status of the bride and to correspond to the rank of the bridegroom. This is why ethnographers tend to report that in societies appropriate for analysis with an unequal bridewealth model, people marry with unequal or variable bridewealth.

4

—————

Understanding Inequality

The first three chapters of this book have presented ideal-typic models for analyzing the organization of inequality in three types of classless societies. In this chapter, I consider the theoretical framework underlying those models. They are not, of course, representations of self-evident truths. They are answers to specific questions. Here, I discuss the questions the models are designed to answer.

On the broadest level, the models are designed to answer the question, how do we understand social inequality? In asking that question, I am presuming that inequality needs explanation. As noted in the Introduction, humans differ in their capacities and attributes, but peoples' privileges and their obligations to others are never simple reflections of biological factors. Inequality is always socially organized.

Because inequality is socially rather than biologically determined, any attempt to understand it must begin with an examination of how people living in particular societies understand the unequal distribution of prestige, power, and privilege. If, as Giddens (1976) and Bourdieu (1977) argue, "the social world, unlike the world of nature, has to be grasped as a skilled accomplishment of active human subjects," then we understand social worlds by "penetrating the frames of meaning which lay actors themselves draw upon in constituting and reconstituting" their worlds (Giddens 1976: 155). In other words, any study of inequality must begin with an analysis of overt cultural values—people's ideas of what is desirable and of the optimal means for achieving goals.

Information on cultural values is easy to find. Field researchers can obtain it directly by asking people what they value and by noting their choices and rationales for action, and indirectly by listening to their stories and gossip or by analyzing the social distribution of rewards and punishments (Robin Williams 1968). Information on values is also easy to obtain from ethnographies. Many studies, particularly those written in the mid-twentieth century, focus primarily on values. Ethnographers of the Comanche, Cheyenne, and Kiowa, for example, record numerous value statements. Wallace and Hoebel write that the "ascribed status" for an adult Comanche male was that of "a warrior, vigorous, self-reliant, and aggressive" (1952: 146); Hoebel writes that "an even-tempered good nature, energy, wisdom, kindliness, concern for the well-being of others, courage, generosity, and altruism" were traits that expressed "the epitome of the Cheyenne ideal personality" (1978: 43); and Richardson writes that "every [Kiowa] man was judged concerning the following personal qualities: physical perfection; wisdom in economic planning; consistent peacefulness and gentle behavior, particularly toward women; generosity in giving horses and gifts; and audacity in war" (1940: 13).

Although any attempt to understand social inequality must begin by identifying the frames of meaning that lay actors draw upon in constituting and reconstituting their worlds, no analysis can end there. To record cultural values is not to penetrate frames of meaning. The analyst, therefore, must ask two further questions. First, what is the relationship between overt cultural values and the distribution of social rewards such as prestige, power, and privilege? Second, why do peoples have the particular cultural values they do?

Few social scientists have bothered to ask the first question because they assume that cultural values determine the allocation of social rewards. It seems only logical that people who perform valued behaviors and activities or exhibit valued attitudes should be rewarded with prestige, power, and privilege. Ethnographers of nineteenth-century Plains societies make this assumption. Wallace and Hoebel write that "war honors provided the basis of the whole system of rank and social status in Comanche society" (1952: 245); Llewellyn and Hoebel write that a Cheyenne chief was "appointed to his station because he approached the ideal qualities of leadership—wisdom, courage, kindness, generosity, and even temper" (1941: 73); and Richardson writes that "war record was the single most important determinant of status in Kiowa life. It was the *sine qua non* of all the great rewards of the culture" (1940: 14).

Though few social scientists ask the first question, there is a well-known answer to the second. Many social scientists argue that people have the particular values they do because such values promote social survival—the welfare of the group. Davis and Moore (1945) suggest that societies cannot survive unless someone is prepared to perform various socially necessary, but difficult or dangerous, activities. As a result, social survival demands that the people who carry out these activities be motivated by rewards. On the assumption that values determine the allocation of rewards, they conclude that cultures value those difficult behaviors and activities that must be performed if society is to survive.

Oliver (1962) offers such a functionalist explanation for the values of Plains societies. After concluding that "unquestionably, the crucial status determinants on the Plains were military skill and the possession of horses" (1962: 65), he tries to account for these values. In answering the question of why Plains peoples valued military skill, he observes that they were "quite literally fighting for their lives": Plains peoples had to reward warriors to ensure that they would have the incentive to fight (1962: 63). And in seeking an explanation for why Plains peoples valued the possession of horses, he observes that well-mounted hunters could kill more bison than men with poor mounts (1962: 63).[1] Oliver thus posits that societal needs for protection and food explain why military skill and possession of horses were so highly valued.

Functionalist explanations may seem compelling to people in capitalist societies, where common sense leads one to assume that wages reflect the value of a person's labor, but some social scientists have advanced an alternate explanation for why people have the values they do. Dahrendorf (1968) suggests that valued behaviors and activities are not those most beneficial to society as a whole. Rather, valued behaviors, activities, and attitudes are those that people in power can perform and exhibit more easily than members of powerless groups can. Dahrendorf agrees with the functionalists that people who perform valued behaviors and activities receive rewards, but he disagrees with their notion that rewards determine the distribution of power, prestige, and privilege in society. The functionalists assert that the distribution of social rewards reflects the value of what people do for society (Parsons 1940; Davis & Moore 1945). Dahrendorf asserts that the value placed on what people do reflects the distribution of social rewards, particularly power. He argues that "in the last analysis, established norms are nothing but ruling norms, i.e. norms defended by the sanctioning agencies of society and those who control them" (1968: 174).

In reversing the functionalists' causal arrow, Dahrendorf not only provides a different answer to the question of why people have the values they do but also suggests a different answer to the question of how values are related to the distribution of social rewards. Whereas functionalists assume that values regulate the distribution of such rewards, Dahrendorf suggests that their distribution determines the nature of values.

Dahrendorf's two answers offer a more satisfying explanation of inequality in Plains (and other) societies than those suggested by functionalists and Plains ethnographers. Although there is no reason to doubt ethnographers' descriptions of cultural values, or to doubt that high rank was positively correlated with the performance of valued behaviors and activities, there is reason to doubt that the causal arrow for this correlation runs from behaviors to rank. Oliver (1962) is undoubtedly right that Plains peoples were fighting for their lives and that bison were more easily hunted with a good horse than a poor one, but military skill and possession of horses were not the crucial determinants of status on the Plains. The available evidence suggests the opposite. War honors and generosity did not determine a man's rank; rather, a man's existing social obligations determined his opportunities for acquiring war honors and the valuables he would then give away.

Although ethnographic evidence supports Dahrendorf's argument that "established norms are nothing but ruling norms, i.e. norms defended by the sanctioning agencies of society and those who control them" (1968: 174), his argument raises a serious question. If, as he asserts, inequalities in power precede and shape value systems, then how do we explain the unequal distribution of power? Dahrendorf recognizes this problem but offers no solution. He observes in a footnote that "what an explanation of inequalities of power might look like is hard to say" (1968: 172 fn. 19).

By assuming that inequalities in power exist prior to value systems, Dahrendorf implies that power exists apart from, and prior to, cultural systems of meaning. In particular, his separation of power from values suggests that power is based on real things, such as physical force or control of the means of production, whereas value systems belong to the epiphenomenal realm of the symbolic. But force and control are not acultural verities. Given that social systems exist only as they are realized by the actions of living people (Bourdieu 1977), power, too, must be "grasped as a skilled accomplishment of human subjects" (Giddens 1976: 155). Nor are symbolic systems without their material aspects. Knowledge organizes the distribution of power (Foucault 1980). As a result, power and values are not related to one another as the material to the symbolic. Power, as Dahrendorf asserts, may exist prior to overt systems of cultural values, but the establishment of power, like that of values, is a cultural process, just as values, like power, are realized in the everyday activities of living people.

Dahrendorf's approach poses the central theoretical question of this book: How do we preserve Dahrendorf's recognition of power as existing prior to overt cultural values without treating power as an acultural verity? It is important to preserve Dahrendorf's separation between power and values because, without it, we would have to return to our commonsense assumption that overt cultural values organize inequality—that cultural systems of social evaluation are, in themselves, systems of social stratification. We would thus lose Dahrendorf's insight that overt values reflect not the bases of inequality but only those behaviors, activities, and attitudes that people already in power can perform and exhibit more easily than others. In preserving Dahrendorf's separation, however, we must avoid falling into the trap of treating power as existing apart from, or prior to, cultural systems of meaning.

In this chapter, I briefly review the various approaches to understanding the relationship between power and values that I considered when constructing the models presented in this book. I begin with Dahrendorf's reversal of the functionalists' causal arrow and then consider the three sanctioning mechanisms isolated by Malinowski (1926): publicity, reciprocity, and coercion. The chapter ends with a brief comparison of the three models that illustrates their common theoretical framework.

Misrecognition

Although Dahrendorf (1968) has no theory of power to explain how powerful people gain control of the sanctioning agencies of society to reward their own behaviors, his observation that overt cultural values reflect not the bases of inequality but only those behaviors, activities, and attitudes that powerful people can perform and exhibit more easily than others suggests a starting point for investigating power as culturally established. Specifically, Dahrendorf's formulation suggests that people "misrecognize" the bases of social inequality in their societies. Perhaps we can understand inequality if we investigate the basis of this misrecognition.

Before investigating the basis of misrecognition, however, we have to establish that people do in fact misrecognize. In this section, therefore, I will draw on examples from Comanche, Cheyenne, and Kiowa societies to briefly illustrate the sense in which overt cultural values reflect not the determinants of status but only those behaviors, activities, and attitudes that people who already enjoy high status can perform and exhibit more easily than others. There is no reason to doubt that Oliver correctly describes overt cultural values when he writes that "unquestionably, the crucial status determinants on the Plains were military skill and the possession of horses" (1962: 65). But, as I will show in this section, it was actually a man's status that determined his opportunities for demonstrating military prowess and acquiring horses.

In Chapters 1–3, I provided ample evidence that status determined a Comanche, Cheyenne, or Kiowa man's opportunities to acquire war honors and horses. Since "raiding was everywhere the principal method of acquiring horses" as well as war honors (Mishkin 1940: 6), men's opportunities to perform valued activities and thus to gain status were determined by their opportunities to join raiding parties. And opportunities to join raiding parties were, in turn, determined by a man's obligations to hunt and herd. Men who were obliged to hunt and herd had to stay near camp. Only those without such obligations were free to absent themselves for weeks or months of raiding (Mishkin 1940: 46).[2]

In the previous chapters, I suggested that marriage was the social mechanism that kept men at home hunting and herding while others went off in search of horses and glory. In each society, the men who stayed home were those on whom obligations to wife-givers weighed most heavily. They had good reason to fear losing fiancées or wives. But because marriages were validated differently in each society, Comanche, Cheyenne, and Kiowa men differed in their obligations toward wife-givers, and thus in their opportunities to join raiding parties.

Opportunities to join raiding parties were most equally distributed among the egalitarian Comanche. Because hunters distributed their meat widely, and captive children herded horses, any man who so wished could leave camp to join a raiding expedition without having to worry about who would herd horses or provide meat for his kin.[3] As a result, age was probably the best predictor of both war record and status. Older men, because they had been alive longer, had had more opportunities than younger men to join raiding parties and so to acquire war honors and horses. And older men were more likely than younger ones to be securely married and to receive credit for giving women away. It thus seems reasonable to conclude that in Comanche society, the valued activity of reciting many heroic deeds at public ceremonies was one that older men were able to perform more easily than young men who had been on fewer raiding expeditions.

Opportunities to join raiding parties were probably less equally distributed in Cheyenne society, where sons and sons-in-law hunted for their uxorilocal extended families. It seems reasonable to conclude that men from large households with many hunters had more opportunities to absent themselves from camp than did men from small households, and that older sons-in-law were favored over newly married men. Acts of generosity, not acquisition of war honors or horses, however, were the most valued behaviors in Cheyenne society (Hoebel 1978: 43). And such acts, as noted in Chapter 2, could be carried out only by men who already headed large extended family households. Among the Cheyenne, as among the Comanche, the most valued behavior was thus one that high-ranking men could perform more easily than others.

Opportunities to join raiding parties were very unequally distributed in Kiowa society. Men from high-ranking families who had lower-ranking sisters' and daughters' husbands to hunt and herd for them could join many raiding parties. Lower-ranking men, who could not refuse wife-givers' requests, tended to have poor war records "largely because they could not go to war as often" (Richardson 1940: 15). In Kiowa society, rank determined a man's opportunities to join raiding parties, and thus his opportunities to perform the valued behaviors of acquiring war honors and horses.

The data from Comanche, Cheyenne, and Kiowa societies presented in Chapters 1–3 thus suggest that Dahrendorf is correct in reversing the causal arrow functionalists draw between behavior and rewards. The performance of valued behaviors in these societies did not determine the distribution of social rewards. Rather, the distribution of social rewards, particularly power to command others' labor, determined men's opportunities to perform valued behaviors and activities.

This conclusion is supported by ethnographic evidence not presented in the chapters on models. In Comanche, Cheyenne, and Kiowa societies, men's opportunities to have their war honors validated and to receive captured horses were also determined by their existing status.

Among the Comanche, heroic deeds were validated by members of the raiding party, preferably before they returned to camp. Wallace and Hoebel report that on returning from a raid, the war party chief called together his warriors and had each recite his heroic deeds. The assembled warriors then "either publicly recognized the deed as a coup or rejected the claim" (1952: 248). When the war party entered the camp, they rode in order of established bravery. "The leader and any other person receiving special recognition led the way. Behind them were those who had shown the greatest courage, counted coups, or performed creditable acts. The remaining warriors came next" (Wallace & Hoebel 1952: 270).

The Comanche apparently did not quarrel over coup claims. Hoebel reports that Comanche informants remembered no instances of such disputes, and he notes that "the Comanches do not seem to have had any oath ritual for settling disputed coup claims as did the Cheyenne and other Plains Indians" (1940: 105).

The Cheyenne also validated coup claims before returning to camp. Grinnell describes a meeting of war party members very like that held by the Comanche, in which each man recited his war deeds and other warriors either validated or rejected his claims (1923, 2: 32). Members of Cheyenne raiding parties also entered the camp in order of established bravery (1923, 2: 21). Grinnell's description, however, suggests that the Cheyenne, unlike the Comanche, had frequent disagreements over coup claims. When such disagreements occurred, "A man who believed he had accomplished something made a strong fight for his rights, and was certain to be supported in his contention by all his friends, and especially by all his relatives" (1923, 2: 33). This report would seem to indicate that men with many recognized relatives[4] were more successful than men with few in having their claims of heroic deeds validated by others.

In writing about the Kiowa, Mishkin emphasizes the relationship between family rank and the publicizing of heroic deeds. He notes:

> The warrior who has been successful in accomplishing certain heroic acts must capitalize upon them immediately. He does not automatically attain the rating of a [great warrior] by merely performing his deeds and then modestly belittling them or refusing to speak of them at all. Extensive publicity of his attainments is essential and recognition of his attainments must be tribal in scope. . . . Perhaps the most effective manner of publicizing deeds because it is more spontaneous and direct revolves around kinship ties. Especially at the beginning of his career the young warrior is dependent upon his relatives to give him a 'build-up.' (1940: 40–41)

On the basis of Mishkin's observations, we can conclude that a youth from a high-ranking family had many more opportunities to have his deeds publicized than a youth from a family of low rank.

The rules of the Comanche, Cheyenne, and Kiowa for distributing captured horses among raiding party members exhibit greater intersocietal variation than their practices for validating heroic deeds.

Hoebel reports that Comanche distribution rules favored those who were brave. When horses were divided after a raid, the group leader ranked each member according to the bravery, industry, and willingness he exhibited during the venture.

> To the man who excelled, [the leader] allowed first choice of the horses. Each member of the party chose in turn according to his service as determined by the chief. The leader took his pick *of what remained.* Then the succession of choices was repeated in the same order as before. If there was an acute shortage of horses, the cook was always taken care of. A nice adjustment, this: the cook had been burdened with the meat supply. If there were too few horses, only the bravest got any return. The leader, no matter what his deeds, got nothing at all if there were not enough horses to go around. (1940: 25, italics his)

Comanche distribution patterns thus favored the daring whatever their age or marital status, did not penalize the cook, and granted no special advantage to the already prestigious war party leader.

Cheyenne distribution patterns seem considerably less egalitarian. According to Llewellyn and Hoebel,

> unless it was agreed otherwise beforehand, each horse [captured on a raid] went to the man who first struck a coup on it. This gave great advantage to the man with a fast horse. To equalize this, the Cheyennes often agreed before the raid to divide equally, in which event the leader of the raid took first choice, then named the succession of choice for the rest of the party. . . . If there was no agreement calling for equal division, then a man who saw horses off to one side, and ran them in himself, took all for himself without any obligation to divide. This was Stump Horn's dictum. No cases were obtainable to prove or disprove it. Again, in the absence of the equality distribution, scouts out on duty who missed out on the take, missed out on the booty! Nor did the cooks receive any special preference for their labors. (1941: 223)

Such patterns favored those who already enjoyed prestige and access to good horses; they did not favor those who performed necessary, but nonheroic, services for the group.

Kiowa distribution patterns appear to have resembled those of the Cheyenne. Richardson reports that a war party leader "received and distributed all booty gathered" (1940: 8), but she also notes that the custom of handing over all horses to the leader for distribution was "not very well established, and conflicted with a feeling that the horse was the property of him who took it or saw it first" (1940: 127). Kiowa customs probably resulted in a less egalitarian distribution of captured horses than Cheyenne customs, however, because opportunities to join raiding parties were less equally distributed in Kiowa society. Mishkin's statement that "if [Kiowa captives] were taken on war parties, they were compelled to do the drudgery, attending to camp duties, cooking, etc." (1940: 43) suggests that if low-ranking men did join raiding parties, they were the cooks, who received few horses, if any, when captured animals were distributed.

In summary, ethnographic evidence suggests that among the Comanche, Cheyenne, and Kiowa, there was a correlation between the amount of power, prestige, and privilege a man enjoyed and his reputation for military skill and for having acquired many horses. But the evidence also suggests that contrary to Oliver's assumption that "military skill and the possession of horses" determined a man's status (1962: 65), it was a man's status (his kinship obligations and privileges) that determined his opportunity to acquire horses and a reputation for military skill. In each society, the men on whom obligations to wife-givers weighed most heavily had least opportunity to join raiding parties or to acquire horses by other means,[5] whereas men who had hopeful grooms and insecure husbands to hunt and herd for their domestic groups had the most opportunity to acquire horses, perform heroic deeds, and publicize their military exploits. A comparison of the three Plains societies also reveals that opportunities to acquire military honors and horses were most equally distributed among the egalitarian Comanche, and least equally distributed among the ranked Kiowa.

Publicity

Evidence from Plains societies may support a conclusion that these people misrecognized the bases of inequality in their societies, but is misrecognition what actually occurred? Do people really misrecognize the bases of inequality? There can be no doubt that Plains informants talked and acted in ways that led ethnographers to conclude that "unquestionably, the crucial status determinants on the Plains were military skill and the possession of horses" (Oliver 1962: 65). But did Plains peoples actually believe that military skill and acquisition of horses were the determinants of status? Did they fail to recognize that these were only behaviors that high-ranking men could perform more easily than others?

There can be no definitive answer to the question of whether Plains peoples were deceived or misled. But rather than assume that people misrecognize the bases of inequality in their societies, and then ask why they do so, perhaps we should ask what people are talking about when they make statements ethnographers interpret as meaning that the performance of valued behaviors and activities determines rewards. When, for example, Plains informants made the statements Oliver (1962) and other ethnographers interpreted as assertions that military skill and possession of horses were the crucial determinants of male status, what were they talking about?

Dahrendorf (1968) offers one answer to the second question: because people who have power use the sanctioning agencies of society to reward behaviors that they can perform more easily and frequently than others, the performance of valued behaviors does, in people's everyday experience, bring rewards. Dahrendorf's answer provides one explanation for why Plains peoples might have told ethnographers that military heroes and those who acquired many horses were rewarded with more prestige and power than were others. The sanctioning agencies of their societies did, in fact, reward heroes and those who had acquired many horses.

Dahrendorf's answer suggests a conspiracy theory of society, however. It implies that only power holders act; others simply react. Yet our own experience, confirmed by the findings of social scientists, tells us that power holders are not the only ones to praise and reward individuals who perform valued behaviors and activities. Everyone celebrates the achievements of such individuals.

Bourdieu's (1977) theory of practice is an alternative to Dahrendorf's conspiracy theory. Because Bourdieu links what ordinary people say to what ordinary people do in pursuing the interests assigned to them by the organization of production, he provides a framework for understanding why the powerless, as well as power holders, join in celebrating those who perform valued behaviors. His theoretical framework emphasizes a social *system* rather than an elite social *group*.

Bourdieu suggests that when people make statements ethnographers interpret as meaning that cultural values determine the distribution of rewards, they are not simply reporting the truth; they are actively trying to influence the distribution of social rewards. His theory of practice leads us to conclude that if we are to understand overt cultural values in any society, we must know what people in that society want or fear. If people who refer to cultural values are actively trying to influence the distribution of social rewards, then we must ask what rewards exist and what processes organize their distribution.

Bourdieu (1977) implies that sanctioning mechanisms, such as the publicizing of heroic deeds, cannot be understood apart from their total social contexts. In Plains societies, for example, "the method of 'scoring' war records in one tribe did not differ materially from that operative in another" (Mishkin 1940: 3). A Kiowa warrior could recite his war deeds to an appreciative Cheyenne or Comanche audience, and vice versa. But Comanche, Cheyenne, and Kiowa reciters of war honors could not have been *doing* the same thing. The actual rewards available to heroes were too different. More power was available to a Kiowa hero than to his Comanche counterpart.

These nineteenth-century Plains societies appear to have resembled the societies of Highland Burma, as described by Leach (1965: 281). The Great Plains, like the Kachin Hills, was an area where people had a common ritual language for making statements about relative rank, but where the ability of high-ranking people to obtain compliance varied according to the political realities of their particular social systems. Comanche, Cheyenne, and Kiowa heroes who recited their war deeds may have used the same method of scoring, but they were making very different claims.

Evidence from the Comanche, Cheyenne, and Kiowa societies supports Bourdieu's alternative to Dahrendorf's conspiracy theory. If we examine these peoples' interests, as assigned by the organization of production, we see that informants who implied that military skill was a major determinant of male status were not merely reporting that elites used sanctioning agencies to reward their own behaviors; they had specific goals they hoped to accomplish.

In discussing the brideservice model, I noted that a Comanche man's ability to enjoy the self-reliance so highly valued in his society depended on having a wife. Wallace and Hoebel assert that "war honors provided the basis of the whole system of rank and social status in Comanche society" (1952: 245), but my analysis suggests that wives, not war honors, were the basis of men's privileges. In Comanche society, the organization of production gave each man an interest in acquiring and keeping a wife. War honors were the idiom men used to talk about their claims to wives.

Although Comanche men acquired wives by fulfilling obligations toward in-laws and by building affectionate ties with women (a slow process), their success in warfare was publicly linked to their claims to women in three ways. First, raided horses were the most publicized gifts a groom could give his in-laws during the time he was courting (Wallace & Hoebel 1952: 272). Second, "the one outstanding factor around which the settlement of a dispute [over women] turned was not the question of the right or wrong of the situation, but rather the relative bravery in warfare of the two parties involved" (Hoebel 1940: 54). Third, men whose poor war records made them unable to prevent others from stealing their wives were reduced to the status of dependent bachelors. In Comanche society, therefore, men who were attempting to establish, defend, and account for men's claims to women talked about military exploits. Comanche men of all ages and marital statuses stressed their war records in pursuing their objective interest of establishing claims to the women whose labor freed them from direct obligations to other men.[6]

Because Bourdieu's (1977) theory of practice focuses attention on what people hope to accomplish when they make particular statements, it helps to explain why people do not fall into the trap of believing their own rhetoric. People talk while pursuing their objective interests. They do not mistake talk for interests.

Comanche men, for example, may have had ample cause to talk about their war records, but there is no reason to believe that they acted as if war honors, and not claims to women, were the basis of a married man's privileges. Direct evidence about nineteenth-century Comanche behavior is not available,[7] but evidence collected by ethnographers who have observed people in other brideservice societies reveals that men in such societies do not accumulate more war honors, or hunt more animals, than they need to realize particular and quite realistic goals. Bachelors are commonly reported to be lazy and cowardly (see Draper 1976; Siskind 1973; Chagnon 1968). As long as a man lacks a wife, he has little reason to demonstrate his capacity to fight potential seducers. Therefore, we might conclude that people do not, in fact, misrecognize the bases of inequality in their societies. People may *say* things that lead ethnographers to believe that hunting and raiding are the bases of male privileges in brideservice societies, but people *act* as if they understand that enjoyment of rewards both permits and requires performance of valued behaviors.

Cheyenne men also recited their war deeds to appreciative audiences on ceremonial occasions, but an examination of men's objective interests suggests that these Cheyenne heroes and their Comanche counterparts were engaged in different activities when they told of their exploits. In Cheyenne society, as indicated by the equal bridewealth model, the organization of production gave each man an objective interest in establishing and maintaining advantageous long-term status relationships with others. Men established and maintained them not by acquiring war honors but by fulfilling the obligations of the status they wished to assume. But the acquisition of war honors did testify to a man's ability to perform favors for others. By reciting war deeds, Big Men could justify their right to expect political support from members of other households, and husbands and fathers could justify their rights to appropriate the labor products of wives and children.

Hoebel reports that "there [were] at least a hundred different situations in the ritual life of the [Cheyenne] people that [invited] ceremonial coup counting by an outstanding warrior" (1978: 75). Counting coup was an integral part of the ritual because coup had to be counted for ritual action to proceed. When the Cheyenne ritually tanned a rare white bison hide, for example, every action performed with regard to the hide had to be preceded by recitation of a similar coup. Only a warrior who had scalped an enemy could skin the bison's head; only a warrior who had lifted an enemy or a friend onto his horse could so lift the bison hide; only a man who had pulled an enemy from his horse could take down the hide (Grinnell 1923, 2: 200–204). Each man who counted coup, therefore, did a favor for the person sponsoring the ceremony. An outstanding warrior, who could recite many heroic deeds, was thus able to perform many favors.

Heroic deeds were linked to privilege in at least two other ways that also involved doing things for others. First, audacious horse stealing was a way of acquiring animals to give away (see Grinnell 1923: 2: 1–2). Second, an excellent war record established that a man had access to cosmic energy. Although raiding was not a way of acquiring energy but rather of expending it, success in warfare was taken as proof that a man had established the spiritual contacts necessary to obtain and renew cosmic energy (J. Moore 1974a: 181). Successful warriors could pass energy on to others, particularly to women and children who were not able to contact the spirits by themselves. The Cheyenne believed that "a young son is kept alive by his father's power," and that women were "sustained by the cosmic power received by their husbands" (J. Moore 1974a: 179). A man with an outstanding war record thus had reason to refer to it in justifying his right to appropriate the labor products of his wives and children.

Although Cheyenne ceremonies provided men with many occasions in which to perform favors for others by reciting heroic deeds, there is no reason to assume that Cheyenne men acted as if performing such favors were the basis of privilege. People not in a structural position to reap the rewards of performing particular favors probably did not try to force their favors on others.

Ethnographers of Kiowa society have posited a direct relationship between war record and a man's rank. Richardson writes that "war record was the single most important determinant of status in

Kiowa life" (1940: 14). But war record could not have been the most important determinant of a Kiowa man's rank. The unequal bridewealth model suggests that rank was established through gift exchanges between affines.

War record was the idiom men invoked when contesting claims to rank with near equals, however.

> If any debate arose over the relative position of two individuals rather closely matched, it was usually settled by a recitation of the two coup-counts. Sometimes there was difficulty in arriving at a decision, for it was in the nature of the Plains individualistic warfare that no two episodes were exactly alike, and therefore not strictly comparable. If a decision could not be reached on the basis of coup-counts, the warriors recited the number of captives and horses taken, and the horses given away. (Richardson 1940: 16)

In Kiowa society, the organization of marriage gave each man an objective interest in claiming as high a rank as possible so that he could either avoid having to work for his in-laws if he was of low rank, or acquire sisters' and daughters' husbands to work for him if he was of high rank. Each man, therefore, had an objective interest in reciting as many heroic deeds as possible because it was by doing so that he challenged his immediate superior and advanced upward in the hierarchy.

Men's efforts to acquire war honors must have reinforced and perpetuated the organization of inequality in Kiowa society. Each man's opportunities to join war parties depended on his place in the social hierarchy. Men who already enjoyed high rank were able to attract sisters' and daughters' husbands to work for them, thus enabling them to join more raiding parties. Men of low rank tended to have the poor war records that compelled them to continue working for in-laws. The composition of each raiding party thus tended to perpetuate the conditions that had made that composition possible (see Bourdieu 1977: 70).

Kiowa informants may have made statements that led ethnographers to conclude that war record was the single most important determinant of a man's status, but there is no reason to believe that Kiowa men acted as if war records were the basis of status privileges in their society. Richardson describes third-rank men as "immune to insult because [they had] little honor to defend" (1940: 120). In Kiowa society, it would have made little sense for a third-rank man to respond violently to insults.

These brief examples from Comanche, Cheyenne, and Kiowa societies support Bourdieu's contention that the meaning of a particular act, such as reciting war honors, can never be ascertained solely by analyzing that act. Rather, it must be determined by analyzing the total social context in which the act occurs. When Comanche, Cheyenne, and Kiowa warriors recited their heroic deeds, they were doing much more than simply informing others of their past activities. They were making specific claims. To understand what those claims were—that is, to understand what Comanche, Cheyenne, and Kiowa warriors were talking about—it is necessary to examine both the privileges available to individuals and the interests assigned to them by the organization of production.

In summary, ethnographic evidence suggests that Comanche, Cheyenne, and Kiowa informants were not deceived or misled when they made the statements ethnographers interpreted to mean that military skill, as revealed in accumulated war honors, was a major determinant of rank. Bourdieu's theoretical framework suggests that informants were not disengaged observers who commented on the working of their societies. Rather, they were actively pursuing their objective interests: they were trying to increase their social prerogatives vis-à-vis particular others.

Some people in Plains societies may have drawn incorrect conclusions from the correlation between war honors and rank, just as some Americans draw an incorrect conclusion from the correlation between education and income when they assert that more education for poor people will eradicate poverty. If such people were to analyze the organization of inequality in their societies, they would probably realize that their conclusions are wrong. But few people have the time or incentive to analyze their societies; they are too busy pursuing practical ends. When asserting, contesting, or just talking about claims to prestige, power, and privilege, people have no reason to discuss the organization of inequality that establishes the rewards available to those who perform valued behaviors and activities. When men in Plains societies recited their war honors, the Comanche did not mention women's obligation to feed families, the Cheyenne did not talk about juniors' obligation to obey the seniors who supported them, and the Kiowa did not discuss the obligations of wife-takers. As Bourdieu's theory of practice suggests, what people do not say is more significant than what they do say.

Bourdieu emphasizes significant silences when discussing the perpetuation of inegalitarian social relations over time (1977: 159–71). He notes that what is never said is never open to challenge and therefore not open to change. "What goes without saying" becomes "what cannot be said for lack of an available discourse," and subsequently becomes what most people cannot even think (1977: 170). The source of a social system's legitimacy is that which is taken for granted: "the absolute form of recognition of legitimacy" occurs as a result of "misrecognition of arbitrariness" (1977: 168). Bourdieu thus implies that people at all levels of a social system act in ways that perpetuate that system because it never occurs to most of them that things could be otherwise.

Bourdieu's emphasis on significant silences raises a new problem. It seems empirically wrong to conclude that Plains peoples were unaware of the arbitrariness of their social systems, in view of the frequent contact between the Comanche, Cheyenne, and Kiowa—three societies with such different ways of organizing inequality. Perhaps it is the silences that need investigation. How did people maintain silences in the face of constant evidence of such arbitrariness? Although Bourdieu asserts that significant silences perpetuate unequal relationships, he also suggests that the content of what is never said derives from what is said: the "universe of the undiscussed [and] undisputed" is "negatively constituted by the constitution of a *field of opinion*, [which is] the locus of the confrontation of competing discourses" (1977: 168, italics his). What people take for granted are the shared assumptions that make it possible for them to make the statements they do. Therefore, if we are to understand the content of what is never said, and to understand the bases of social inequality, we must examine the universe of discourse. I begin that examination in the next section by focusing on reciprocity, the second sanction isolated by Malinowski (1926). In particular, I analyze transfers of valuables in classless societies in an attempt to determine what people talk about when they exchange goods and services.

Reciprocity

Any analysis of reciprocity—defined here as the mutual exchange of goods and services—must consider both how people come to *have* what they concede to others and why people *need* or *want* the goods and services others provide. When Oliver writes that "possession of horses" was a major determinant of men's status on the Plains (1962: 65), for example, what does he mean? In what sense could a Comanche, Cheyenne, or Kiowa man "possess" a horse? And why should "possession of horses" have granted status? Why might it not have merely required an owner to spend more of his time herding horses?

Capitalist common sense, coded in English words, hinders rather than facilitates our attempt to understand reciprocity in classless societies. If we are to grasp the role of valuables in relations between people, we must first clear away the misconceptions inherent in English, a language long associated with capitalism. In this section I use information from ethnographies of nineteenth-century Comanche, Cheyenne, and Kiowa societies to criticize capitalist commonsense assumptions about ownership and need, and to show that Plains people could not have owned horses in the way people in capitalist societies own things. It was not possession of horses that Plains people talked about as determining status. The valued activity was giving the animals away. But because "giving away" is no more transparent an activity than "possessing," I consider other theoretical approaches to answering the questions of how men could have horses to give away and why others should want the animals.

Ownership

Even a cursory reading of Plains ethnographies reveals that neither possession of horses nor military skill, could have meant the same thing for the Comanche, Cheyenne, and Kiowa. The rewards available to men who acquired horses were different in the three societies. Moreover, ownership in Plains societies could not have meant what the word means in commonsense English. Ownership is never a relation between a person and a thing; it is always a relationship between people in respect to things (Hoebel 1954: 47). Ownership, therefore, must differ when social relations differ. The Comanche, Cheyenne, and Kiowa must have had different forms of ownership, and ownership in all three Plains societies must have been different from the kinds of relations people in capitalist or agrarian societies have with one another in respect to things.

Because ethnographers who have written about ownership of horses in specific Plains groups have used words that can easily be misunderstood as meaning that Plains peoples could own horses in the way we own things, a consideration of what it meant to own a horse in nineteenth-century Plains societies must begin by asking why ethnographers have described ownership in these terms.

An examination of ethnographies reveals that ethnographers writing in the 1930's and 1940's were participating in a debate over whether native Americans practiced primitive communism. As a result, ethnographers who have written that Plains peoples recognized individual ownership of animals were not arguing that ownership on the Plains was similar to ownership in capitalist or agrarian societies. Rather, they were arguing that Plains peoples did not practice primitive communism.

Hoebel, for example, reports that among the Comanche, "horses were individually owned by both men and women" (1940: 14). Llewellyn and Hoebel similarly report that "with the Cheyennes, as indeed among all American Indians who had them, horses were individually owned" (1941: 223). And Richardson writes that among the Kiowa, "a strong sense of private ownership prevailed [in respect to horses] with individual rights recognized within the family" (1940: 125). But these statements cannot be taken to mean that the Comanche, Cheyenne, and Kiowa owned horses in the way people in capitalist societies own things. Nor did ethnographers mean that the Comanche, Cheyenne, and Kiowa had the same concept of ownership—for they report differences in other contexts. Ethnographers meant, quite correctly, that the Comanche, Cheyenne, and Kiowa did not practice some idealized (and unspecified) form of primitive communism.

Anthropologists writing after 1950 who compared Plains societies seem to have overlooked the fact that to earlier ethnographers, individual ownership meant only "not primitive communism" rather than what individual ownership means in commonsense English. This confusion probably occurred because these anthropologists were participating in a debate over whether the introduction of horses into egalitarian Plains societies led inevitably to the development of social classes based on differential herd sizes. This debate could have led anthropologists to wonder what it meant to own a horse on the Plains, but instead they focused on factors that influenced herd sizes.

This tendency to focus on factors that influenced herd sizes is particularly obvious in Oliver's (1962) attempt to reconcile the two sides of the debate. Oliver accepts the idea that the introduction of horses led to class formation. He writes that "among the Blackfoot, the introduction of the horse brought about a change from a relatively classless society to a society with three loosely defined social classes" (1962: 63). But Oliver is more interested in showing why classes failed to develop in many groups. He therefore searches for factors that prevented the formation of economic classes because they militated against the development of permanent inequalities in herd sizes. The factors he lists are constant warfare, which meant that horses were easily acquired and lost; cultural patterns requiring division of captured horses among raiding party members and division of a man's herd at his death; cultural requirements that "a man who had a lot of horses was supposed to give horses away to less fortunate persons"; and ecological conditions suggesting that groups in which all hunters were well mounted would have more food (1962: 63–64).

Oliver is correct in asserting that many factors militated against the development of permanent inequalities in herd sizes on the Plains. But the more important issue is whether differential herd sizes determined status inequalities. In searching for factors that militated against the development of permanent inequalities in herd sizes, Oliver assumes that such inequalities correlate with inequalities in status privileges: that societies in which horses were most unequally distributed should also have exhibited the greatest status differentials.

My reason for questioning the relationship between horses and status derives, of course, from my theoretical framework, but it is also true that what empirical evidence exists does not support Oliver's unstated assumption of a positive correlation between inequalities in herd sizes and inequalities in status privileges. Rather, this evidence suggests the reverse.

Although estimates of herd sizes for nineteenth-century Plains tribes cannot be relied upon (Roe 1955: 282–86), ethnographers' descriptions of ideal herd sizes suggest that the most inegalitarian society required the smallest herd sizes and that the most egalitarian society allowed the largest discrepancy in number of horses. Among the inegalitarian Kiowa, who "were among the wealthiest people in the Plains" (Mishkin 1940: 19), "a herd of twenty or thirty was considered a proper size"; to keep more horses "showed stinginess" (Richardson 1940: 14).[8] Among the somewhat more egalitarian Cheyenne, a prestigious family kept 40 or 50 good riding horses (Hoebel 1978: 29). But among the egalitarian Comanche

(I could find no statements about their ideal herd size), some prestigious warriors apparently had no horses, for they gave them all away (Wallace & Hoebel 1952: 131); and Hoebel writes about a Comanche man, too fat to ride a horse, who died leaving an estate of 1,000 to 1,500 horses (1940: 123; see also Linton 1936: 297). That there was an unequal distribution of horses in the most egalitarian society is, as indicated by this evidence, the opposite of what one would expect, given Oliver's assumption of a positive correlation between inequality in herd sizes and inequality in status privileges.

From the ethnographic evidence we can conclude that ownership in Plains societies could not have meant what ownership means in capitalist societies. Merely noting this fact, however, does not help us to understand why ethnographers report that possession of horses was a crucial determinant of male status. Ethnographers who have assumed that Plains peoples had a capitalist concept of ownership are wrong. But if we want to find out why they are wrong—so that we can avoid repeating their mistakes—we need to examine their explanations for why horse ownership determined status.

Oliver's reasons for assuming that status differentials correlated with differential herd sizes are not incorrect, they are simply inadequate. He asserts that men who were mounted on good horses, presumably because they had many horses to choose from, could kill more bison and enemies than men with poor or tired horses: "a Blackfoot hunter on a good horse could kill four or five buffalo in a single chase, but a man on a poor horse couldn't kill any at all" (1962: 63). Mishkin (1940) offers a more complete argument. He notes that men could not derive the hunting and raiding benefits to be expected from maintenance of large herds unless they could mobilize other men to herd for them while they were away. A man who was out hunting and raiding could not simultaneously herd the rest of his horses. Instead of focusing on what a man could do with his horses, therefore, Mishkin focuses on relations between people. He concludes that status differentials correlated with herd sizes not because men who had many horses killed many bison but because men who lacked horses of their own worked for horse owners, thereby freeing horse owners to join many raiding parties.

Mishkin is obviously correct in noting that horse owners could not herd their horses while they were hunting and raiding, but his explanation of why some men herded horses and hunted for others is problematic. He suggests that because horses were useful for hunting and transporting belongings, men who did not have horses of their own worked for those who could lend them animals (1940: 45). But the question is not, what were horses good for? The question is, what would people be willing to give in return for access to horses? Horses have obvious uses, but men on the Plains would not have worked for others—particularly if such work kept them from raiding for horses of their own—if they had had other means of acquiring the animals. In short, Mishkin's explanation is problematic because it assumes that men who owned horses could deny other men access to the animals. Only this assumption can account for the unequal terms of exchange Mishkin posits when he concludes that men who lacked horses gave labor in exchange for the mere *use* of other men's animals.

Mishkin never states that ownership of horses on the Plains involved the right or ability of horse owners to deny nonowners access to the animals. Had he made that statement, he probably would have realized it was wrong. But such an assumption is necessary to make sense of his explanation of why horse borrowers worked for horse owners. Horse owners could use their animals to obtain access to others' labor only if nonowners were prevented from obtaining access to horses on terms other than giving their labor in exchange. Nonowners who could borrow horses without working for others would not have herded owners' horses. And nonowners who were given horses, rather than the mere use of horses, in return for their labor would soon have become owners and had no further need to borrow the animals. Mishkin's assumption that herders worked in return for the use of horses is tenable, therefore, only if owners could control the terms of their exchange with nonowners by being able to deny them access to the animals.

Ethnographic evidence reveals that ownership of horses in Plains societies did not involve the right of owners to deny others access to their animals. The Comanche may have recognized "individual ownership" of horses, but because "*ability* to possess was 'nine points of the law' " (Hoebel 1940: 66), it seems reasonable to assume that a Comanche man could prevent another from using a horse only if he was prepared to physically repel the intruder. Cheyenne horse owners did not have the right to withhold horses. Llewellyn and Hoebel report that until 1830, it was acceptable for one Cheyenne to borrow another's animal without asking permission (1941: 127–29). And Richardson reports that "the strong sense of private ownership" among the Kiowa "ran counter to the general feeling that possessions and commodities, though not communally owned really, were for the free use of all the kindred" (1940: 125). In summary, neither Cheyenne nor Kiowa horse owners could legitimately deny others use of their horses, and if a Comanche man wished to prevent another from borrowing an animal, he had to enforce the ban himself. In all three societies, the most effective way of preventing another from taking a horse was to kill the animal, an act that the Comanche often carried out (see Hoebel 1940: 126; Llewellyn & Hoebel 1941: 224; Richardson 1940: 128). In no Plains society could horse owners deny others access to their animals; therefore, in no Plains society could horse owners have enjoyed the kinds of privileges that people who live in capitalist societies associate with private ownership of the means of production.

Status Obligations

I have been arguing that individual ownership of horses on the Plains could not have meant what individual ownership means in commonsense English. In this section I consider what ownership of horses did mean in nineteenth-century Comanche, Cheyenne, and Kiowa societies. We have seen that horse owners were not able to prevent others in their society from borrowing their animals, and that when the three societies are compared, cultural prescriptions for ideal herd sizes varied inversely with inequality of status. The evidence also indicates, however, that horse owners could claim reciprocal goods and services from those in their society to whom they gave (not lent) animals, and that when the three societies are compared there is a positive correlation between inequalities in *access* to horses and inequalities in status privileges.

In Plains societies, it was not the number of horses a man kept in his herd but the number he gave away that allowed him to claim status privileges. Richardson suggests this when she writes that among the Kiowa, "wealth had to be kept moving through one's hands by continual give-aways and even by conspicuous display. Generosity in giving horses was vastly more important than the possession of horses itself" (1940: 14). But because giving is no more transparent an activity than owning, we should examine what men received in return for gifts of horses.

Although ethnographers report that horses were used as a medium of exchange on the Plains, they also report that within societies, horses were transferred primarily in social rather than economic transactions; the animals were used as gifts and not for barter. Mishkin, for example, writes that "in most economic manipulations [on the Plains] horses alone or horses plus other items were the principal counters" (1940: 22). But it makes less sense to view horses as money (a universal standard) than as valuables—"precious objects" that exhibit a "dual nature" in "primitive societies" (Godelier 1977: 128).

Valuables are "both goods and non-goods, 'money' and gifts, according to whether they are bartered between groups and circulate within the group" (Godelier 1977: 128). On the nineteenth-century Plains, horses were bartered across ethnic boundaries and with whites in exchange for guns, agricultural produce, and ornaments—probably at fairly fixed exchange rates. Within ethnic groups, horses were given away to create or confirm social ties such as marriages and to validate the acquisition of ritual knowledge or blessing. Because horses were "demandable in settlement of damage suits at law" (Hoebel 1940: 15), they were used to heal breaks in social relations. And when given by high-ranking people to low-ranking people, horses established and symbolized a superior social position (see Godelier 1977: 128)[9]

This linking of gifts to status obligations recalls Malinowski's (1926) linkage of reciprocity with status obligations in his analysis of Trobriand Island law. He describes Trobriand social structure as "founded on the principle of *legal status*" (italics his), by which he means that "the claims of chief over commoners, husband over wife, parent over child, and vice versa, are not exercised arbitrarily and one-sidedly, but according to definite rules, and arranged into well-balanced chains of reciprocal services" (1926: 46). Malinowski's analysis, when applied to Plains societies, suggests that what horse owners received in return for giving away animals was a function of the reciprocal services they believed were required of people in particular status relationships, not of bargains negotiated between individuals.

Malinowski views reciprocity as a sanction that makes "it impossible for the native to shirk his responsibility without suffering for it in the future" (1926: 59). He argues that if obligations are organized into "well-balanced chains of reciprocal services," then self-interest will motivate people to conform to social rules. Each person would know that the obligations associated with his or her particular status have to be fulfilled to ensure that others fulfill their obligations in return (1926: 67). Malinowski also notes that if reciprocal services are arranged into "well-balanced chains," then there will be "premiums for an overdose of fulfillment" (1926: 58). This observation is interesting because it implies that people who give away more than their existing status obligations require may claim more goods or a higher status in return.

Gluckman's (1968) observations provide a broader framework than Malinowski's for understanding the rewards available to people who give things away. In discussing ownership in tribal societies (which he defines as those where simple tools are used to produce primary goods for immediate consumption), he observes that property law defines not so much the *rights* of one person as against those of all other persons in respect to things, but rather the *obligations* concerning things owed between people who are related to one another in "specific, long-standing ways" (1968: 75).

Gluckman also observes that "if new relationships are being established, this is done through transfers of property, which create and define these relationships" (1968: 75). In tribal societies, people who acquire goods can justify making claims to others' products and services by using those goods to fulfill the obligations associated with a specific long-standing status relationship they wish to establish or confirm.

Gluckman's observations help to explain why ethnographers of the Comanche, Cheyenne, and Kiowa report that possession of horses was a crucial determinant of male status. In Plains societies, men who acquired horses could give them away to validate marriages, fulfill the obligations of parenthood, acquire ritual knowledge, and demonstrate chiefly generosity. They could use horses to acquire the privileges associated with the statuses of husband, father, ritual leader, and chief. But Gluckman's observations do not provide an answer to the question of why people had a concept of statuses with defined reciprocal obligations. The privileges enjoyed by husbands, fathers, ritual leaders, and chiefs could in no way be due to their gifts of horses. Horses could be used to obtain desired status privileges only if the concept of long-term status relationships with defined reciprocal obligations existed prior to any given transaction. Gifts of horses to a woman's brother could bring husbandly privileges only if people already conceived of marriage as a long-term status relationship in which a husband was obliged to provide horses for his wife's brothers and a wife was obliged to serve her husband.

This discussion of status obligations recalls Bourdieu's discussion of significant silences. When giving away horses, as when reciting war honors, men in Plains societies did not mention the status obligations that made horse givers' and heroes' rewards possible.

Partial Representations

At the end of the section on publicity, I implied my agreement with Bourdieu's (1977: 168) assertion that silences can be understood by focusing on what is said. Here I discuss Gluckman's analysis of what people talk about. In discussing the "property law" of tribal societies, Gluckman (1968) observes that people talk about relationships, not rights, when arguing over property. People handle property disputes not by deciding who owns the object in question but by determining the relationship between the parties, and therefore what each party owes the other. As a result, tribal peoples tend to have "no clear definition of ownership," in the sense of rights vested in individuals or status groups (Gluckman 1968: 75). But (except for brideservice peoples) they do tend to have well-developed notions of the kinds of specific, long-standing relationships that can exist between people.

Gluckman is correct in observing that people in tribal societies talk about relationships rather than rights, but I do not agree with his analysis of why tribal peoples do so. He attributes the emphasis on obligations to the low level of technology: tribal peoples are condemned to a life of economic dependence on their kin. But it seems more reasonable to relate the distinction between reciprocal status obligations and individual or group rights to the differences between stateless societies, where denial of reciprocity is the primary sanction, and state-based societies, which have organized coercive power.[10]

Malinowski (1926) emphasizes the importance of denial of reciprocity in the Trobriand Islands, but he leaves unanswered the question of whether denial of reciprocity is the Trobriand equivalent of the organized coercive power that (supposedly) compels obedience in states, or whether reciprocity is a universal sanction to which states merely add the extra compulsion of coercion. The latter interpretation has predominated since the publication of *Crime and Custom in Savage Society* because it does, in fact, make more sense. As Malinowski has pointed out, "no society can work in an efficient manner unless laws are obeyed 'willingly' and 'spontaneously' " (1926: 13). The expectation of reciprocity, or the fear of its denial, are potent inducements for conformity.

But if we are to understand the consequences of denial of reciprocity in stateless societies, we have to interpret denial of reciprocity as the stateless society's equivalent of state power. We can then see that property law in stateless societies concerns obligations owed between people who are related to one another in specific long-standing ways because it is negotiated in social contexts where the most salient sanction is denial of reciprocity by an individual. In state-based societies, by contrast, where state power is available—at least in theory—to enforce the rights of one individual or status group as against those of all others, property law concerns individual or group rights.

In state-based societies, the existence of organized coercive power allows people to own things, in the common meaning of the term. Because people assume that they can call on the power of the state, they can conceive of the possibility of denying others access to things they claim.[11] As a result, people in state-based societies (or living just outside state boundaries) come to understand their relations with others as derived from peoples' relations to things. Serfs work for their lord, sharecroppers work for landowners, and employees work for their employers because lords, landowners, and employers own the land or tools workers use, and thus can deny workers access to them unless the workers pay with goods and labor.

In stateless societies, however, where denial of reciprocity by an individual is the most salient sanction, people can demand only that specific others fulfill their obligations. People cannot deny all others access to things. They can demand only that the particular others who accept things from them fulfill the obligations associated with such acceptance. In societies where quarrels over things can be phrased only in terms of disputants' mutual obligations, those who quarrel over things are forced to negotiate the nature of their relationship with one another.

The interpretation that denial of reciprocity is the stateless society's equivalent of state power may explain why social relations in stateless societies are discussed in terms of reciprocal status obligations rather than in terms of rights held by individuals or status groups. But the cultural representation that status relationships entail reciprocal obligations is a partial one. However well-balanced the chains of reciprocal services in the Trobriand Islands (Malinowski 1926: 46), Trobriand commoners are not the equals of their chiefs, nor are children the equals of their parents. Reciprocal status obligations appear balanced only because the parties are already unequal. How, then, do we explain this inequality?

When criticizing Mishkin's analysis of why some men on the nineteenth-century Plains herded others' horses, I noted that an exchange of labor for mere use of horses could appear to be balanced only if horse owners were able to ensure the neediness of nonowners by preventing them from obtaining access to the animals on more favorable terms. This observation suggests that if we are to explain why apparently balanced exchanges do not balance status inequalities but actually perpetuate them, we have to examine the forces responsible for creating unequal needs. People in stateless societies lack the state power necessary for enforcing the rights of individuals against those of all others. Therefore, what power do people have to enforce their rights against those of other individuals?

The answer to this question is initially simple, and ultimately complex, for the power that allows people to assert their rights against those of other individuals is the power of women's kin to deny men access to wives. In all three types of classless societies considered in this book, men work for those who give them wives—a clearly unequal exchange in that husbands give labor whereas wife-givers give women, whom they produce only in a metaphorical sense. How, then, can wife-givers be considered to have the women they give away? And how can men be considered to need wives, since sexually mature men and women seem to have no problem getting together? These questions are considered in the next section.

Coercion

Ethnographers who search for law in classless societies inevitably discuss men's quarrels over women, whether or not they conclude that such societies have law. In classless societies, quarrels over women between men, or between husbands and women's kin, are endemic. Ethnographers interested in Comanche, Cheyenne, and Kiowa law apparently heard many lurid and detailed accounts of men's disputes over women, though they had difficulty obtaining information about disputes over horses or other property (Hoebel 1940: 118; Llewellyn & Hoebel 1941: 229; Richardson 1940: 125–29). Women seem to have been the major bones of contention among the Comanche (Hoebel 1940: 49) and the Kiowa (Richardson 1940: 131). Even the sexually repressed Cheyenne described many instances of elopement, adultery, and wife stealing.[12]

In classless societies, marriage is—on the surface—an exchange of women (or their social equivalents) between men (or their social equivalents). Comanche, Cheyenne, and Kiowa men, for example, formally obtained wives by providing gifts for the women's brothers (Gladwin 1948: 83; Hoebel 1978: 33; Richardson 1940: 65).

In all human societies, marriage is a relationship between men with respect to women, but it is also always a relationship between a man and a woman with respect to things and others, and a relationship between women with respect to men. Marriage is all these relationships simultaneously. But the quality of these relationships varies according to the nature of available enforcement mechanisms. In modern American society, where the state supposedly protects peoples' right to own things, marriage is legally defined as a relationship between a man and a woman in respect to things and others—property, children, and outsiders. But in classless societies, where denial of reciprocity is the strongest sanction available, people perceive marriage as primarily a relationship between men (or their social equivalents) in respect to women and women's children.

Lévi-Strauss (1969) locates the origin of human culture in the taboo on brother-sister incest and argues that social order in classless societies is constituted by alliances between men (or groups or men) established and maintained through exchanges of sisters for wives. He analyzes kinship as derived from three same-generation roles: a woman, her brother, and her husband.

Because Lévi-Strauss's theory parallels the understanding of people in many classless societies, it provides a logical starting point for my analysis. However, his explanation of why a man deserves compensation or services in return for making his sister available to another man is ultimately incorrect for the same reason that Mishkin's (1940) explanation of why horse owners could expect hunting and herding services from horse borrowers is problematic. Both Lévi-Strauss and Mishkin assume that the value of the object to be exchanged is determined by the object itself.

In discussing why a man who observes the incest taboo should receive compensation or another woman in return for giving up his sister, Lévi-Strauss alludes only to women's sexual attractiveness and to their performance of necessary tasks in societies where labor is divided by sex (1969: 37–41). But the question is not What are women good for? Women—and men—do useful work and are sexually desirable to the opposite sex. Rather, we should ask why, given their mutual attractiveness and usefulness, men and women do not just get together and live happily ever after. Why should a man have to compensate, or work for, his wife's brother? Or, given the sexual desirability and usefulness of men, why does a woman not have to compensate or work for her husband's sister?

In short, Lévi-Strauss, like Mishkin, takes for granted what is most perplexing: that people can have rights to objects or objectified others in the first place. Because Lévi-Strauss uses " 'exchange of women' [as] a shorthand for expressing that the social relations of a kinship system specify that men have certain rights in their female kin, and that women do not have the same rights either to themselves or to their male kin" (Rubin 1975: 177), his analysis raises the question of how men come to have such rights. However desirable or useful women might be, what men are willing to give in return for access to them is a function of prior relations between men that establish their opportunities to obtain access to women. In what sense, then, can brothers have rights in sisters? To answer this question we must examine the remedies available to women's kin in situations where their rights are violated, for it is by examining remedies that we discover the origin and content of rights.

In classless societies, women's kin have rights to women because the marital bond is initially fragile. The remedy available to women's kin in situations where their rights are violated is to support a woman against her husband. Because women's kin have influence over sisters and daughters, they have the power to deny men access to wives.

In all human societies the marital bond is initially fragile. To explain why marital instability is the basis of social inequality in classless societies we cannot focus on the universal fact of fragility. We must instead focus on the particular nature of marriage in classless societies.

To understand what marriage *is* in such societies, we have to understand what it *is not*. We must therefore add another character to Lévi-Strauss's triad consisting of a woman, her brother, and her husband: her lover. In classless societies, marriage, as a relationship between men in respect to women, takes its meaning from the relationship between lovers. Marriage and its opposites—fornication and adultery—are mutually defined.

An examination of ethnographies from classless societies reveals that people dramatize the contrast between a woman's brothers and her husband, but are relatively silent about the role of a woman's lover. Ethnographies of the Comanche, Cheyenne, and Kiowa show that these cultures presented women with a clear contrast between husbands and brothers as men who did, and did not, beat them, respectively. In each of these societies, husbands were granted the socially approved right to beat or mutilate unfaithful or uncooperative wives (Hoebel 1940: 49; Llewellyn & Hoebel 1941: 197; Richardson 1940: 65), and each culture portrayed the brother-sister bond as one involving mutual respect and avoidance of physical contact (Wallace & Hoebel 1952: 130; Hoebel 1978: 33; Richardson 1940: 65).[13]

Although people do not emphasize the role of woman's lover, this role is salient. The cultural representations of classless societies actually present women with three possible relations to same-generation men. With brothers, women engage in voluntary exchanges of goods and services, but do not have sexual relations. With lovers, women engage in direct and voluntary exchanges of goods, services, and sex. And with husbands, women have sexual relations, but engage in exchanges of goods and services that are forced.

Women's exchanges with husbands are forced not because of anything inherent in the exchanges themselves, but because of their contrast to women's exchanges with lovers. Husbands cannot engage in direct and voluntary exchanges with wives because a husband must distribute his products according to prior obligations.[14]

In classless societies, marriages are unstable because the contrast between women's lovers and women's husbands defines marriage as an unequal relationship in which wives owe obligations to husbands whereas husbands owe obligations to others. And the contrast between women's lovers and women's husbands results from actions carried out primarily by men (and women's senior kin) against men. Because men fear losing their wives, men join with seniors to prosecute women's lovers. And because men and women's kin prosecute women's lovers, they establish the contrast between husbands and lovers that defines marriage as an inegalitarian relationship.

Marital instability and the prosecution of women's lovers are therefore mutually established. Because marriages are initially unstable, men heed those seniors who can help them keep their wives. Insecure husbands work for seniors who have influence over the woman and who will join with them in prosecuting the woman's lovers. And because men heed seniors, marriage is an inegalitarian relationship. By working for seniors rather than freely exchanging goods and services with their wives, husbands sustain the contrast between husbands and lovers.

Because legal actions by husbands and seniors against women's lovers establish marriage as an unequal relationship that fosters marital instability, married women's kin have influence with unhappy brides and wives. Women's kin thus come to have rights to women that can be relinquished to husbands in return for labor or goods. It is in this sense that prior relations among men (or their social equivalents) enable women's kin to have rights to women. And because women's kin have these rights, men in classless societies can establish social order (and organize social inequality) by exchanging women.

This point lies at the heart of my argument. It is the central insight informing the models presented in this book. In the first half of this chapter, I discussed the various theoretical approaches that I considered when trying to understand the organization of inequality in classless societies. I began with the concept of misrecognition, which I discarded in favor of significant silences and then of partial representations. My search ends here with the concept of hegemony.

A consideration of coercion has led me to conclude that sanctions are important not for what they encourage or prohibit, but for what they make possible. Sanctions structure the resources available to people in contexts where they negotiate with one another; these resources structure the arguments people use when negotiating. The ultimate force of sanctions is not their ability to compel or prevent action, but their ability to establish meaning. If we understand sanctions we can understand both what people argue about and what they take for granted.

The concept of hegemony developed by Gramsci (1971) is defined by Raymond Williams as "a whole body of practices and experiences, over the whole of living: our senses and assignments of energy, our shaping perceptions of ourselves and our world. It is a lived system of meanings and values—constitutive and constituting—which as they are experienced as practices appear as reciprocally confirming" (1977: 110). Specific distributions of power organize the contexts in which people negotiate the meanings of actions and events, and the "relatively mixed, confused, incomplete, or inarticulate consciousness" that results from such negotiations distributes power and influence in particular ways (Raymond Williams 1977: 108–9).

Comparing the Three Models

Because the concept of hegemony joins meaning and practice, values and power, social scientists who use it to study how inequality is organized cannot treat culture and power as separate analytic concepts whose relationship may be investigated. Instead, they must analyze discourses: ongoing and recurring conversations in which forms of power and types of knowledge (including unacknowledged assumptions and common sense) are realized together (Foucault 1980). This is the strategy I followed in building the three ideal-typic models presented in this book. I analyzed the way particular conversations join particular cultural understandings and unstated assumptions with particular distributions of power and influence.

In this final section, I briefly compare the three models to illustrate the various discourses I analyzed in constructing each one. Because of space limitations, I will not elaborate the contrasts between the models but will merely allude to discussions in earlier chapters.

In the preceding section on coercion, I suggested that marital instability, caused by the unequal relationship between husbands and wives, organizes social inequality in classless societies. Marital instability grants women's kin influence over unhappy sisters and daughters, thereby granting women's kin the power to deny men access to wives. The existence of this power makes necessary, and provides the context for, negotiations between men and women's kin. These negotiations give rise to the commonsense understanding that women's kin have rights to women that they may relinquish to a suitor or husband in return for his labor or gifts. In each of the three types of classless societies modeled here, men who want to marry or whose marriages are unstable work for those who can help them acquire and keep wives.

In all three types of societies, the amount of labor others may appropriate from such men, and consequently the extent of social inequality, varies according to how marital instability is organized. In brideservice societies, little labor can be appropriated from suitors and recent husbands; therefore no one enjoys many privileges. More labor can be appropriated from bachelors and newly married men in equal bridewealth societies, thus allowing some seniors to enjoy the privileges of heading large households. In unequal bridewealth societies, some men spend their lives working for others; consequently the men they work for are able to spend their lives pursuing prestige-enhancing activities.

In discussing each of the three models, I suggested that the amount of labor privileged people may appropriate from suitors and men with unstable marriages is related to how long marriages remain unstable. For each model, the length of time marriages remain unstable is related to how much labor is appropriated from women's suitors and from women's husbands. The more labor is appropriated from such men, the longer marriages remain unstable, and conversely. Recognition of this vicious circle is a critical first step in building models of social inequality in classless societies. This circle provides the context for conversations in which people negotiate the meaning of marriage, work, and gifts.

Because marital instability, which grants power to women's kin, is the ultimate determinant of social inequality in the three types of classless societies discussed here, I began my discussion of each model by examining what people talk about in contexts where bachelors seek brides and abandoned husbands negotiate for the return of runaway wives. I noted that cultural representations of affinal relations reflect not how affines actually treat one another but rather how people talk about the affinal relationship. Cultural representations of marriage do not reflect actual relations of power and dependence as organized by marital instability. They reflect what people say in the process of claiming, justifying, contesting, and manipulating the privileges that power relations make possible.

In brideservice societies, for example, women's kin cannot reclaim a mature daughter from her husband and thus cannot claim to give her away; as a result, suitors stress what they provide for wife's kin. In equal bridewealth societies, women's kin are able to keep a married sister or daughter from her husband; they therefore talk as if they had the ability to give women away. In unequal bridewealth societies, women's kin can refuse to take back an unhappily married daughter or sister; they talk as if they had the right to reclaim a married woman from her husband.

These cultural representations shape people's understandings of how men acquire and keep wives. In brideservice societies, people say that men earn their wives through their own efforts. In equal bridewealth societies, people portray young men as receiving wives from their own senior kin, who obtain the wives by negotiating with a woman's senior kin. In unequal bridewealth societies, people say that men acquire and keep wives by being able to fulfill wife-givers' requests for goods and services.

Brideservice peoples understand a young man's ability to acquire and keep a wife as a function of his own capacities. In the experience of equal bridewealth peoples, young men acquire wives through the beneficence of their parents or guardians. In unequal bridewealth societies, young men perceive their ability to acquire a wife by providing goods instead of services as a function of sharing patterns within their sibling sets.

These cultural understandings of how men acquire wives grant power to certain individuals, and by structuring the contexts in which some people work for others, they elicit conversations in which people posit the factors responsible for determining the fates of individuals. In brideservice societies, people credit men (and women) with forging their own destinies. In equal bridewealth societies, people perceive themselves as dependent on the beneficent help of seniors and supernatural beings. In unequal bridewealth societies, people consider hereditary rank the most important determinant of a person's fate.

Cultural understandings of how men acquire wives, by structuring the contexts in which some people work for others, also structure the conversations in which people develop culturally acceptable justifications for appropriating the labor of others. In brideservice societies, where men earn their brides, no one can justify appropriating the labor of any other. As a result, people control their own labor; they are free to dispose of their labor products as they choose—to use them to fulfill recognized obligations or to exchange them with others. Suitors and husbands are obliged to give the best portions of their meat to their wives' senior kin, thus allowing women's kin to enjoy privileged access to the products of others. But women's kin have no cultural justification for claiming a man's meat before the meat is actually delivered. They may grumble when meat is not provided, but they have no grounds for claiming that a suitor's labor is theirs to command.

In equal bridewealth societies, where men receive wives from their senior kin, socially defined parents may claim unquestioning obedience from the children they beneficently support. As a result, parents can direct children's labor and thus may claim as already belonging to them anything a child produces, even before the goods are produced. In actuality, parents in equal bridewealth societies are most successful at directing the labor of courting bachelors and unhappily married children, but in theory, parents may claim unquestioning obedience from children of any age.

In unequal bridewealth societies, where men acquire wives (or rather, manage to keep them) by fulfilling wife-givers' requests for goods and services, women's kin claim rights to the labor and products of kinswomen's husbands on the grounds that they are not exercising their right to take their kinswomen back again. People assume that a man can never refuse a request from his wife's kin. Thus it is by permitting a marriage to continue (i.e. by renouncing their right to break up a man's marriage) that women's kin justify their right to claim the products and labor of a particular kinswoman's husband.

In shaping the cultural representations available to people for justifying appropriations of labor, understandings of how men acquire wives simultaneously shape people's perceptions of the reciprocal status positions involved in labor appropriation, thus influencing people's understanding of how production units are organized. In brideservice societies, where no one may justify claiming another's labor or products, women feed their families and men distribute their meat throughout the group. In equal bridewealth societies, where socially defined parents may claim unquestioning obedience from children, production units appear to be extended families composed of parents, their socially defined children, and those children's spouses and children. In unequal bridewealth societies, where women's kin claim rights to the labor and products of men married to their socially defined sisters, production units appear to be extended sibling sets composed of full brothers, their half, classificatory, and pact brothers, and the husbands of their full, half, classificatory, and pact sisters.

The organization of production units provides a context for understanding how women experience marriage and therefore for analyzing the duration and distribution of marital instability. In brideservice societies, where no one can justify claiming another's products or labor, women experience marriage as an inegalitarian relationship only until they become mothers. As long as a woman is childless, her husband's demands for daily food, shelter, and sexual fidelity seem to restrict her freedom to avoid work and take lovers. But once a woman has borne a child for whom she must provide daily food and shelter, her husband's demands seem less onerous, and she welcomes his help in child care.

In equal bridewealth societies, where production is carried out in households that vary in size and productivity, both women and men benefit from accumulating children who will work for them. As a result, mothers seek out men who can help advance their children's careers and play husbands off against their natal kin to the advantage of their children. Young husbands have little to offer their wives, but they must demand things from them if they are to advance their own careers. Young husbands thus have insecure marriages. Older men who have achieved respect find women flocking to them; those who have lost respect find their women turning to others.

In unequal bridewealth societies, women's possibilities for success depend on the rank of their full brothers. Some women have low-ranking brothers who are easily co-opted by high-ranking men who want to give them away. Such women must either cooperate with their brothers' benefactors or face the world without supportive male kin. A woman might thus agree to live with a low-ranking, undesirable man for as long as her brothers' benefactor requires. The organization of women's choices ensures that a high-ranking man can acquire and keep wives without difficulty. A low-ranking man may keep his consort only so long as he complies with her kinsmen's requests for labor.

The preceding analysis of the duration and distribution of marital instability, which helps to explain the powers available to people when they negotiate marriages and appropriations of labor, also helps to explain what people talk about as they exchange goods and services. Because marital instability structures the organization of production units, it organizes the distribution of valuables and the cultural meanings that people attribute to gifts.

In brideservice societies, where marital instability is primarily a function of age, people understand men's activities as also being a function of age. Young men appear to be concerned with proving themselves as hunters and warriors. Although they give away almost everything they acquire, they appear to be forever wanting something in exchange. Adult men, in contrast, appear to practice generalized reciprocity, giving things away without expectation of immediate return. And old men, who seem to have no needs, may be credited with generously giving away even women.

In equal bridewealth societies, women's need to advance their children's careers puts young men in the position of having to work for elders who can help them marry and keep their wives. Young men lack the goods they need to acquire respect, whereas respected seniors receive many goods from eager juniors and also appropriate the labor products of their wives and children. As a result, young men appear to need goods, and seniors have goods for giving away. Respected seniors are thus able to provide juniors with the objects they need to present to seniors in return for brides and ritual knowledge, or in payment of compensatory damages. Household heads visibly provide for their dependents, and Big Men have access to the goods they need to generously support less fortunate household heads.

In unequal bridewealth societies, some men have unstable marriages, and so spend their lives working for those who give or lend them wives. The men they work for have access to many goods for giving away and thus can enjoy the secure marriages associated with high rank. High-ranking men can provide gifts, instead of labor, to their wife-givers, and they may also use their goods to help half, classificatory, and pact brothers acquire and keep wives.

As a result, such men may acquire many socially defined brothers and thereby acquire many sisters whose husbands can never refuse their requests.

The duration and distribution of marital instability organize the circulation of valuables, but people seem rarely to comment on this fact. They are understandably more interested in speculating about and trying to influence what they or others can expect in return for gifts and services and therefore focus on how gifts determine relationships. They seldom have reason to sit back and contemplate how interpersonal relations determine individuals' possibilities for gift giving. People thus come to think of gifts as establishing and validating relationships involving reciprocal rights and obligations.

In brideservice societies, where men with secure marriages enjoy freedom from obligations to others, people take a man's ability to hunt and raid as proof of the potency that makes possible such independence. In equal bridewealth societies, where socially defined parents may claim obedience from children, people consider the provision of children with the goods they need to marry, acquire ritual knowledge, and pay compensatory damages evidence of parental status. In unequal bridewealth societies, where wife-takers may never refuse wife-givers' requests, people assume that a man's offer to help another man acquire the gifts he needs to marry or to reclaim a wife is proof of a brotherly relationship.

The second and third sections of Chapters 1–3 (on marriage and on production and circulation) focused on what people talk about in situations structured by marital instability. In discussing marriage negotiations, I noted that what people say does not reflect actual relations of power and dependence; it reflects people's justifications for the behaviors that power relations make possible. Those who are credited with giving (or earning) wives do not give women, for women are not objects; rather, they are the individuals who wield power during marriage negotiations. And in discussing circulation patterns, I noted that people talk about gifts as determining relationships. They seldom have occasion to contemplate how existing relationships determine individuals' ability to give gifts.

In these sections I implied that there are two critical displacements of meaning in the constitution of commonsense knowledge—in the realm of marriage, and in the realm of circulation. In brideservice societies, common sense suggests that (1) men earn wives by hunting and raiding, rather than by waiting for women to become mothers, and (2) married men's independence is due to their abilities as hunters and raiders. Few people have cause to comment that a wife's services permit her husband's freedom. In equal bridewealth societies, common sense suggests that (1) women's kin have the ability to give women in marriage, not merely the ability to keep them from their husbands, and (2) socially defined parents have the right to claim obedience from children they support. Few people have cause to comment that children's labor supports their parents. In unequal bridewealth societies, common sense suggests that (1) women's kin have the right to reclaim women from their husbands, rather than the ability to refuse women shelter, and (2) men who share valuables are brothers. Few people have cause to comment that low-ranking men's labor enables high-ranking men to acquire the valuables they share.

The silences that result from these displacements of meaning are of two different types. The first silence, which occurs during negotiations of marriage, involves basic assumptions that ordinary people probably find difficult to question. A person in an equal bridewealth society would probably have as much difficulty accepting the proposition that women's kin cannot really give women in marriage as would an ordinary American who was told that things do not have value in and of themselves (whether value is determined by an object's inherent usefulness, its scarcity, or the labor required for its production).

This silence about fundamental assumptions shapes the basic distribution of possibilities. In equal bridewealth societies, for example, the assumption that women's kin can give them in marriage casts women and men as having different possibilities for achieving power and privilege. Socially defined women are people who cannot give themselves; a woman's kin reap the benefits of her gift to others. Socially defined men can exchange women. In capitalist societies, where things appear to have value in and of themselves, control of things allows control over people.

The second silence concerns information that people undoubtedly recognize and can obtain for themselves, but which they probably find useless for dealing with social reality. Many people in equal bridewealth societies must recognize that young men lack the valuables they need to marry only because they cannot exchange labor for valuables, either because their labor already belongs to parents or because valuables are exchanged only for rights to women. But this information is of little use to someone deciding how to act. It does not help a bachelor to know that he lacks valuables because social processes prevent him from acquiring them by his own labor. He still needs valuables if he is to become the socially recognized husband of a woman.

The second silence shapes what people may hope for and their strategies for achieving goals. In equal bridewealth societies, the understanding that socially defined parents have the right to claim obedience from children they support establishes (1) a differentiation between men who acquire children by acquiring wives and women who acquire children by bearing and feeding them, and (2) a differentiation between seniors who have acquired many socially recognized children and those who have few or none. The second silence establishes the rules of the game that people must follow—consciously or not—if they wish to enjoy social rewards and avoid social sanctions. People may recognize that the rules are arbitrary and unfair, but individuals are hardly able to create an entirely new game, or even to withdraw from the one in which they are involved.

In discussing each model, I noted that the falsity of the two critically displaced meanings is protected from exposure by people's sense of reality (see Bourdieu 1977: 164). People who are not in a structural position to claim rewards seldom bother to exhibit the behavior common sense defines as necessary to reap them. In brideservice societies, bachelors are notoriously lazy. In equal bridewealth societies, bachelors do not arrange their own marriages even if they acquire valuables. In unequal bridewealth societies, low-ranking men seldom respond angrily to insults.

Because the displaced meanings are used by people in everyday life, they are the foundation of most public knowledge. In the final two sections of Chapters 1–3 (on political processes and cultural representations), I examined some of the many contexts in which people apply and elaborate commonsense understandings. I did not search for the definitive context or meaning of dominant cultural representations. Because people have many contexts in which to apply and elaborate commonsense understandings, a particular cultural representation may be explained in several ways. I therefore examined only some of the situations in which people use and elaborate common cultural idioms so that I might suggest ways to understand why ethnographers describe peoples' ideas and institutions as they do.

Ethnographers of societies appropriate for analysis with a brideservice model frequently report that people handle conflicts by staging contests between the disputants. Drawing on my analysis of commonsense knowledge in the second and third sections of Chapter 1 (the brideservice model), I suggested that people appear to stage contests because they understand conflict as calling into question a man's ability to take and keep what he claims as his (i.e. his wife). As a result, everyone involved in a dispute focuses on the relative prowess of the disputants, rather than on the rights and wrongs of their grievances.

Ethnographers of equal bridewealth societies commonly report that people handle disputes by negotiating compensatory payments for victims. My analysis of circulation patterns indicates that people understand conflict as arising from incomplete exchanges. The legal systems of such societies appear to be based on principles of strict liability, self-help, and collective responsibility because incomplete exchanges establish a relationship between the disputants regardless of their intentions and actions. And people settle disputes by negotiation rather than by contests or adjudication because conflicts can end only when both sides appear to agree on the nature of their relationship.

In considering the conflict-management procedures of unequal bridewealth societies, I proposed that people understand conflicts as calling into question the ranking of the disputants. Because a person's rank is determined by the person's access to valuables for giving away, people handle conflicts by mobilizing sibling sets to display their sharing patterns.

Because people use their commonsense assumptions to understand and manage conflict, commonsense assumptions about how men acquire wives and people get ahead in the world become self-fulfilling prophecies, and therefore appear to be undeniably true. Because conflict can occur only between individuals who have contact with one another and whose actions affect one another's lives, the meanings that people attribute to actions and events during the process of conflict management do, in part, serve to determine the distribution of rewards and penalties between the disputants. An unintended consequence of conflict-management procedures is to create a world in which actions and events have expected outcomes—a world in which individuals may plan strategies and careers (see Comaroff & Roberts 1981).

In the process of handling conflicts, people develop recognized vocabularies for pressing claims and voicing desires that distribute power in particular ways.[15] In brideservice societies, for example, where people focus on the relative prowess of contestants, women are inherently disadvantaged in pressing their claims because they never have to earn wives through demonstrations of prowess. They never appear to have the prowess that ensures a concerned audience for angry bachelors and injured husbands. In equal bridewealth societies, where conflicts are perceived as incomplete exchanges, women involved in marital disputes are considered objects rather than subjects. Angry wives may complain of their husbands' failings, but women lack the vocabulary for questioning the right of their kin to give them away. In unequal bridewealth societies, where conflicts call into question the ranking of disputants, women have fewer opportunities than men to mobilize their sibling sets.

The analysis of conflict-management procedures provides a context for understanding leadership patterns. Ethnographers of brideservice societies often report that leaders lack the power to give orders and that men strive "to achieve parity, or at least to establish a status that announces 'don't fool with me' " (Fried 1967: 79). In a society where the outcome of conflicts appears to turn on the bravery of disputants, each man wants to establish his ability to take and keep what he wants. Since inequality incites violent attempts to prove parity, it is little wonder that respected leaders do not give orders and that no one strives for dominance. But if leaders lack the power to give orders, the paradigms of argumentation developed in conflict-management procedures do grant authority to men who have turned from collecting women to giving them away. In societies where each man must maintain a status that announces "don't fool with me," men who give women away can be credited with offering disinterested advice that combatants may heed without appearing to sacrifice their self-reliance.

Ethnographers of equal bridewealth societies commonly describe leaders as Big Men who acquire power by generously giving things away (Sahlins 1963). Men who head large households and have debtors in other households command the valuables that allow them to handle conflicts by negotiating compensatory payments for others, as well as to organize major rituals, trading expeditions, and warfare. Such men have considerable power to affect the fates of others, but they seldom hold offices that give them recognized authority over groups of people. Each leader must collect his own followers, who disperse upon his senility or death. The paradigms of argumentation confer authority on people who have access to the valuables needed for establishing or reestablishing social relationships. People without valuables must ask others to establish relationships for them.

Ethnographers of unequal bridewealth societies frequently write that hereditary or quasi-hereditary chiefs rule over their lower-ranking subordinates. In such societies, men born to high-ranking mothers never have to perform necessary, but degrading, tasks; therefore, some men enjoy a privileged lifestyle from birth. And the impossibility of equality ensures that high chiefs have only subordinates. Because rank appears to determine the outcome of disputes, high-ranking people, particularly men, wield authority, and low-ranking men know that it makes little sense for them to respond violently to insults.

The actions of political leaders shape people's understandings of the gestures and speech mannerisms that connote authority. Authority is evidenced by a self-reliant stance in brideservice societies, by generous or officious direction of others' affairs in equal bridewealth societies, and by the unruffled demeanor of high-ranking individuals in unequal bridewealth societies. The actions and utterances of those who, because of sex, age, or prior commitments, cannot exhibit the behaviors associated with authority are treated as being of lesser consequence.

An analysis of conflict-management procedures also provides an explanation for ethnographers' reports of how people understand their social system. Societies vary considerably in the degree to which people develop explicit or elaborate folk models of social structure. But when people do develop such models, they appear to build on the commonsense assumptions they use in everyday life to justify, claim, and negotiate privileges.

Ethnographers of brideservice peoples commonly report that they recognize few rules and understand personal power as the basis of social relations. The contests they use for handling disputes provide people few opportunities to discuss rules, but many contexts in which to discuss the relative prowess of disputants. Brideservice peoples celebrate men's capacity for violence, but they also fear its disruptive effects. They thus venerate those men who, by appearing to give women, turn hostile competitors into cooperative brothers-in-law.

Equal bridewealth peoples, in contrast, often develop bodies of recognized norms. Because they handle disputes through negotiation, they have many opportunities to state and elaborate social rules. Many equal bridewealth peoples come to think of their world as rule-governed. Some, such as the Cheyenne, posit a mechanistic universe.

Unequal bridewealth peoples elaborate notions of hereditary rank. Because their procedures for handling conflicts call upon disputants to display their rank, people have many occasions to contemplate how rank organizes social relations.

Folk models of social structure, based on peoples' understandings of the causes and consequences of conflict, provide the vocabularies individuals use to monitor their own actions and their relations with others. Such models establish narrative conventions for constructing the individual and collective histories that are constitutive of social identity. In brideservice societies, where contestants' bravery appears to determine the outcome of disputes, attempts to interpret or predict a person's actions focus on the person's intentions and capacities. Consequently, brideservice peoples come to think of themselves and others as "following their hearts." In equal bridewealth societies, where disputants justify their actions as counteracting opponents' previous wrongs, attempts to predict or interpret a person's actions focus on that individual's past and present relationships with others. Each person thus comes to be understood not as a bounded, autonomous being but as a web of relationships. In unequal bridewealth societies, where disputants try to establish their ranks, people understand behavior as determined by rank. So they tend to develop notions of how people of particular ranks can be expected to behave.

The ideas people use in daily life to interpret actions, make claims, justify privileges, manipulate others, and plan strategies are the ones they elaborate in rituals. These ideas need elaboration and frequent repetition because they are continually contradicted by everyday events. Because commonsense assumptions are actually displaced meanings, as just discussed, reality inevitably contradicts dominant cultural representations. In every society, the wide variety of contexts for elaborating commonsense assumptions ensures that some elaborations will contradict others. And because such assumptions encode notions of inequality, they inevitably provoke resistance. The undeniable presence of conflict, disorder, and evil in the world gives people good reason to state and elaborate, again and again in ritual, their ideas of how things should be.

In every society, the grand syntheses that people express in rituals, which anthropologists call world view and structural marxists call ideology, are always both revelations and mystifications. They are revelations because they impose order on the contradictory, contested, and partial representations of everyday life by suggesting the ultimate regularity of confusing reality. Grand syntheses are mystifications because they are bound to misrepresent crucial areas of peoples' experience.

Rituals in brideservice societies commonly celebrate male prowess—Man the Hunter who both kills and gives life. Men's apparent capacity to earn wives and to forge cooperative relationships by giving women is dramatized in myth and ceremony. Although men's marriages create social order, they also establish the inequality between unmarried and married men that breeds conflict. And the notion that men earn wives through proofs of prowess conflicts with elaborations of sister-exchange marriage based on the notion that men create social order by giving each other women.

In many equal bridewealth societies, ancestral cults dramatize the notion that those who come after are dependent on those who came before (Meillassoux 1972: 99–100). Young men, in particular, appear to be dependent on senior men for knowledge of how to maintain the universe and protect it from feminine pollution. But in celebrating the knowledge of senior men, equal bridewealth peoples classify young men with women and thus misrepresent the vast difference between powerless young men and powerful senior women. And among peoples who develop elaborate ideas of a mechanistic universe, the notion that ritual actions, in themselves, constitute effective forces contradicts the idea that spirits are not required to grant human requests.

In unequal bridewealth societies, rituals commonly dramatize the role of rank in organizing social life. Consequently, they frequently provoke status confrontations that disrupt social order. Peoples' belief that rank is hereditary also conflicts with the notion that rank is based on individual achievement.

Conceptions of gender also reflect people's commonsense understandings. Gender conceptions are never simply reflections of biological sex differences or of what men and women do. Rather they reflect aspects of the wider cultural systems of meaning according to which people interpret and manage their worlds (Collier & Rosaldo 1981). In brideservice societies, both men and women appear to perceive themselves as autonomous agents who "follow their hearts," but men are credited with having capacities that women never acquire. Man the Hunter is accompanied by a curiously undefined wife, although women, in their rituals, celebrate the sexual attractiveness that ensures them a choice of lovers. In equal bridewealth societies, women's capacity to bear the children all people desire is both celebrated and feared. Woman the Mother and Source of all Life is also the source of chaos and death. Men, to restore and preserve cosmic order, must separate themselves from women. But masculinity is a fragile force, forever in danger of being overwhelmed by potent femininity. Unequal bridewealth peoples seem less concerned with gender than with rank. For both men and women, rank appears to be the most important aspect of personhood.

Although I concluded my description of each model with a discussion of gender conceptions, I did not intend to portray such conceptions as determined by more fundamental social processes. Marital instability, which I discussed before considering production and circulation, political processes, and cultural representations, does not determine economy, polity, or beliefs. Because marriages are made by socially defined women and men, conceptions of gender and generation affect the constitution of marital and kinship relations, as well as the constitution of economic and political relations. Social systems exist only as they are realized in the skilled performances of living women and men.

In brideservice societies, men, as autonomous agents, earn brides by performing services for women's kin and by demonstrating their ability to establish and maintain a status that announces "don't fool with me." Women, as equally autonomous agents, resist settling down with unwanted husbands and use their sexual attractiveness to establish and maintain relationships with lovers.

In equal bridewealth societies, both youths and maidens perceive femininity as dangerous. Both thus rely on their senior kin to arrange the marriages that will enable them to become successful parents. Young men work for seniors who will help them acquire and keep wives, and young women turn to those kin who will help ensure that their children survive and prosper.

In unequal bridewealth societies, men and women who are contemplating marriage perceive themselves as bearers of particular ranks with particular prerogatives. Women refuse to consort with low-ranking men, thus forcing them to work for high-ranking men who can help them acquire and keep female companions.

In this chapter I have identified a variety of discourses. Because power and knowledge are inevitably linked in discourse (Foucault 1980: 100), social scientists trying to understand the organization of inequality in human societies need a vocabulary to describe the varieties of ongoing and recurring conversations in which particular cultural understandings and silences are joined with particular distributions of power. This book is intended as a contribution to the effort of building such a vocabulary.

Conclusion

Models of the type presented in this book have obvious limitations. In this Conclusion, I briefly review some of the limitations and then discuss why constructing ideal-typic models seems, nevertheless, a worthwhile—indeed indispensable—project.

By discussing only models of uncentralized, classless societies, I may have conveyed the impression that centralized societies or those with classes cannot be modeled in the same way. Although I have not developed models of such societies, I believe they can be constructed. As mentioned in the preceding chapter, I distinguish between societies in which the principal sanction is denial of reciprocity and those with organized coercive power, but this distinction does not require that the two types be analyzed with different theories of society. Therefore, the three models presented in this book should be thought of as part of a larger set that includes, at the minimum, a model of chiefdoms and at least two models of societies in which the state, not marriage, organizes inequality. Wallerstein's "world empires," in which the state allocates economic resources, should be distinguished from his "world economies," in which no single state controls economic allocations (1974: 15); see also Giddens's distinction between "class divided" and "class" societies (1981).[1]

The three models developed here are limited in that they necessarily group in the same category societies whose differences may seem more striking than their similarities. Any model, such as the brideservice model, that is presented as being equally appropriate for analyzing the "fierce" Yanomamo (Chagnon 1968) and the "harmless" Bushmen (Thomas 1959), necessarily treats as similar two societies many people prefer to regard as polar opposites. The equal bridewealth model, which is presented as being equally appropriate for analyzing kinship-based societies in Africa and New Guinea, provides no method for analyzing the important distinctions in lineage organization noted by Barnes (1962). The unequal bridewealth model does not distinguish societies such as the Kiowa, where high-ranking men acquired workers by lending sisters and daughters, from societies such as the Kpelle of Liberia, where chiefs lent out surplus wives. Ideally, therefore, each model should be presented not as a single system, as I have done, but rather as a set of variations on a theme.

In addition, models should ideally include a description of the possibilities for change inherent in each system. Brideservice societies may vary from egalitarian to apparently hierarchical and gerontocratic, depending on the rate of polygyny and senior men's tolerance of their wives' adulteries. Some equal bridewealth peoples may live in such small households that leaders have little power, whereas others may develop such large production units that some household heads appear to enjoy the powers of village or regional chiefs. Unequal bridewealth societies may vary from fragmented and egalitarian to centralized and hierarchical, depending on the degree of consensus as to a single ranking scale. The extent of inequality in all three types of society may change, depending on existing circumstances.

Finally, each model should ideally contain a description of its own limits—the points at which it becomes inapplicable to particular social groups. I have implicitly identified, but have not stressed, some of these limits. The unequal bridewealth model, for example, is useful for analyzing only those societies where wife-takers or wife-borrowers are expected to work for wife-givers or wife-lenders. Some fragmented unequal bridewealth societies, such as the *Gumlao* Kachin of Highland Burma (Leach 1965), may seem indistinguishable from equal bridewealth societies, but as long as people maintain that wife-takers cannot refuse wife-givers' requests, the unequal bridewealth model facilitates a more reasonable estimate of the society's possibilities than does the equal bridewealth model. Similarly, a centralized unequal bridewealth society may seem indistinguishable from a chiefdom, but until it develops a conical clan structure (see Friedman 1975), the unequal bridewealth model affords more and deeper insights than would a chiefdom model.

The models presented here are also of limited utility for understanding historical ethnic groups. As noted in the Introduction, any historical group is necessarily too complex for all of its aspects to be analyzed by an ideal-typic model. All of the experiences from which people draw their understandings of the world cannot be considered in constructing models. People are not limited to the cultural representations discussed in this book. Some ethnic groups may seem to be self-perpetuating units with distinct institutions and homogeneous cultural traditions, but all historical groups live surrounded by other peoples whose actions influence them. And people in every group may always draw on the understandings of residual and emergent cultural traditions (see Raymond Williams 1977).

The historical Comanche, Cheyenne, and Kiowa, for example, were far more complex societies than I have suggested in this book. Cheyenne social institutions underwent rapid and extreme changes during the nineteenth century (Llewellyn & Hoebel 1941). These peoples first had to adapt to a nomadic life on the Plains and then faced the westward advance of the whites, who killed bison and disrupted Indian trade networks. Their dominant cultural tradition (which was, I believe, the one I have sketched here) was challenged in the second half of the nineteenth century by an emerging one. John Moore (1974b) proposes a "dualistic model" for analyzing nineteenth-century Cheyenne society. He asserts that "uterine forces," exemplified by the Council of Forty-Four Chiefs, were struggling for power with emerging "agnatic forces" exemplified by the Dog Soldier Society, whose members constituted a single band. Dog Soldiers lived together and, unlike other Cheyenne men, distributed their produce throughout the group rather than hunting for their extended family households. The wives of Dog Soldiers, who were separated from their natal kin (Petersen 1964), fed their husbands and children. The dominant Cheyenne tradition, appropriate for analysis with an equal bridewealth model, was thus apparently challenged by an emerging tradition more appropriately analyzed with the brideservice model.[2]

A brief review of Plains history suggests that a brideservice organization of inequality was expanding at the expense of more unequal forms of organization. The Comanche ethnic group, with an estimated population of 10,000 to 12,000 (Ewers 1973), far out-numbered the Cheyenne and the Kiowa, although the Comanche evidenced the low reproductive rates common to foraging peoples (see Wallace & Hoebel 1952: 142). Incorporation of people from other societies may account for the large Comanche population. It is reasonable to conclude that a low-ranking Kiowa man, aware that he could never refuse a request from his wife's kin, would be attracted by the possibility of becoming a Comanche and being able to earn a wife for himself. Such a change of ethnic identity would have not have been difficult, since the Kiowa and Comanche were allies on the southern Plains and Comanche was the dominant language of the region.

The models presented in this book may be ahistorical, but they are not static. Because I follow Giddens (1976, 1979) and Bourdieu (1977) in viewing "the production and reproduction of society . . . as a skilled performance on the part of its members" (Giddens 1976: 160), I believe that "change, or its potentiality, is . . . inherent in all moments of social reproduction" (Giddens 1979: 114). Social institutions exist only to the extent that people, pursuing their own subjective ends, realize them by their actions. The relationship between system and activity is truly dialectical. System and activity are either realized together, or both are transformed. A theory of history is thus basic to each ideal-typic model.

This theory of history does not include a concept of evolutionary change, however, either within types or between them. My models do not imply a necessary direction to change. An equal bridewealth society may become more or less egalitarian, depending on whether the size of households decreases or increases over time. And particular equal bridewealth peoples may adopt a brideservice form of organization, as the Cheyenne Dog Soldiers apparently did, or they may adopt an unequal bridewealth form, if wife-takers come to be seen as indebted to wife-givers. But because the models presented here reveal the complex relationships between different societal aspects, they provide a framework for analyzing historical processes and for understanding how particular environmental or historical forces may have affected specific peoples.

The argument of this book is based on the assumption that no social practice—be it a way of validating marriages, a mode of exploiting the land, a productive system, an exchange pattern, a way of reckoning kinship, or the use of force—has meaning in and of itself. Every social practice has a meaningful construction whose interpretation requires an analysis of context. In every society, people carry out actions we call marrying, exploiting the land, producing goods, giving gifts, or using force, but such labels tell us little because we cannot understand peoples' actions unless we understand the sociocultural system that gives them meaning.

If a social practice has no meaning in and of itself, and cannot be analyzed independently of the total system of which it is a part, then we cannot presume to know what a social practice is without analyzing the total system that encompasses it. Without such knowledge, we cannot compare institutions across societies in the hope of discovering sociological laws. Evans-Pritchard recognized this dilemma when he said that "there is only one method in social anthropology, the comparative method—and that's impossible" (reported in Needham 1975: 365).

One possible solution to the problem that holism poses for anthropology is to abandon the comparative enterprise in favor of studying particular, unique ways of life. Geertz has noted that anthropologists have turned "from trying to explain social phenomena by weaving them into grand textures of cause and effect to trying to explain them by placing them in local frames of awareness" (1983: 6). Instead of trying to discover sociological laws applicable to several societies, many anthropologists have turned to examining "the ways in which the world is talked about—depicted, charted, represented—" by particular peoples (1983: 4).

However promising the abandonment of comparative analysis for the study of particular, unique ways of life, this solution to the problem of holism is untenable. Not only does a focus on particular societies have the disadvantage of fostering extreme cultural relativism but such an analysis is, in fact, impossible to carry out without using the comparative method. To write about a people's way of life using English or another language not used by that people is implicitly to compare their beliefs and practices with those of the analyst's society or professional group. Anthropologists may have turned from searching for sociological laws to translating local discourses, but Evans-Pritchard was right. There is only one method in social anthropology. We cannot translate without comparing.

Given that translation requires comparison, thoughtful comparison is doubtless preferable to the thoughtless variety. The richer our comparative vocabulary, the richer our translations are likely to be.[3] If we use only a "them/us" comparison, we are able to note only the ways in which "they" are or are not like "us." We reinforce, and thus contribute to the persistence of, the "West and the Rest" dichotomy that condemns others to perpetual, and undifferentiated, otherness. We all know that others are not undifferentiated. But without a vocabulary for talking about the differences between others, we can only discuss, over and over, the ways in which "they" are different from "us" (see Strathern 1985).

Ideal-typic models of societal types offer a solution to the problem of developing a comparative vocabulary. If no social practice has meaning apart from the total system of which it is a part, then we need a method for comparing wholes. As representations of social wholes, systemic models of societal types provide a principled method for deciding what social practices are, and therefore for determining which practices of different societies are comparable.

A set of models allows us to detect crucial differences that underlie apparent similarities. Comanche, Cheyenne, and Kiowa grooms may all have presented horses to their bride's kin, but because such apparently similar practices occurred in different total systems, they had different meanings and different consequences for social relations. Although men in many societies validate their marriages with substantial gifts to a woman's kin, we would reach misleading conclusions if, for analytical purposes, we treated the payment of "brideprice" by a traditional Chinese peasant and the payment of "bridewealth" by a traditional Nuer as the same kind of transaction (see Goody 1973) because these transfers occur in totally different social and political contexts.

Models of total systems also allow us to detect the similarities that underlie apparent differences. Ethnographers write that Comanche grooms were expected to give horses to bride's kin and that !Kung Bushmen grooms were expected to provide services. The brideservice model suggests that Comanche gifts and Bushmen services are more similar than might appear, however. An analysis of the total systems in which the exchanges occurred reveals that a Comanche groom's gifts and a Bushman groom's services were both understood as proof of the groom's willingness and ability to fight potential seducers of his bride. Similarly, a set of systemic models can lead us to conclude that traditional Chinese dowries and European dowries may be fruitfully compared, even though Chinese dowries were only a father's gift, whereas European daughters received an inheritance. Because both presentations were made in class-based, agrarian societies, both types of dowry were understood as displays of a bride's family's wealth, and hence social position (see Goody 1973).

By allowing us to appreciate differences and similarities between practices followed in societies far apart in space or time, a set of ideal-typic models offers us the possibility of comparing the beliefs and practices of the particular group we are studying with those of societies other than our own. We are no longer condemned to discuss only how "they" are different from "us." The historic Comanche, for example, were indubitably different from the modern Bushmen of the Kalahari Desert, but a comparison of the Comanche and the Bushmen may illuminate aspects of Comanche belief and practice that would remain obscure if our only basis for comparison were our own society or other Plains societies.

I am only one of the many anthropologists who have proposed ideal-typic models as a solution to the problem holism poses for comparison. Feminist anthropologists, particularly those arguing against theories of universal sexual asymmetry, have advocated the use of societal typologies as a way of understanding qualitative variations in women's lives. Marxist feminists have proposed typologies based on forms of access to the means of production (e.g. Leacock 1978; Sacks 1979; Etienne & Leacock 1980; Caulfield 1981). Other feminists have used typologies based on productive activities (e.g. Friedl 1975; Martin & Voorhies 1975; Schlegel 1977a; Whyte 1978). All, however, have suggested that since women's lives and activities cannot be understood apart from the total systems that give them meaning, we must begin our analyses with a typology of such systems.

Although many anthropologists have advocated or used typologies of social systems, all have not constructed the same kinds of systemic models. The models presented in this book differ from many proposed models in that I postulate the existence of neither functional integration nor determining traits. My aim in constructing ideal-typic models is not to discover scientific sociological laws but to develop tools for interpreting and understanding the activities and ideas of particular historical peoples. As a result, the models I construct bear more resemblance to Weber's ideal types than to those of Durkheim (see Smelser & Warner 1976).

The reader will recognize that I do not describe social systems as being functionally integrated. The systems I describe are marked by silences, conflicts, inconsistencies, and contradictions. Like Bourdieu (1977), I understand social institutions not as fulfilling societal, class, or individual needs but rather as the outcomes of countless actions by individuals pursuing subjective ends. Most institutions are not even intended by the people whose actions realize them. Peoples' everyday activities give rise to the clusters of interacting and interrelated elements that we call social systems, but such systems are not functionally integrated.

My theoretical framework also precludes the positing of determining traits. If no social practice has meaning in and of itself, then no social practice can exist prior to the system of which it is a part. Many theorists consider technology a determining variable (e.g. Gluckman 1968). I do not deny the importance of technology. It determines the amount of goods a group can produce and shapes the division of labor. But technology should not be treated as an independent variable. Social factors affect its development and its adoption. Even capitalist folk wisdom predicts that no one will invent a better mousetrap unless the inventor can expect to profit from the effort.

The models presented here focus on discourses—ongoing and recurring conversations that join power and knowledge including commonsense assumptions. In developing ideal-typic models of three different types of classless, uncentralized societies, I analyzed power relations to show the ways in which power provides the context of and necessity for particular conversations. And I analyzed conversations in an attempt to reveal how the knowledge they require and transmit distributes power and influence in particular ways. By examining discourses, I traced the complex connections between ways of validating marriages, methods of organizing production, understandings of conflict, leadership patterns, folk models of social structure, and conceptions of the cosmos and of the gendered self.

The concept of social system I used in this study is that developed by Bourdieu (1977) and by Giddens (1976, 1979). People in the process of pursuing their own subjective ends carry on the conversations and realize the social institutions that shape the experiences from which they draw their understandings of the world. People act under conditions they did not choose and may not fully understand (as suggested by the existence of recognizable types of societies), but in the last analysis, people make the worlds they live in.

Reference Matter

Notes

Introduction

1. In common anthropological usage, the terms "brideservice" and "bridewealth" belong to the set that includes dowry, gift exchange, token bridewealth, sister-exchange, and absence of gifts. Within this set, brideservice is the "mode of obtaining a wife" through "substantial material consideration in which the principal element consists of labor or other services rendered by the groom to the bride's kinsmen," whereas bridewealth involves the "transfer of substantial consideration in the form of livestock, goods, or money from the groom or his relatives to the kinsmen of the bride" (Murdock 1967: 47). I began using these two terms according to their common meanings, but I soon found that I was, in fact, using them not to differentiate between services and goods, but rather to distinguish between societies where men could marry without having to borrow from kin (brideservice) and societies where men had to borrow from kin (bridewealth). Later, I realized that I was using the terms less to distinguish forms of marriage than to label models of entire social systems. The latter usage is the one employed in this book. When I write about actual marriage transactions, I tend to use different words. Although my misuse of the terms "brideservice" and "bridewealth" has led some readers to misunderstand my arguments, I continue using those terms because I have already used them for labeling models in previously published articles (Collier & Rosaldo 1981; J. Collier 1984; J. Collier 1987) and because others have used the terms in referring to those articles (e.g. Strathern 1985).

2. Many feminists have criticized Meillassoux's analysis of women's role in lineage-based societies (see O'Laughlin 1977; Edholm, Harris, & Young 1977; Harris & Young 1981). Although my thinking has been influenced by these feminist critiques, I do not discuss them here because my aim in this Introduction is not to criticize Meillassoux but rather to raise the questions my models are intended to answer.

Chapter 1

1. Other groups I believe might be fruitfully analyzed with the brideservice model include Australian aborigines (Elkin 1938; Kaberry 1939; Hiatt 1965; Goodale 1971; Hart & Pilling 1960; Maddock 1972; Warner 1937); Eskimos (Balikci 1970; Briggs 1970; Chance 1966); foragers of northern North America such as the Montagnais-Naskapi (Leacock 1954; Lips 1947); Basin-Plateau peoples (Downs 1966; Steward 1938; Whiting 1950); hunter-horticulturists of the South American tropical forest (Biocca 1971; Lévi-Strauss 1967; Chagnon 1968; Holmberg 1969; Murphy & Murphy 1974; Siskind 1973); Philippine hunter-horticulturists (M. Rosaldo 1980; R. Rosaldo 1980); New Guinea hunter-horticulturists (Kelly 1976); and African foragers (Thomas 1959; Lee & Devore 1976; Marshall 1976; Shostak 1981; Turnbull 1961; Woodburn 1968a, 1968b, 1970, 1972).

2. No ethnographer of Comanche society has commented on the fact that women were obliged to feed their husbands and children, probably because ethnographers have taken it for granted.

3. Men's and women's obligations are not equal. Women must feed their families every day, whereas men need hunt only sporadically. Similarly, men can hope to be free of their obligation to provide meat for senior in-laws because those seniors will ultimately die, whereas women can never expect to be free of the obligation to feed their families.

4. The Comanche appear to have delegated herding chores to captured Mexican youths and children purchased from the Shoshone Indians (Hoebel 1940: 15). Each of the three Plains peoples discussed in this book took captives, but the status of a captive appears to have differed depending on the wider system of social inequality. Comanche captives, at least as children, were apparently considered a separate group that was forced to assume herding chores. In Cheyenne society, male captives became socially recognized sons of their captors. And in Kiowa society, male captives became sisters' and daughters' husbands who married without gift exchanges. In all three societies, female captives did women's chores, thus becoming subordinate chore wives of their captors. But what it meant to be a chore wife varied according to what it meant to be a wife.

5. The discussion of Comanche improvidence by Wallace and Hoebel (1952: 76) provides a good example of the problems anthropologists encounter when they use the generic masculine. In attempting to explain why the Comanche failed to "make provision for the future" by storing food, they write only about men. They observe that Comanche men could subsist on little food and practiced self-denial. But men were not the ones who would have stored food had food been stored. The preparation, storage, and transportation of food were women's tasks. Therefore, the reasons why Comanche failed to store food cannot be discovered by analyzing men's capacities and preferences. A search for reasons requires attention to the constraints and incentives that shaped women's lives. In Comanche society, women had little incentive to preserve food because a woman could ask any returning hunter for meat, because there was no reason for anyone to keep more than everyone else had, and because Comanche

women (in contrast to Cheyenne and Kiowa women) had little to gain from feeding others. Evidence indicates that Comanche co-wives did not divide labor to increase output, for they were more interested in minimizing labor than in maximizing production. The head wife in a set of Comanche co-wives used her privileged position to escape women's work altogether: she became her husband's constant companion and carried his shield on the march (Wallace & Hoebel 1952: 141–42).

6. Wallace and Hoebel also describe a fifth form of marriage in Comanche society: "Occasionally an up-and-coming youth who was industrious and showed promise as a warrior was sought out by a father or brother and asked to marry a girl in their family. Such a man was usually a captive: a fullblood Comanche would consider it disgraceful for him to accept advances from the girl's family (1952: 138)." This form of marriage, as we will see in the chapter on the unequal bridewealth model, resembles a form practiced by the Kiowa that was also considered "disgraceful." I imagine that for the Comanche, however, the disgrace came from a man's being given a wife rather than having to earn her for himself.

7. My analysis, in contrast to that of Service (1962), suggests that bands are often matrilocal. Men tend to spend more of their lives living in wives' bands than women do living in husbands' bands. Men who must spend years living near in-laws, however, tend to dream of the day when in-laws are dead and they may settle near their father and brothers. Demographically, bands may show a matrilocal bias. But ideologically, patrilocality is the ideal.

8. Meillassoux (1972: 99) attributes the fact that "hunters, once they share the common product, are free from any further reciprocal obligations or allegiance" to the hunting process. Because hunters use land only as a "subject of labor," not as an object in which they invest work, their immediately available output allows a process of sharing to take place at the end of each enterprise. I, in contrast to Meillassoux, attribute hunters' freedom from reciprocal obligations and allegiance to the fact that their wives feed them and provide for all their daily needs.

9. Seemingly disproving my assertion that parents in brideservice societies cannot reclaim a married daughter from her husband, Linton (1936: 260) writes about a Comanche woman who reclaimed her daughter from a cowardly husband, and Hoebel describes one case in which a Comanche informant reported telling another man that he would reclaim that man's wives if that man insisted on claiming the speaker's favorite horse: "I told him not to forget that he was married to two of my 'daughters' (they were daughters of my brother). In these words I spoke to him. 'If I accept these terms, and you insist on that horse, you can have it. But if you do, you will lose your two wives. I will take back my daughters from you. You are my son-in-law and yet you are not caring what you say; you are trying to get the horse I love' " (1940: 57). The speaker never had to make good his threat. I doubt he could have done so. In Comanche society there were no recognized procedures for a man to reclaim his wife from her kin; this suggests that Comanche women's kin had no regularized procedures for taking a daughter away from her husband. In my view, the informant's

threat is best interpreted as an attempt to remind the other man of their affinal relationship, as revealed in his statement that his opponent "had forgotten about being my son-in-law in that way" (1940: 57). And Linton's report of a woman reclaiming her daughter is best interpreted as a cowardly man's loss of his wife.

10. Hoebel does not mention elopement in his discussion of Comanche law (1940), but he and Wallace do mention it in their ethnography of Comanche society (Wallace & Hoebel 1952). They begin their paragraph on elopement with the statement, "When a girl learned that a rich suitor whom she did not care to marry was about to propose, she might elope with the man she loved" (1952: 136). Wallace and Hoebel thus suggest that elopement was, in fact, understood less as an offense against the girl's parents than as an offense against the man to whom they hoped to marry her.

11. Hoebel presents no evidence that rejected Comanche suitors revenged themselves by abducting the women they were denied. Such actions are reported with regard to other brideservice peoples, however. A particularly noteworthy example is described by Hoebel: a rejected Eskimo suitor systematically killed "the father, mother, brothers and sisters [of his desired bride], seven or eight in all, until only the girl survived, whereupon he took her to wife" (1954: 85–86).

12. In some brideservice societies, a few biological females may assume a male gender role—they hunt and marry wives (see Landes 1971; Blackwood 1984). In this book, however, I do not discuss gender crossing by either sex in any type of society, even though Plains societies are famous for the male berdache role (see Whitehead 1981; Callender & Kochems 1983). When I use the words "woman" and "man," I refer to socially defined gender, not to biological sex. As a result, when I write that women in brideservice societies cannot marry wives, I mean that people with a feminine gender identity cannot do so.

13. Hoebel (1940: 113) does report one case in which a cuckolded husband demanded horses from the father of two youthful seducers. The father gave two horses. But when the youths' older brother returned from a raid and discovered what his father had done, he so objected to the settlement that he went to the cuckold's herd and shot the two horses dead. This refusal by the youths' older brother to acquiesce in what his father had done suggests that the Comanche, unlike the Cheyenne and Kiowa, did not expect a senior relative to pay compensatory damages to those injured by a young person.

14. Although no ethnographer of Comanche society has written that peace chiefs maintained large herds, this inference seems plausible, given Hoebel's observation that the Comanche peace chief had "just one single definite power: that of deciding the time and place of camp moving" (1940: 18). If peace chiefs did maintain large herds, then they would control the horses that people needed for moving their possessions. It seems reasonable to conclude, however, that women, not men, borrowed animals from peace chiefs. Men traveled lightly during camp moves. They carried only their weapons. Women had responsibility for packing and unpacking the children and household possessions (Wallace & Hoebel 1952: 93).

15. In writing about the causes of conflict in brideservice, equal bridewealth, and unequal bridewealth societies, I discuss only dominant cultural representations of why conflict occurs. In all societies, fights are precipitated by a variety of issues and events, but every society has a dominant idiom for understanding why conflict occurs, and thus for handling it. In American society, where supposedly free, property-holding individuals create social order by contracting with one another, conflict is perceived as resulting from a violation of someone's rights—to property, to the privileges of equal citizenship, or to being treated by others as those others would wish people to treat them. In brideservice societies, where personal prowess appears to be the basis for relationships among men, conflicts are perceived as occurring when some man's reputation for bravery has been called into question. In equal bridewealth societies, where the giving and accepting of gifts seem to define social obligations, conflicts are understood as debts. And in unequal bridewealth societies, where a person's rank appears to determine his or her possibilities, all conflicts appear to be disputes over the relative ranking of two individuals or groups.

16. The Comanche "champion-at-law" who prosecuted cases of adultery and wife stealing for brotherless men of low status is a famous figure in the anthropology of law. The man who asked or allowed a champion-at-law to prosecute for him may have obtained revenge or the return of his wife, but he also proved his own cowardliness and consequent inability to maintain a status that announced "don't fool with me."

17. In Comanche society, favorite horses were equivalent to people; some men reacted to the killing of a favorite horse as they reacted to the killing of a male kinsman—by committing a vengeance killing (Hoebel 1940: 67). For a cuckold to kill his cuckolder's horse was therefore a brave and defiant act (but see Linton 1936: 428–29).

18. Hoebel describes the Comanche champion-at-law as motivated by a sense of "noblesse oblige" (1940: 64). I believe this term is not only inaccurate but inappropriate. "Noblesse oblige" pertains to a political system with a landed aristocracy. The Comanche had an egalitarian society without vast differences in wealth and power.

19. I do not think that the Comanche, or members of any brideservice society, are adolescent. Brideservice peoples tend to portray desire as the cause of action because they lack contexts in which to develop elaborate concepts of duty and obligation. And they do not describe thought about consequences as intervening between desire and action because, unlike modern Americans, they do not live in a society where vast inequalities exist despite an ideology of equality. Therefore, they lack contexts in which to develop justifications for why people who supposedly enjoy equal opportunities should end up so unequally.

20. Brideservice peoples appear to believe that might makes right and that society is made up of autonomous individuals, each of whom, like the "natural man" of social contract theory, is bent on taking what "he" wants and keeping what "he" has. The cultural representations of brideservice societies thus allow Western observers to conclude that these people exhibit the avariciousness social contract theory attributes to human nature.

Hoebel, for example, describes Comanche men as "striving for accumulated war honors, horses, and women" (1954: 131). The behavior of brideservice peoples contradicts the conclusion of natural avariciousness, however. Comanche men may have strived to acquire war honors, horses, and women, but they gave away all three.

21. A survey of societies appropriate for analysis with a brideservice model suggests the hypothesis that male violence against women is a function of the amount of aggression among men. When intergroup violence escalates, men try to avoid fights with needed allies and to make peace with former enemies; consequently, they seek to control the women whose adulteries would turn allies into enemies and whose marriages would turn enemies into cooperating brothers-in-law. It seems no accident, therefore, that male violence against women appears most extreme in those modern brideservice groups living in areas where, during the nineteenth century, agents of capitalist expansion wittingly or unwittingly caused members of some brideservice groups to exterminate others (Australia), enslave them (Amazon Basin and the Western rim of the Great Plains), or steal their furs (northern North America). In contrast, male violence against women appears mild or nonexistent in those modern brideservice groups that have long been surrounded by, and have been partially integrated into, societies for which a brideservice model is not appropriate (e.g. Pygmies, Bushmen, Hadza, Semang).

22. The difference in the amount of violence reported by anthropological observers and described in informants' accounts is evident from a comparison of Shostak's life history of a !Kung woman (1981) with the observations about !Kung daily life made by ethnographers such as Thomas (1959), Marshall (1976), and Draper (1975).

23. Murphy and Murphy report that they "could not find a shred of evidence [among the Mundurucu of tropical South America] to indicate that men think that women are inherently, biologically, and irredeemably inferior or submissive" (1974: 91). The same seems true of most societies appropriate for analysis with a brideservice model. When people explain why women do not have as much prestige and influence as men, they describe women as lacking the skills or achievements that supposedly earn men wives—such as hunting, raiding trophies, or spiritual knowledge— but not as having qualities that make them inferior to men.

Chapter 2

1. Among the societies I believe can be profitably analyzed with an equal bridewealth model are the Nuer (Evans-Pritchard 1940; Gough 1971), the Tiv (Bohannan 1957), the Kaguru (Beidelman 1971), the Plateau Tonga (Colson 1962), the Sebei (Goldschmidt 1967), the Arusha (Gulliver 1963), and the Ndembu (Turner 1957) of sub-Saharan Africa; the Cheyenne (Grinnell 1923; Llewellyn & Hoebel 1941; Hoebel 1978; J. Moore 1974a) and the Hopi (Schlegel 1977b; Dozier 1966) of North America; the Zinacantecos (Vogt 1969; J. Collier 1968, 1973) of Mesoamerica; and the Kapauku (Pospisil 1958) and the Jalemo (Koch 1974) of New Guinea. I believe

that this model is also appropriate for understanding the Trobriand Islanders (Malinowski 1926; Weiner 1976) even though they, unlike all the other societies mentioned, have a concept of rank. There are, of course, many other groups in Africa, the Americas, and Melanesia that can be profitably analyzed with an equal bridewealth model. I have listed only those societies that have contributed most to my understanding.

2. In a footnote to the phrase "food is prepared in the mother's lodge, each daughter taking her share to her own lodge," Eggan mentions one explanation of why Cheyenne and Arapaho daughters continued to cook with their mothers after marriage: "Kroeber (*The Arapaho*, 1: 12–13) intimates that this is because the daughters do not know how to cook yet" (1955: 61). For reasons that will become obvious later in the chapter, this footnote is one of my favorites in the anthropological literature.

3. Sahlins (1963) suggests that Big Men control many valuables because they finesse the relationship of reciprocity required among close kin. My analysis suggests, instead, that Big Men do not need to finesse any relationships. They have many goods because they have many workers in their households. I also disagree with Sahlins as to the reason why accumulation is limited. He suggests that cheated exchange partners finally rebel. I suggest that Big Men's households dissolve upon the senility or death of their founders.

4. In this paragraph I am deliberately vague about the sex of seniors and juniors and refer primarily to men. But as will become clear in the remainder of this chapter, women are also divided into seniors and juniors.

5. I imagine that in almost all human societies, women's parents can portray themselves as giving a wife to their son-in-law. The question, therefore, is not whether women's kin say they give women, but rather what they mean. As a result, I explore in this chapter the contexts that give "gifts of women" their meaning.

6. For convenience, I refer to the relationship between senior and junior consanguines in equal bridewealth societies as the "parent-child" bond. This is the bond in which the major appropriation of labor takes place: adolescent and young adult "children" work for the "parents" who support them. Parents need not be, and often are not, the biological parents of the children who work for them. Rather, parents are those who fulfill cultural requirements for the role. In most equal bridewealth societies, parents are those who rear a child. In some matrilineal societies, however, a child who reaches the age to do useful work may be expected to live with, and work for, a maternal uncle. Among the matrilocal Cheyenne, young men worked for the parents who reared them; after marriage, they were expected to live with their in-laws.

7. The difference in child-rearing practices discussed in this paragraph is usually explained as resulting from different ecological adaptations. Foragers need to train their children in autonomy; horticulturists and pastoralists need to train their children in responsibility and obedience. I attribute the child-rearing difference to differences in the organization of inequality, however. Brideservice peoples, even when they have horses to herd, as did the Comanche, or are horticulturists, as are the Sharanahua

of lowland South America (see Siskind 1973: 59, 80), seldom appropriate the labor of children and teenagers. Equal bridewealth peoples, in contrast, continually stress responsibility and compliance even when hunting is a major activity, as it was among the Cheyenne.

8. Wallace and Hoebel write that Comanche girls followed their mothers everywhere and were "given small tasks" as they grew older. (1952: 125). But there is no indication that Comanche mothers continually admonished, exhorted, and trained their daughters, as Hoebel reports Cheyenne mothers did (1978: 34).

9. Parents in equal bridewealth societies seem to be more successful in obtaining useful labor from children and adolescents than their counterparts in brideservice societies—probably because equal bridewealth parents expect children to obey. They therefore issue frequent commands and actively seek out wandering or disobedient children. Hoebel reports that Cheyenne girls were "continually" admonished and exhorted by their mothers (1978: 34). Parents in brideservice societies seem to direct few commands at children—probably because they do not expect obedience. Children in brideservice societies seem to escape parental demands by staying far enough away from parents so that they cannot hear the few commands that parents do issue (see Draper 1976; Siskind 1973: 59). Children in equal bridewealth societies probably lack this option. When performing chores, they can easily be found by parents who want to give more commands. Parents also probably seek out children they suspect of avoiding chores.

10. Ethnographers use the word "debt" as the closest English translation of a concept that has no English equivalent. Equal bridewealth peoples do not have the governmental structures that invest the English concept of debt with a notion of the possible legal enforcement of its payment by agents of a state who claim a monopoly on coercive force. This difference in meaning between the English concept of debt and the one common among equal bridewealth peoples may explain why Llewellyn and Hoebel conclude that debt was not an important concept in Cheyenne society. The Cheyenne clearly did not have debt in the English (legal) sense; "the poor, instead of being driven into the hands of the capitalist by debt, wage-dependence, or clientage, seem rather to have sponged somewhat upon the chief, the lucky hunter, the succession of celebrant givers; . . . there happens not to be in the cases a single instance of a long-term obligation for a fixed return; outside of family and marriage relations, *continuing* obligations running between any parties were most unusual" (Llewellyn & Hoebel 1941: 233), italics theirs).

11. Injuries are also understood as debts, for the person who harms another takes something—the use of an eye, an arm, or a leg, or even a life—from the person harmed. The offender must therefore repay the victim or assume obligations equivalent to the repayment.

12. Ethnographers of equal bridewealth societies often report that people hold contradictory attitudes toward petty thieves. Informants say that thieves not only should be allowed to keep what they have stolen but

should be showered with gifts. Llewellyn and Hoebel report that the Cheyenne believed it "was not good taste to make too much fuss about 'stolen' articles of minor value" (1941: 226). Rather, the victim of a theft was supposed to express a willingness to give the object to the thief. A Cheyenne informant told Llewellyn and Hoebel that "if one found such a transgressor, one upbraided him in public and shamed him by saying, 'If you had come in the day, I would have given it to you'" (1941: 226). However, the same people who express the first attitude will sometimes say that petty thieves not only should have to return what they have stolen but should have to give an equivalent amount and/or be punished in addition. These contradictory attitudes may co-exist because both seem reasonable to people who live in equal bridewealth societies. A person who makes too much fuss over a minor theft is considered ungenerous, whereas a person who proclaims a willingness to give away the stolen object receives credit for giving without expecting anything in return. And a thief who is showered with gifts is humiliated. People feel a deep resentment toward thieves, however. Thieves obtain something from another person without assuming the obligations to the person that would accompany acceptance of a gift. They should therefore be punished for their perfidy, made to return double what they have stolen, and perhaps publicly humiliated as well.

13. The Cheyenne seem somewhat extreme in the passivity they expected of cuckolds. But the cultural logic underlying such passivity is common to most societies appropriate for analysis with the equal bridewealth model.

14. Llewellyn and Hoebel report that "there seems to have been no public knowledge of what took place . . . in a session of the Council of Forty-Four when it was giving consideration to a sentence of banishment" (1941: 136). I suggest that there was no public knowledge because the council did not, in fact, consider sentences of banishment. It decided whether to hold a ceremony to renew the Sacred Arrows of the tribe, with a decision to renew constituting a public announcement that a murder had polluted the Sacred Arrows. A sensible murderer then banished himself (or herself) for fear of a vengeance killing.

15. This is the case of a man who killed another in a drunken brawl (Llewellyn & Hoebel 1941: 12–13). Llewellyn and Hoebel report that the peace chiefs ordered him away for having committed the murder, although they also report that the victim's kin vowed to kill the murderer if they saw him. He stayed away for three years. Then he initiated settlement procedures by sending a horse loaded with bundles of tobacco as a gift to the peace chiefs. They sent some of the bundles to the soldier chiefs, asking their opinion, and called in the father of the victim. The victim's father finally agreed to allow the murderer to return (i.e. the father agreed to renounce his desire for vengeance). Although Llewellyn and Hoebel do not emphasize the point, it is clear that some of the tobacco was intended as a gift to the murderer's kin, for the murderer's father is reported to have said: "As far as that stuff of his is concerned, I want nothing that belonged to him. Take this share you have set aside for me and give it to someone else"

(1941: 13). By asking that his share be given to someone else, the victim's father was, of course, accepting it, for a person must have something to be able to give it away. (See also 1941: 135).

16. The power associated with having knowledge suggests to me that the Cheyenne Council of Forty-Four Chiefs was a body of religious, not secular, leaders. Hoebel writes that the council decided "such matters as camp moving and tribal war policy" (1978: 52), that it acted as a judicial body in murder cases, and that it assigned particular soldier societies to police summer bison hunts. Each of these powers can be attributed to their control of sacred knowledge, for the Cheyenne believed that supernatural aid was vital to success in war; that murder was, by definition, an act that polluted the Sacred Arrows; and that camp moving and policing the summer bison hunt came under the control of sacred chiefs because the summer camp represented "a symbolic tipi with the open door facing the rising sun" (Llewellyn & Hoebel 1941: 74). I do not believe that Cheyenne chiefs held political offices. They were Big Men whose personally established followings granted them prestige and access to the goods necessary for acquiring the highest levels of ritual knowledge, and whose claim to such knowledge allowed them, in concert with other chiefs, to decide matters affecting the running of the universe.

17. When I was interviewing people in Zinacantan, Chiapas, Mexico, about instances of conflict (J. Collier 1973), I found that informants usually described an accused wrongdoer as having acted in counteraction to a previous wrong. Zinacanteco stories of conflict were thus in marked contrast to the stories that people tell in brideservice societies and to the ones that I collected from Stanford students (J. Collier 1980), in which a wrongful action is usually portrayed as motivated by the agent's feelings or desires. Zinacantecos did, on occasion, portray wrongful acts as resulting from drunkenness or describe offenders as simply bad people. But if pushed, Zinacantecos usually related a story about a past conflict between the drunk or bad person and the victim. When I pushed Stanford students to explain a wrongdoer's actions, they tended to resort to popular psychology.

18. In all human societies, people tell unflattering stories about others who are not present, but this type of gossip seems far more prevalent in some societies than in others. In brideservice societies, gossip does not seem to play an important role in social life (see R. Rosaldo 1978). In a society where people supposedly "follow their hearts" and "hearts" are affected by the immediate social context, scurrilous stories about a person's past would seem to be of little use for predicting a person's behavior. But in equal bridewealth societies, gossip provides people with important information about past actions. In some of these societies, such as the Maya of Zinacantan, "hearts" are also credited with determining action, but Zinacanteco hearts, probably in contrast to those of brideservice peoples, harbor thoughts of vengeance for past wrongs (J. Collier 1973).

19. Gluckman attributes people's watchful behavior to technological backwardness. In societies with unproductive agricultural systems, people must rely on their kin to help them in times of need. As a result, they continually watch their kin to ensure that they are displaying the proper

"sentiments of love appropriate to the relationship" (Gluckman 1968: 74). I attribute people's watchfulness not to backward technology but to their system of social relations. Brideservice peoples, whose technology is more backward than that of equal bridewealth peoples, do not seem to watch one another obsessively.

20. In equal bridewealth societies, the amount of power available to socially defined dependents is a function of their ability to play off potential supporters against one another. For this reason, I believe that women appear most organized and powerful in those societies where they, in fact, enjoy the power of being able to play off husbands against brothers. Conversely, women appear most degraded and exploited in those societies where they are rendered powerless by collusion between their husbands and brothers. These statements are tautologies, however. I am merely saying that women have power in societies where they have power and lack it in societies where they do not. But within this context, it is possible to explain Cheyenne women's power by the strong ties that they retained with their natal kin; these ties appear to have given them considerable influence over their sons' careers. The Cheyenne were uxorilocal; young men were therefore separated from their mothers at marriage. Nevertheless, young men probably remained dependent on their parents after marriage, particularly their mothers, for access to the gifts they needed for giving to teachers of ritual knowledge. The Cheyenne practice of having married daughters cook in their mother's lodge and then take home with them only what their husbands and children needed to eat and to wear (Eggan 1955: 61) suggests that young husbands were not able to obtain appropriate gifts from their own incipient households.

21. Llewellyn and Hoebel pitied Stump Horn for having a swarm of relatives camping on him. Stump Horn probably was to be pitied, since he was living on the reservation, under a capitalist system, at the time he was being interviewed. But when the Cheyenne were still living under a system appropriate for analysis with an equal bridewealth model, the man who had a swarm of relatives camping on him was fortunate indeed.

22. The Cheyenne differed from most equal bridewealth peoples in their apparent concern for preserving a girl's virginity. In most of these societies virginity is not an issue. However, the Cheyenne also appear to have differed from most of the other societies known to have "virginity complexes." Unlike people in chiefdoms, for example, the Cheyenne had no concept of rank; they did not guard high-ranking girls' virginity to prevent lower-ranking men from seducing them (see Ortner 1981). Unlike people in traditional agrarian states, the Cheyenne lacked a concept of private property; they were not worried about guaranteeing the legitimacy of heirs to family estates. In this context, it seems significant that a Cheyenne man whose sister eloped against his will might commit suicide, but he did not first chase after his sister to kill her and her seducer (Llewellyn & Hoebel 1941: 174–77) as a Mediterranean brother or father was expected to do (see Campbell 1964). And unlike the Victorian bourgeois, the Cheyenne did not think of male sexuality as a dangerous force, in need of a "pure" woman to tame and sublimate it. This bourgeois conception of

virginity may provide a basis for understanding why nineteenth-century whites were so interested in Cheyenne women's chastity. For a white man to write that Cheyenne women were pure was to tell his fellow whites that Cheyenne men were also good, and so should not be massacred.

23. Although Llewellyn and Hoebel's Cheyenne informants agreed that husbands had the right to put adulterous wives "on the prairie" to be raped by any man (1941: 202), women's kin seem to have contested the husband's right in almost all of the cases discussed by Llewellyn and Hoebel—that is, they appear to have considered a husband's attempts to have his wife raped by a gang as a wrong that required a counteraction.

24. The opposition between masculinity and femininity is, as I hope is obvious, cultural rather than natural. This culturally created opposition is then used to order what people perceive in their world. The masculine/feminine opposition need not be mapped onto what we consider the biological difference between males and females. In many equal bridewealth societies (e.g. the Nuer), women can assume masculine roles. They can acquire wives with bridewealth. And in some societies (e.g. the Trobriand), young men can be assigned feminine roles; they can be given as wives to men by a family that wishes to establish an affinal bond but presently lacks young women.

Chapter 3

1. Some of the societies I think might be profitably analyzed with the unequal bridewealth model are the Yurok of California (Kroeber 1926) and perhaps other peoples of the American Northwest Coast (Drucker 1965); the Ifugao of the Philippines (Barton 1919); the peoples of western Malaya (Gullick 1958); the Kachin of Highland Burma (Leach 1965); the Burundi of East Africa (Albert 1971); and the Kpelle of West Africa, whom Gibbs describes as having three "incipient classes" (of men)—"wife-lenders, wife-keepers, and wife-borrowers" (1965: 215; see also Bledsoe 1980). I do not believe the model is appropriate for analyzing Polynesian and African chiefdoms, or the native American chiefdoms of Central and South America.

2. The English words "chief," "king," "aristocrat," "noble," "commoner," "slave," and "debt bondsman" necessarily misrepresent the privileges and disabilities that accompany the statuses held by people in unequal bridewealth systems, but they are the terms used by ethnographers and are the best available. By the end of this chapter, however, readers should have an understanding of what these terms mean in an unequal bridewealth society.

3. Leach observes that for the Kachin, the brideprice corresponds to the status of the groom; a chief charges only a "moderate" brideprice when he marries one of his daughters to a political subordinate. He also describes a case in which a wealthy, but formally lower-ranking man, paid a "bride price of staggering dimensions" for the daughter of a chief (1965: 151–52). Leach's example supports my contention that the amount a groom pays establishes his status. In Kachin society, a groom who pays a moderate brideprice for the daughter of a chief becomes and/or remains the chief's

political subordinate, subject to the chief's commands, whereas the man who pays a staggering brideprice affirms his equality with or superiority over the wife-giver.

4. In societies where men try to marry women of equal or higher rank, families in the middle ranks usually receive fewer goods from the kin of daughters' and sisters' husbands than they need for giving to the kin of brothers' and sons' wives. In the long run, this creates a situation in which some families necessarily lack access to the valuables needed to ensure that all sons escape labor obligations to in-laws. Men who find themselves working for in-laws, in turn, have fewer opportunities to acquire gifts, and so ensure that their sons will face the same situation. Consequently, at any one time, there will always be some families under such stress that they try to recoup their fortunes by marrying a sister or daughter to a high-ranking man as his secondary wife. And at any one time, there will necessarily be some men who lack access to marriage-validating goods. The particular men who fall in the category of outcast, slave, or debt bondsman may have done so as a result of their own misdeeds or misfortunes, but the social category of men who have only their labor to give in return for women is a product of wider social processes.

5. Some ethnographers of societies appropriate for analysis with an unequal bridewealth model report that marriages are validated with token gifts, standard bridewealth, variable bridewealth, gift exchanges, or no exchanges at all. There is also some evidence that affines in unequal bridewealth societies, unlike their equal bridewealth counterparts, exchange different types of gifts at weddings. The relatives of a Kiowa groom, for example, may have given "male" things, such as horses, saddles, weapons, blankets, and buckskin goods, and the relatives of the bride may have returned "female" things, such as dishes, flatware, water buckets, cooking outfits, and tablecloths (see Corwin 1958: 153).

6. As will become clear in the remainder of this chapter, it seems reasonable to conclude that a high-ranking man, who could easily persuade women to run away with him, might readily desert a wife whose kin demanded too many favors.

7. Mishkin assumes that Kiowa "class" relations were based on private ownership of the means of production (horses), but unlike other ethnographers of Kiowa society, he is not content to accept the idea that "there was no single criterion of status"—that "each man had a niche in a number of separate systems" (Richardson 1940: 12). Mishkin is concerned with demonstrating relations among the various components of Kiowa ranking. He agrees with Richardson that "war record was the single most important determinant of status in Kiowa life" (Richardson 1940: 14), but Mishkin argues that relative wealth, as measured by the number of horses owned, mediated the relationship between heroic deeds and rank. Mishkin's argument, stated in simple terms, is that the introduction of horses to an egalitarian hunter-gatherer society led to a distinction between "haves" (men who were the first to be successful at capturing horses) and "have-nots." This original distinction was perpetuated because men without horses could not hunt bison or transport their belongings without borrowing

horses from relatives who demanded certain services in return. Borrowers "were expected to hunt for their benefactors or turn over a part of their kill as well as spend considerable time herding horses for them" (Mishkin 1940: 45). Men who had to borrow horses had little time to raid for animals and thus had little chance of acquiring their own herds. Men who had horses to lend were freed from the drudgery of hunting and herding and therefore could devote their time to rustling more horses and to performing the heroic deeds that brought prestige. Over time, according to Mishkin, this division of labor between haves and have-nots led to the development of a hereditary elite—an aristocratic caste. There are many problems with Mishkin's assumption that there was private ownership of the means of production, most of which are touched on in this book. Nevertheless, I am deeply indebted to him for posing the question that I, too, try to answer: Why did some Kiowa men work for others?

8. Donald Collier writes that "the obligation of a woman to her husband's sister is similar to that of a man to his wife's brother, although it is not so binding and the term *heido* [downgrade, no stopping, i.e. not refundable] is not applied to it" (1938: 94). There is no indication that a wife who refused to obey her husband's mother or sister might lose her husband. Collier writes that if a Kiowa wife's "mother-in-law abuses her she will go home to her family. Under such circumstances her husband will have to go and live with her family if he wants to keep her as his wife" (1938: 99).

9. Donald Collier reports that the captives, most of whom were women, made up 6 to 7 percent of the Kiowa population (1938: 87); Mishkin observes that Kiowa men commonly gave their wives captive women to perform chores for them (1940: 44).

10. High-ranking Kiowa families, like many unequal bridewealth peoples (see Barton 1919), had a custom of favoring one child in a sibling set. Richardson describes the "favored child" complex as "a custom of concentrating the entire family's attentions and wealth on one child, pampering and dressing him up, relieving him of all work-a-day activities, and giving away in his honor quantities of horses and objects at the most trivial opportunity. These children were legally recognized as [favored] and had special advantages over other relatives" (1940: 12). Ethnographers of Kiowa society view this custom as detrimental to the interests of non-favored children (see Mishkin 1940: 51). My analysis, however, suggests that, far from being hurt by the favoritism shown a sibling, Kiowa non-favored siblings gained access to horses as a result of having a favored full brother or sister who had given away so many of the animals that the favored sibling's access to horses was indisputable.

11. Donald Collier (1938) does not provide information about the other 13 suicides. Although not enough evidence is available to permit a comparison of Comanche, Cheyenne, and Kiowa suicide patterns, the suicides described by ethnographers indicate that cultural justifications for male suicides were different in the three societies—as would be expected because of their different systems of inequality. Hoebel (1940: 116) tells of two Comanche bachelors who killed themselves after being refused food by

their sister's husband (signifying the husband's refusal to engage in sister-exchange marriage?). Llewellyn and Hoebel (1941: 174) write about a Cheyenne man who committed suicide after his sister refused to marry the man he had chosen; signifying the sister's refusal to help further the brother's career?). Donald Collier reports that rejection by a brother was a major cause of suicide in Kiowa society (1938: 57–58).

12. On Hoebel's (1954) scale, the Comanche rank third (lowest) because they had only "champions-at-law" who prosecuted for individuals. The Kiowa rank second because they had powerless medicine-bundle owners who could intervene to halt violence. The Cheyenne rank highest because, Hoebel believes, the Cheyenne Council of Forty-Four Chiefs acted as a judicial body in murder cases.

13. If either side disapproved of an elopement, however, real violence might erupt. Donald Collier writes that "the girl's family will express disapproval of the boy in an elopement marriage by destroying, as well as taking, property in the elopement raid. This destruction usually takes the form of chopping up the tipi poles and cutting the tipi up. This serves forceful notice to his family that they disapprove of the boy. The boy's family expresses their disapproval of the girl by hiding property before the elopement raid. Only rarely (probably when the son has been disowned) would the boy's parents resist the raiders. This is so because of the sanction underlying the elopement raid, and because resistance causes the raiders to destroy property without mercy, and possibly beat the boy's parents as well. As these raiding parties are often large and it is customary for the women to be equipped with butcher knives and hatchets for the occasion, resistance would be apt to prove disastrous" (1938: 100).

14. It probably was most prestigious for a man to abscond with a high-ranking wife of a high-ranking man. Absconding with one of a polygynous high-ranking man's low-ranking wives might bring the absconder some prestige, for it would show that the woman preferred her lover over her husband, but a high-ranking man's status was not really threatened by the desertion of one of his low-ranking wives. Richardson quotes a high-ranking Kiowa cuckold: "The woman is rather silly to run away from me, but it is not worth making a scene about. After all, I am *onde* [highest rank]; I can get any woman I want" (1940: 121). The reported tendency of men of the highest rank not to prosecute absconding cases vigorously, if at all (Richardson 1940: 121), may indicate that would-be absconders had more success in seducing low-ranking wives than high-ranking ones.

15. Ethnographers of Kiowa society portray the Kiowa system of named, apparently hereditary ranks as an elaboration of the general Plains custom of "counting coup"—of treating some valorous deeds as more prestigious than others (Richardson 1940: 14; Mishkin 1940: 37). Richardson and Mishkin had no reason to view the Kiowa ranking system as unique because they were writing before ethnographies of the Comanche (Hoebel 1940; Wallace & Hoebel 1952) and the Cheyenne (Llewellyn & Hoebel 1941) were published. Hoebel, writing in 1954, did emphasize the cultural differences between the Kiowa, Comanche, and Cheyenne. He portrayed the Kiowa ranking system as "unique" (1954: 170) in that the Kiowa

thought of rank as hereditary, and they ranked women as well as men. Although the Kiowa ranking system was unique to Plains bison hunters, it may have had analogues among settled agriculturalists. Skinner reports, for example, that "among the Ioway of olden times, three grades of marriage were recognized, namely those of the chiefs, or 'royalty,' the braves, or 'nobility,' and the ordinary 'commoners' " (1926: 251).

16. William Murphy, who has done fieldwork among the Kpelle of Liberia, once commented to me that he understands what Berger and Luckmann meant in titling their book *The Social Construction of Reality* (1966). In Kpelle society, people visibly construct reality every day.

17. The Kpelle of Liberia, like the Kiowa, may interpret acts of giving and receiving in contradictory ways, depending on how the interpreter views the series of exchanges of which the present exchange is a part. A Kpelle informant told me that a woman whose brothers request valuables from her husband always tries to interpret her husband's gifts as a loan her brothers will repay, whereas the woman's husband often interprets his gifts to his wife's brothers as installments of bridewealth that strengthen his claim to his wife.

18. Ethnographers of Comanche and Cheyenne societies could probably have obtained similar lists of famous women if they had thought to ask, but the fact that they did not suggests that the listing of famous women with their accomplishments was more appropriate for the Kiowa than for the other two societies.

19. Donald Collier discusses a possible Kiowa analogue of the Cheyenne women's quilling society, but he describes it as a "work guild which [had] no formal organization" and that was concerned with tanning and tipi making (1938: 16). There is no indication that this "work guild" enjoyed the prestige and power of the Cheyenne women's quilling society, although the women were feasted by those for whom they performed services.

20. Ethnographers of Kiowa society have apparently resisted the idea that marriage can be as ambiguous as rank. They are more familiar with a society in which the state defines people as either married or not and whose folk model of social structure defines the family as a natural unit on which the rest of society is based. Richardson, for example, recognizes that Kiowa elopement and absconding cases were concerned with rank, but she avoids the implication that marriage and rank were mutually defining. She reports that top-ranking men "seem to have absconded as much as anyone in the tribe" and declares: "It should not be thought, however, that absconding was an every day occurrence for these men or anyone. For every case of absconding, there were hundreds of men who lived in lifelong happiness and partnership with one or two wives" (1940: 121).

Chapter 4

1. Oliver stresses "three interrelated factors" in explaining why Plains peoples valued military skill and the possession of horses. "First, there was the fluidity and mobility of the band . . . [which] tended to reduce the

importance of kinship as an organizing device" (1962: 62). "Second, there was the military situation in the Plains." Because Plains peoples were "quite literally fighting for their lives," warriors had to be rewarded with prestige, power, and privilege as an incentive to fight (1962: 63). "Third, there was the crucial importance of horses in the Plains situation." Not only were well-mounted hunters able to kill more bison than men with poor mounts, but in a nomadic society, the ideal form of property was one that could transport itself and bear burdens (1962: 63).

2. I owe to Mishkin (1940) the insight that in nineteenth-century Plains societies, a man's war record and the number of horses he captured depended less on his individual capacities as a warrior and raider than on his opportunities to join raiding parties. Like Mishkin, therefore, I ask why some men stayed home hunting and herding so that other men could have free time to join raiding parties.

3. Although a Comanche man could leave camp for long periods without having to worry about who would hunt and herd for his kin during his absence, it seems reasonable to assume that young men married to sexually mature women who were not yet mothers (i.e. who wanted lovers, not husbands) were more likely to stay in camp than either bachelors or men whose wives had borne children. Men with reluctant brides would not only want to keep an eye on them but would also want to ensure the support of in-laws by assiduously hunting for them.

4. In Cheyenne society, the number of recognized relatives a man had probably depended less on the fertility of his kinship group than on the number of wedding exchanges in which he or his immediate kinsmen had participated. People who had enough valuables to participate in many exchanges had many recognized relatives. People who had few valuables were forced to refrain from cementing possible kinship relationships for lack of gifts to give.

5. Other opportunities for acquiring horses in ways that did not involve incurring obligations to a living person, such as capturing wild horses, the natural increase of a herd, or inheritance, were also unequally distributed in Comanche, Cheyenne, and Kiowa societies. Opportunities to join expeditions to hunt wild horses were probably as unequally distributed as opportunities to join raiding parties. The opportunity to acquire horses through the natural increase of a herd was available only to those who already had herds. The available information on inheritance rules is incomplete, but it suggests that opportunities to inherit were most equally distributed in Comanche society: the horses of a dead man were killed, distributed among all who came to mourn, or given to his widow (Hoebel 1940: 120–25). In Cheyenne society, a widow acquired "title" to her dead husband's horses (Llewellyn & Hoebel 1941: 216); her household benefited from retaining the animals or from giving them to others. Inheritance of Kiowa herds was apparently confined to the patriline (D. Collier 1938: 53).

6. In Comanche society, women also had reason to celebrate men's war honors. Because men distributed their meat widely, the relationship between husband and wife was not characterized by a direct and equal ex-

change of male and female products. But women could initiate direct exchanges with men by serenading departing or recently returned warriors, in return for which they received a share of the warriors' booty (Wallace & Hoebel 1952: 251, 272). These exchanges also dramatized the culturally postulated relationship between a man's success in war and his success in love.

7. Hoebel's statement that "the self of the [Comanche] male is realized in striving for accumulated war honors, horses, and women" (1954: 131) implies that nineteenth-century Comanche men accumulated war honors, horses, and women. Ethnographic evidence, however, clearly reveals that men gave away all three. The self of the Comanche male was realized in *striving* for war honors, horses, and women. It was not realized in *accumulating* them.

8. Mishkin makes a statement that appears to contradict Richardson's description of Kiowa herd sizes: "Although the Kiowa were among the wealthiest people in the Plains, horses were as unevenly divided among the individual members of the tribe as anywhere in the area. Not a few families owned no horses at all, there were many with six to ten horses, well-to-do families owned herds numbering 20 to 50 animals, and a few very rich men could count hundreds of heads in their herds" (1940: 19). Later in his monograph, however, Mishkin writes in a footnote that "[band headmen] were not the richest men in the tribe; they seldom owned more than 50 to 60 horses" (1940: 42fn. 12). Mishkin's statement casts doubt on Richardson's assertion that the Kiowa considered the proper size of a herd to be 20 to 30 animals; however, his footnote suggests that the most powerful men in the tribe kept smaller herds than did Cheyenne and Comanche peace chiefs.

9. Godelier describes gifts of valuables in "primitive societies" as serving to (1) create or validate social ties, (2) heal breaks in social relations, and (3) symbolize superior social position (1977: 128). I have used these categories in this paragraph.

10. My analysis diverges from Gluckman's at this point because he contrasts tribal and modern societies within the framework of Maine's (1972) distinction between status and contract, whereas I contrast stateless and state societies within a framework that distinguishes between two types of sanctioning mechanisms, denial of reciprocity and organized coercive power. I do not distinguish between societies in which rights and obligations inhere in status and societies where rights and obligations are assumed through contracts. Rather, I distinguish between societies in which rights and obligations are held in respect to *particular* other people and societies in which individuals or status groups hold rights and obligations in respect to *all* other people. This distinction is derived from Gluckman's (1968) contrast between tribal property law as concerning obligations and modern property law as concerning rights, but it does not correspond to the distinction between status and contract.

11. Although I believe that the concept of private property can be invented only in a state with coercive power, the concept can survive the

demise of any particular state and it may be borrowed by stateless societies. Many apparently stateless societies, particularly in Eurasia and North Africa, now have a concept of private property and thus have true classes (see Barth 1959).

12. Sociobiologists have attributed men's fights over adultery in classless societies to men's desire to ensure that the children they support are genetically theirs. This explanation, however, is falsified by the data. Men in foraging societies may fight other men who seduce their wives, but men seem quite willing to lend their wives to men who so request, or to share wives during rituals marked by general promiscuity (see Fried 1967: 75–78).

13. This casting of husbands as wife-beaters seems common in many classless societies. When I did fieldwork in Zinacantan, Chiapas, Mexico, the first question every woman asked me was, "Does your husband beat you?" Wife beating is, of course, found in many cultures, but no American—or Spaniard—has ever asked me if my husband beats me. Ironically, the cultural portrayal of husbands as wife-beaters has the effect of putting husbands in a position where they must heed the commands of wife-givers, though women still suffer from the blows.

14. My analysis of marriage is, in many ways, based on Friedl's discussion of theoretical alternatives to marriage (1975: 21); she emphasizes the role of in-law relations in organizing production and distribution.

15. I am grateful to Nancy Fraser for identifying what she terms "the socio-cultural means of interpretation and communication," which include "the officially recognized vocabularies in which one can press claims; the idioms available for interpreting and communicating one's needs; the established narrative conventions available for constructing the individual and collective histories which are constitutive of social identity; the paradigms of argumentation accepted as authoritative in adjudicating conflicting claims; the ways in which various discourses constitute their respective subject matters as specific sorts of objects; the repertory of available rhetorical devices; the bodily and gestural dimensions of speech which are associated in a given society with authority and conviction" (1985: 1).

Conclusion

1. Lenski's (1966) discussion of agrarian societies read in conjunction with Goody's (1973) analysis of Eurasian societies with dowry, provides, I think, a good starting point for developing an ideal-typic model of class societies in which the state (or the most powerful social group) allocates economic resources. In such highly stratified societies, people perceive their opportunities as determined by the status group into which they are born.

2. In contrast to John Moore (1974b), I suggest that the conflict in Cheyenne society was not between "uterine" and "agnatic" forces but between an equal bridewealth system that happened to be characterized by uxorilocal rather than virilocal residence and a brideservice system that was not agnatic but in which people celebrated male prowess.

3. Bernstein, following Gadamer, argues that reason and tradition are not opposed. Rather, "all reason functions *within* traditions" (1983: 130, italics his). Given that our thinking is circumscribed by the cultural traditions we inherit, we can learn new things only by using our present understandings to rethink and revise our traditions.

Works Cited

Adams, Richard N. 1975. *Energy and Structure: A Theory of Social Power*. Austin: University of Texas Press.

Albert, Ethel. 1971. "Women of Burundi: A Study of Social Values," pp. 179–216 in Denise Paulme, ed., *Women of Tropical Africa*. Berkeley: University of California Press.

Balikci, Asen. 1970. *The Netsilik Eskimo*. Garden City, N.Y.: Natural History Press.

Bamberger, Joan. 1974. "The Myth of Matriarchy: Why Men Rule in Primitive Society," pp. 263–80 in Michelle Z. Rosaldo and Louise Lamphere, eds., *Woman, Culture, and Society*. Stanford, Calif.: Stanford University Press.

Barnes, John A. 1962. "African Models in the New Guinea Highlands." *Man*, 62: 5–9.

Barth, Fredrik. 1959. *Political Leadership Among Swat Pathans*. London: Athlone.

Barton, Roy Franklin. 1919. *Ifugao Law*. University of California Publication in American Archaeology and Ethnology, 15(1): 1–186.

Battey, Thomas C. 1968. *The Life and Adventures of a Quaker Among the Indians*. Norman: University of Oklahoma Press. (First published 1875.)

Beauvoir, Simone de. 1953. *The Second Sex*. New York: Knopf.

Beidelman, Thomas O. 1971. *The Kaguru: A Matrilineal People of East Africa*. New York: Holt, Rinehart & Winston.

Berger, Peter, and Thomas Luckmann. 1966. *The Social Construction of Reality*. Garden City, N.Y.: Doubleday.

Bernstein, Richard. 1983. *Beyond Objectivism and Relativism*. Philadelphia: University of Pennsylvania Press.

Berreman, Gerald D., ed. 1981. *Social Inequality: Comparative and Developmental Approaches*. New York: Academic Press.

Biocca, Ettore. 1971. *Yanoama: The Narrative of a White Girl Kidnapped by Amazonian Indians.* New York: Dutton.

Blackwood, Evelyn. 1984. "Sexuality and Gender in Certain Native American Tribes: The Case of Cross-Gender Females." *Signs,* 10(1): 27–42.

Bledsoe, Carolyn. 1980. *Women and Marriage in Kpelle Society.* Stanford, Calif.: Stanford University Press.

Bohannan, Paul J. 1957. *Justice and Judgment Among the Tiv.* London: Oxford University Press.

Bourdieu, Pierre. 1977. *Outline of a Theory of Practice.* Cambridge, Eng.: Cambridge University Press.

Briggs, Jean. 1970. *Never in Anger.* Cambridge, Mass.: Harvard University Press.

Callender, Charles, and Lee M. Kochems. 1983. "The North American Berdache." *Current Anthropology,* 24(4): 443–70.

Campbell, John K. 1964. *Honour, Family, and Patronage.* London: Oxford University Press.

Caulfield, Mina. 1981. "Equality, Sex, and Mode of Production," pp. 201–20 in Gerald Berreman, ed., *Social Inequality.* New York: Academic Press.

Chagnon, Napoleon. 1968. *Yanomamo: The Fierce People.* New York: Holt, Rinehart & Winston.

Chance, Norman A. 1966. *The Eskimo of North Alaska.* New York: Holt, Rinehart & Winston.

Collier, Donald. 1938. "Kiowa Social Integration." Master's thesis, University of Chicago.

Collier, Jane F. 1968. "Courtship and Marriage in Zinacantan, Chiapas, Mexico." *Middle American Research Institute Publication,* 25: 139–201.

———. 1973. *Law and Social Change in Zinacantan.* Stanford, Calif.: Stanford University Press.

———. 1975. "Legal Processes," pp. 131–63 in Bernard Siegel, ed., *Annual Review of Anthropology,* vol. 4.

———. 1980. "Responsibility for Conflict." Paper delivered at the 1980 meeting of the American Anthropological Association.

———. 1984. "Two Models of Social Control in Simple Societies," pp. 105–40 in Donald Black, ed., *Toward a Genderal Theory of Social Control.* Vol. 2: *Selected Problems.* New York: Academic Press.

———. 1987. "Rank and Marriage: Or Why High-Ranking Brides Cost More," in Jane F. Collier and Sylvia J. Yanagisako, eds., *Gender and Kinship.* Stanford, Calif.: Stanford University Press.

Collier, Jane F., and Michelle Z. Rosaldo. 1981. "Politics and Gender in Simple Societies," pp. 275–329 in Sherry Ortner and Harriet Whitehead, eds., *Sexual Meanings.* New York: Cambridge University Press.

Colson, Elizabeth. 1962. *The Plateau Tonga of Northern Rhodesia (Zambia).* Manchester: Manchester University Press.

———. 1974. *Tradition and Contract: The Problem of Order.* Chicago: Aldine.

Comaroff, John L., and Simon Roberts. 1981. *Rules and Processes.* Chicago: University of Chicago Press.

Corwin, Hugh D. 1958. *The Kiowa Indians: Their History and Life Stories*. Lawton, Okla.

Dahrendorf, Ralf. 1968. *Essays in the Theory of Society*. Stanford, Calif.: Stanford University Press.

Davis, Kingsley, and Wilbert E. Moore. 1945. "Some Principles of Stratification." *American Sociological Review*, 10(2): 242–49.

DiMaggio, Paul. 1979. "Review Essay: On Pierre Bourdieu." *American Journal of Sociology*, 84(6): 1460–74.

Downs, James F. 1966. *The Two Worlds of the Washo*. New York: Holt, Rinehart & Winston.

Dozier, Edward. 1966. *Hano: A Tewa Indian Community in Arizona*. New York: Holt, Rinehart & Winston.

Draper, Patricia. 1975. "!Kung Women: Contrasts in Sexual Egalitarianism in Foraging and Sedentary Contexts," pp. 77– 109 in Rayna Reiter, ed., *Toward an Anthropology of Women*. New York: Monthly Review Press.

———. 1976. "Social and Economic Constraints on Child Life Among the !Kung," pp. 199–217 in Richard Lee and Irven DeVore, eds., *Kalahari Hunter-Gatherers*. Cambridge, Mass.: Harvard University Press.

Drucker, Philip. 1965. *Cultures of the North Pacific Coast*. San Francisco: Chandler.

Edholm, Felicity, Olivia Harris, and Kate Young. 1977. "Conceptualizing Women." *Critique of Anthropology*, 9–10(3): 101–30.

Eggan, Fred. 1955. "The Cheyenne and Arapaho Kinship System," pp. 35–95 in Fred Eggan, ed., *Social Anthropology of North American Tribes*. 2d ed. Chicago: University of Chicago Press.

Elkin, A. P. 1938. *The Australian Aborigines*. London: Angus and Robertson.

Emerson, Richard. 1962. "Power-Dependence Relations." *American Sociological Review*, 27(1): 31–40.

Etienne, Mona, and Eleanor Leacock. 1980. Introduction, pp. 1–24 in Mona Etienne and Eleanor Leacock, eds., *Women and Colonization*. New York: Praeger.

Evans-Pritchard, E. E. 1940. *The Nuer*. Oxford: Clarendon Press.

Ewers, John C. 1973. "The Influence of Epidemics on the Indian Populations and Cultures of Texas." *Plains Anthropologist*, 18(60): 104–15.

Foucault, Michel. 1980. *Power/Knowledge*. New York: Pantheon Books.

Fraser, Nancy. 1985. "Toward a Discourse Ethic of Solidarity." Paper presented at the Conference on Women and Moral Theory, Stony Brook, N.Y.

Fried, Morton H. 1967. *The Evolution of Political Society*. New York: Random House.

Friedl, Ernestine. 1975. *Women and Men: An Anthropologist's View*. New York: Holt, Rinehart & Winston.

Friedman, Jonathan. 1975. "Tribes, States, and Transformations," pp. 161–202 in Maurice Bloch, ed., *Marxist Analyses and Social Anthropology*. London: Malaby.

Geertz, Clifford. 1983. *Local Knowledge*. New York: Basic Books.

Gibbs, James L. 1965. "The Kpelle of Liberia," pp. 197– 240 in James L. Gibbs, ed., *Peoples of Africa*. New York: Holt, Rinehart & Winston.

280   Works Cited

Giddens, Anthony. 1976. *New Rules of Sociological Method*. New York: Basic Books.

————. 1979. *Central Problems in Social Theory*. Berkeley: University of California Press.

————. 1981. *A Contemporary Critique of Historical Materialism*. Berkeley: University of California Press.

Gladwin, Thomas. 1948. "Comanche Kin Behavior." *American Anthropologist*, 50: 73–94.

Gluckman, Max. 1968. *Politics, Law, and Ritual in Tribal Society*. New York: Mentor Books. (Orig. ed., 1965.)

Godelier, Maurice. 1977. *Marxist Perspectives in Anthropology*. Cambridge, Eng.: Cambridge University Press.

Goldschmidt, Walter. 1967. *Sebei Law*. Berkeley: University of California Press.

Goodale, Jane. 1971. *Tiwi Wives*. Seattle: University of Washington Press.

Goody, Jack. 1973. "Bridewealth and Dowry in Africa and Eurasia," pp. 1–58 in Jack Goody and S. J. Tambiah, *Bridewealth and Dowry*. Cambridge, Eng.: Cambridge University Press.

Gough, Kathleen. 1971. "Nuer Kinship: A Re-examination," pp. 79–122 in Thomas O. Beidelman, ed., *The Translation of Culture*. London: Tavistock.

Gramsci, Antonio. 1971. *Selections from the Prison Notebooks of Antonio Gramsci*. Edited and translated by Quintin Hoare and Geoffrey Nowell Smith. New York: International Publishers.

Gregory, Chris A. 1982. *Gifts and Commodities*. New York: Academic Press.

Grinnell, George Bird. 1915. *The Fighting Cheyennes*. New York: Scribner's.

————. 1923. *The Cheyenne Indians: Their History and Ways of Life*. 2 vols. New Haven, Conn.: Yale University Press.

Gullick, John M. 1958. *Indigenous Political Systems of Western Malaya*. London School of Economics Monograph no. 17. London: Athlone.

Gulliver, Philip H. 1963. *Social Control in an African Society*. Boston: Boston University Press.

Harris, Olivia, and Kate Young. 1981. "Engendered Structures: Some Problems in the Analysis of Reproduction," pp. 109–47 in J. Kahn and J. Llobera, eds., *The Anthropology of Pre-Capitalist Societies*. London: Macmillan.

Hart, C. W. M., and A. R. Pilling. 1960. *The Tiwi of North Australia*. New York: Holt, Rinehart & Winston.

Hiatt, Lester Richard. 1965. *Kinship and Conflict*. Canberra: Australian National University Press.

Hoebel, E. Adamson. 1940. *The Political Organization and Law-ways of the Comanche Indians*. American Anthropological Association Memoir no. 54.

————. 1954. *The Law of Primitive Man: A Study in Comparative Legal Dynamics*. Cambridge, Mass.: Harvard University Press.

————. 1978. *The Cheyennes: Indians of the Great Plains*. New York: Henry Holt. (Orig. ed., 1960.)

Holmberg, Allen R. 1969. *Nomads of the Long Bow*. New York: Doubleday.

Hyde, George E. 1959. *Indians of the High Plains*. Norman: University of Oklahoma Press.

Jablow, Joseph. 1950. *The Cheyenne Indians in Plains Trade Relations, 1795–1840*. American Ethnological Society Monograph no. 19.

Kaberry, Phyllis M. 1939. *Aboriginal Woman: Sacred and Profane*. London: Routledge.

Keesing, Roger. 1985. "Kwaio Women Speak: The Micropolitics of Autobiography in a Solomon Island Society." *American Anthropologist*, 87(1): 27–39.

Kelly, Raymond. 1976. "Witchcraft and Sexual Relations: An Exploration of the Social and Semantic Implications of the Structure of Belief," pp. 36–53 in P. Brown and G. Buchbinder, eds., *Man and Woman in the New Guinea Highlands*. American Anthropological Association Special Publication no. 8.

Koch, Klaus-Friedrich. 1974. *War and Peace in Jalemo*. Cambridge, Mass.: Harvard University Press.

Kopytoff, Igor, and Suzanne Miers. 1977. " 'African Slavery' as an Institution of Marginality," pp. 3–81 in Suzanne Miers and Igor Kopytoff, eds., *Slavery in Africa*. Madison: University of Wisconsin Press.

Kroeber, Alfred L. 1926. "Yurok Law," pp. 511–16 in *Proceedings of the 22d International Congress of Americanists*, Rome.

Landes, Ruth. 1971. *The Ojibwa Woman*. New York: Norton.

Leach, Edmund R. 1965. *Political Systems of Highland Burma*. Boston: Beacon. (Orig. ed., 1954.)

Leacock, Eleanor. 1954. *The Montagnais "Hunting Territory" and the Fur Trade*. American Anthropological Association Memoir no. 78.

———. 1978. "Women's Status in Egalitarian Society: Implications for Social Evolution." *Current Anthropology*, 19(2): 247–75.

Lee, Richard, and Irven DeVore, eds. 1968. *Man the Hunter*. Chicago: Aldine.

———. 1976. *Kalahari Hunter-Gatherers*. Cambridge, Mass.: Harvard University Press.

Lenski, Gerhard. 1966. *Power and Privilege*. New York: McGraw-Hill.

Lévi-Strauss, Claude. 1967. "The Social and Psychological Aspects of Chieftainship in a Primitive Tribe: The Nambikuara of Northwestern Mato Grosso," pp. 45–62 in R. Cohen and J. Middleton, eds., *Comparative Political Systems*. New York: Natural History Press.

———. 1969. *The Elementary Structures of Kinship*. Boston: Beacon.

Lewis, Oscar. 1942. *The Effects of White Contact upon Blackfoot Culture, with Special Reference to the Role of the Fur Trade*. American Ethnological Society Monograph no. 6.

Linton, Ralph. 1936. *The Study of Man*. New York: Appleton-Century.

Lips, Julius. 1947. *Naskapi Law*. Transactions of the American Philosophical Society, vol. 37, no. 4.

Llewellyn, Karl, and E. Adamson Hoebel. 1941. *The Cheyenne Way*. Norman: University of Oklahoma Press.

Lowie, Robert H. 1953. "Alleged Kiowa-Crow Affinities." *Southwestern Journal of Anthropology,* 9: 357–68.

——. 1954. *Indians of the Great Plains.* New York: McGraw-Hill.

Maddock, Kenneth. 1972. *The Australian Aborigines.* Australia: Penguin.

Maine, Sir Henry. 1972. *Ancient Law.* London: Everyman's Library. (Orig. ed., 1861.)

Malinowski, Bronislaw. 1926. *Crime and Custom in Savage Society.* London: Routledge and Kegan Paul.

Marshall, Lorna. 1976. *The !Kung of Nyae Nyae.* Cambridge, Mass.: Harvard University Press.

Martin, M. Kay, and Barbara Voorhies. 1975. *Female of the Species.* New York: Columbia University Press.

Mauss, Marcel. 1967. *The Gift.* New York: Norton. (First published 1923–24 in French, in *L'Année Sociologique.*)

Mayhall, Mildred. 1962. *The Kiowas.* Norman: University of Oklahoma Press.

Meillassoux, Claude. 1972. "From Reproduction to Production," *Economy and Society,* 1: 83–105.

——. 1973a. "The Social Organization of the Peasantry: The Economic Basis of Kinship." *Journal of Peasant Studies,* 1: 81–90.

——. 1973b. "On the Mode of Production of the Hunting Band," pp. 187–203 in Pierre Alexandre, ed., *French Perspectives in African Studies.* London: Oxford University Press.

——. 1981. *Maidens, Meal, and Money.* New York: Cambridge University Press.

Middleton, John, and David Tait. 1958. Introduction, pp. 1–32 in John Middleton and David Tait, eds., *Tribes Without Rulers.* London: Routledge & Kegan Paul.

Mishkin, Bernard. 1940. *Rank and Warfare Among Plains Indians.* American Ethnological Society Monograph no. 3.

Mooney, James. 1898. *Calendar History of the Kiowa Indians.* 17th Annual Report of the U.S. Bureau of American Ethnology, pt. 1, no. 2.

Moore, John H. 1974a. *A Study of Religious Symbolism Among the Cheyenne Indians.* Ann Arbor, Mich.: University Microfilms.

——. 1974b. "Cheyenne Political History, 1820–1894." *Ethnohistory,* 21(1): 329–59.

Moore, Sally Falk. 1978. *Law as Process.* London: Routledge & Kegan Paul.

Murdock, George Peter. 1967. *Ethnographic Atlas.* Pittsburgh, Pa.: University of Pittsburgh Press.

Murphy, Yolanda, and Robert Murphy. 1974. *Women of the Forest.* New York: Columbia University Press.

Needham, Rodney. 1975. "Polythetic Classification: Convergence and Consequences." *Man,* n.s. 10(3): 349–69.

O'Laughlin, M. Bridget. 1977. "Production and Reproduction: Meillassoux's 'Femmes, Greniers, et Capitaux.' " *Critique of Anthropology,* vol. 8.

Oliver, Symmes C. 1962. *Ecology and Cultural Continuity as Contributing Factors in the Social Organization of Plains Indians*. University of California Publication in American Archaeology and Ethnology, 48: 1–90.

Ortner, Sherry. 1981. "Gender and Sexuality in Hierarchical Societies: The Case of Polynesia and Some Comparative Implications," pp. 359–409 in Sherry Ortner and Harriet Whitehead, eds., *Sexual Meanings*. New York: Cambridge University Press.

Parsons, Talcott. 1940. "An Analytical Approach to the Theory of Social Stratification." *American Journal of Sociology*, vol. 45.

Petersen, Karen D. 1964. "Cheyenne Soldier Societies." *Plains Anthropologist*, 9(25): 146–72.

Pospisil, Leopold. 1958. *Kapauku Papuans and Their Law*. Yale University Publication in Anthropology no. 54.

Rey, Pierre P. 1975. "The Lineage Mode of Production." *Critique of Anthropology*, 3: 27–79.

Richardson, Jane. 1940. *Law and Status Among Kiowa Indians*. American Ethnological Society Monograph no. 1.

Roberts, Simon. 1979. *Order and Dispute*. New York: St. Martin's.

Roe, Frank G. 1955. *The Indian and the Horse*. Norman: University of Oklahoma Press.

Rosaldo, Michelle Z. 1980. *Knowledge and Passion: Ilongot Notions of Self and Social Life*. New York: Cambridge University Press.

Rosaldo, Michelle, and J. Atkinson. 1975. "Man the Hunter and Woman," pp. 43–75 in R. Willis, ed., *Interpretation of Symbolism*. London: Malaby.

Rosaldo, Renato. 1978. Review of "Gossip, Reputation, and Knowledge in Zinacantan" by John Haviland. *Man*, n.s. 13: 686.

———. 1980. *Ilongot Headhunting, 1883–1974*. Stanford, Calif.: Stanford University Press.

Rubin, Gayle. 1975. "The Traffic in Women," pp. 157–210 in Rayna Reiter, ed., *Toward an Anthropology of Women*. New York: Monthly Review Press.

Sacks, Karen. 1979. *Sisters and Wives: The Past and Future of Sexual Equality*. Westport, Conn.: Greenwood.

Sahlins, Marshall. 1963. "Poor Man, Rich Man, Big-Man, Chief: Political Types in Melanesia and Polynesia." *Comparative Studies in Society and History*, 5: 285–303.

———. 1968. *Tribesmen*. Englewood Cliffs, N.J.: Prentice-Hall.

———. 1972. *Stone Age Economics*. Chicago: Aldine.

Schlegel, Alice. 1977a. "Toward a Theory of Sexual Stratification," pp. 1–40 in Alice Schlegel, ed., *Sexual Stratification*. New York: Columbia University Press.

———. 1977b. "Male and Female in Hopi Thought and Action," pp. 245–69 in Alice Schlegel, ed., *Sexual Stratification*. New York: Columbia University Press.

Scott, Hugh Lennox. 1911. "Notes on the Kado, or Sun Dance of the Kiowa." *American Anthropologist*, 13(3): 345–79.

Service, Elman. 1962. *Primitive Social Organization: An Evolutionary Perspective*. New York: Random House.

———. 1975. *Origins of the State and Civilization*. New York: Norton.

———. 1979. *The Hunters*. 2nd ed. Englewood Cliffs, N.J.: Prentice-Hall.

Shostak, Marjorie. 1981. *Nisa: The Life and Words of a !Kung Woman*. New York: Random House.

Siskind, Janet. 1973. *To Hunt in the Morning*. London: Oxford University Press.

Skinner, Alanson. 1926. *Ethnology of the Ioway Indians*. Bulletin of the Public Museum of the City of Milwaukee, 5(4): 181–354.

Smelser, Neil, and R. S. Warner. 1976. *Sociological Theory*. Morristown, N.J.: General Learning Press.

Steward, Julian. 1938. *Basin-Plateau Aboriginal Sociopolitical Groups*. Bureau of American Ethnology Bulletin no. 120.

Strathern, Marilyn. 1985. "Kinship and Economy: Constitutive Orders of a Provisional Kind." *American Ethnologist*, 12(2): 191–209.

Terray, Emmanuel. 1972. *Marxism and "Primitive" Societies*. New York: Monthly Review Press.

Thomas, Elizabeth. 1959. *The Harmless People*. New York: Knopf.

Turnbull, Colin. 1961. *The Forest People*. New York: Simon & Schuster.

———. 1968. "The Importance of Flux in Two Hunting Societies," pp. 133–37 in Richard Lee and Irven DeVore, eds., *Man the Hunter*. Chicago: Aldine.

Turner, Victor. 1957. *Schism and Continuity in an African Society*. Manchester: Manchester University Press.

Vogt, Evon Z. 1969. *Zinacantan: A Maya Community in the Highlands of Chiapas*. Cambridge, Mass.: Harvard University Press.

Wallace, Ernest, and E. Adamson Hoebel. 1952. *The Comanche: Lords of the South Plains*. Norman: University of Oklahoma Press.

Wallerstein, Immanuel. 1974. *The Modern World System*. New York: Academic Press.

Warner, W. Lloyd. 1958. *A Black Civilization*. New York: Harper. (Orig. ed., 1937).

Weiner, Annette B. 1976. *Women of Value, Men of Renown*. Austin: University of Texas Press.

Wharton, Clarence. 1935. *Santanta: The Great Chief of the Kiowas and His People*. Dallas: Banks Upshaw.

Whitehead, Harriet. 1981. "The Bow and the Burden Strap: A New Look at Institutionalized Homosexuality in Native North America," pp. 80–115 in Sherry Ortner and Harriet Whitehead, eds., *Sexual Meanings*. New York: Cambridge University Press.

Whiting, Beatrice. 1950. *Paiute Sorcery*. Viking Fund Publication in Anthropology no. 15.

Whyte, Martin King. 1978. *The Status of Women in Preindustrial Societies*. Princeton, N.J.: Princeton University Press.

Williams, Raymond. 1977. *Marxism and Literature*. London: Oxford University Press.

Williams, Robin. 1968. "Values," pp. 283–87 in *International Encyclopedia of the Social Sciences*, vol. 16. New York: Macmillan.

Wolf, Eric R. 1981. "The Mills of Inequality: A Marxist Approach," pp. 41–58 in Gerald Berreman, ed., *Social Inequality*. New York: Academic Press.

Woodburn, James. 1968a. "An Introduction to Hadza Ecology," pp. 49–55 in Richard Lee and Irven DeVore, eds., *Man the Hunter*. Chicago: Aldine.

———. 1968b. "Stability and Flexibility in Hadza Residential Groupings," pp. 103–10 in Richard Lee and Irven DeVore, eds., *Man the Hunter*. Chicago: Aldine.

———. 1970. *Hunters and Gatherers: The Material Culture of the Nomadic Hadza*. London: British Museum.

———. 1972. "Ecology, Nomadic Movements, and the Composition of the Local Group Among Hunters and Gatherers: An East African Example and Its Implications," pp. 193–206 in P. J. Ucko, R. Tringham, and G. Dimblely, eds., *Man, Settlement, and Urbanism*. London: Duckworth.

Index of Authors Cited

In this index an "f" after a number indicates a separate reference on the next page, and an "ff" indicates separate references on the next two pages. A continuous discussion over two or more pages is indicated by a span of page numbers, e.g., "pp. 57–58." *Passim* is used for a cluster of references in close but not consecutive sequence.